Thumb Culture

In Memory of Professor Peter Glotz
(1939-2005)

PETER GLOTZ, STEFAN BERTSCHI, CHRIS LOCKE (EDS.)

Thumb Culture.
The Meaning of Mobile Phones for Society

[transcript]

Bibliographic information published by Die Deutsche Bibliothek
Die Deutsche Bibliothek lists this publication in the Deutsche Nationalbibliografie; detailed bibliographic data are available on the Internet at http://dnb.ddb.de

Layout by: Kordula Röckenhaus, Bielefeld
Typeset by: Justine Haida, Bielefeld
Printed by: Majuskel Medienproduktion GmbH, Wetzlar
ISBN 3-89942-403-4

Distributed in North America by:

Transaction Publishers
New Brunswick (U.S.A.) and London (U.K.)

Transaction Publishers	Tel.: (732) 445-2280
Rutgers University	Fax: (732) 445-3138
35 Berrue Circle	for orders (U.S. only):
Piscataway, NJ 08854	toll free 888-999-6778

Contents

Section Three—Industry Perspectives

Conclusion—Delphi Report

Foreword

When I approached René Obermann, the CEO of T-Mobile International, about financing this study in my former capacity as Director of the Institute for Media and Communications Management at the University of St. Gallen, I found him immediately receptive. Our thesis was that the mobile phone, this piece of hardware that is sometimes inconspicuous, sometimes gaudy, sometimes used exclusively for business purposes and sometimes only for building up personal networks, and sometimes even employed cleverly in a wide variety of ways, is changing the culture of communal life: The thing is an artefact, just like the Roman viaducts or the immense water tanks which the missionaries of India's culture used to render the plains of Ceylon fertile. 'The only thing is: The mobile phone is international,' I said. 'But it is used differently in different cultures,' he answered. And then, René Obermann used the term 'thumb culture', a word originally coined in Japan. This term has now become the title of this volume.

Our work progressed through a variety of stages: Desk research, an international expert workshop in London, a Delphi survey, and the editorial work on this book. We identified a scientific community of communications researchers, sociologists, philosophers, and psychologists in the United States, Great Britain, Germany, Italy, Switzerland, Hungary, and elsewhere, all addressing the new cultural patterns created by the mobile phone. Our introduction presents the perspectives which changed the lives of billions of people—the acceleration mega-trend, the individualisation of communication networks, the changes that the language undergoes when short messages are sent—remember the terrorist attacks of New York, Madrid, and London?—, the customisation of the mobile phone and its transformation into a fetish, and the process of mobile communication in itself. No more than two decades ago, when pioneers (such as the late Axel Zerdick, a communications researcher from Berlin, or Ithiel de Sola Poole of the MIT) began to investigate the telephone as a means of communication, many believed that this instrument (exclusively served by landline networks at the time) was nothing but a utility channel for communication. Communication by telephone seemed uninteresting because it appeared to have no influence on 'the public' or on 'public opinion' (whatever that may be). Apart from campaigning, the telephone was not used for propaganda purposes. Today, international communications research has developed a methodology to demonstrate that both the telephone and the Internet are subverting people's communication habits on the sly. Paul Lazarsfeld's classical term 'personal influence' is acquiring a new meaning. An important segment of communication is shifting to the 'new media', circumventing mass communication which was supposed to be the subject proper of communications studies a few decades ago. This development in the history of science is something that cannot be commented on in other but ironical terms.

Falling in with our suggestion was a courageous act on the part of T-Mobile because the ground-breaking technological developments associated with the mobile phone have spawned both positive and negative utopian fantasies, both euphoria about progress and cultural criticism, particularly in Europe. Global corporations sometimes incline towards a philosophy of silent enjoyment or, in other words: Sell but don't discuss problems. This is more wrong than right. Societal discussions catch up with the economy frequently enough, and large enterprises should aim for thought leadership to secure their economic success, which of course is due to smart business models and marketing, for a long time to come.

I should like to thank Stefan Bertschi, the project manager of this study, Chris Locke, who co-edited the book, and Beat Schmid, the Managing Director of the MCM Institute, who held sheltering hands over our heads whenever necessary. Needless to say, I owe a particular debt of gratitude to T-Mobile International which proved itself a wise and unobtrusive sponsor.

August 2005
Peter Glotz

Introduction

Peter Glotz, Stefan Bertschi and Chris Locke

The mobile phone is becoming an increasingly ubiquitous part of everyday life—not only in developed countries where penetration levels suggest there are more handsets than people in some countries, but also around the rest of the globe. Handset manufacturers are now turning their attention away from the saturated European markets to countries such as China, which boasts the largest mobile subscriber base in the world, and increasingly to developing countries, where cellular technology is often leapfrogging the roll-out of stable fixed-line telephone networks. With this ubiquity comes a change in the role of the mobile phone as a social artefact.

We already know how it enables simple social communication, but increasingly it plays a number of sophisticated roles in social interaction and everyday life. It is an enabler of social interactions, hierarchies and communication. It is a fetishised object that reinforces a sense of individual identity. It is a transformative technology that changes the way we do business. It is a device that changes how we manage space and time. It is a tool for text-messaging. It is a supercomputer in our palm, able to perform more computational tasks than the Apollo rockets. It is simply a voice-machine, its advanced features neglected by the vast majority of its users. It is all these things, and yet more besides.

Perhaps most of all, the mobile phone is coming to be associated with *presence*. With fixed-line telephony we call a place; with mobile telephony we call a person. We increasingly expect the person to be on the other end of the line, and become frustrated if the call is not answered or if we are redirected to voicemail—a typical frustration explored further in the research in this volume. Tragically, in recent times we have become most aware of how closely mobile phones are associated with presence by the shock of their sudden association with absence. In recent terrorist atrocities, mobile phones have played many critical roles, starkly indicating how tightly woven they are into our social and cultural being. Most tragically of all in the Madrid bombings of 2004, mobile phones were used to trigger the bombs and then, subsequently, mobile phone records were used to trace the bombers themselves. In the London bombings of 2005, mobile phones were used amidst the confusion of the aftermath to check on the wellbeing of loved ones—to check their presence in the world—at such dense levels of usage that the networks struggled to manage the volume of calls. In the days after the bombings, mobile phones were also called into service as witnesses, when first the news networks and then the London Metropolitan Police themselves called for mobile phone photo and video evidence of the atrocities to be submitted, and were deluged. Some of the most shocking, and most repeated, images of the bombings are the grainy, dim images taken by passengers immediately after the event via their mobile phones. It is a perverse validation of the centrality of the mobile phone in our lives that when faced with catastrophe, it is the small hand-held device in our pockets we turn to, both to re-connect ourselves with our loved-ones in the outside world and also to capture the events we are part of. It expresses a double interpretation of our presence in the world—both '*I* am here' and 'I am *here*'.

As the role of the mobile phone in society has changed—rapidly developing in complexity as subscriber numbers leapt exponentially during the late 1990's in Europe and Asia—we have seen a rapidly developing body of research into its social and cultural effects. It is this explosion of research that this volume aims to capture, from both academic and industry perspectives. At times, the social research into mobile phones has been dwarfed by the concurrent social research into the Internet. The past decade has seen two simultaneous technological revolutions in communication, and we are rapidly heading towards the convergence of them both. The new century has seen a steadily growing body of research into the mobile phone develop, lead by the writers in this volume, that establishes some clear basic tenets for our understanding of the crucial role the mobile phone plays in people's everyday lives.

The over-arching theme of this volume is to investigate the effects of the mobile phone on its user's life and on society as a whole. The book's aim is to reveal their meaning. Its title emphasises the current mode of interaction with the device: the user dials numbers, types text messages, takes pictures or navigates a mobile Internet portal like i-mode in Japan: "Young Japanese have become so adept at their phones—manipulating a set of cursor keys or a button-sized joystick by thumb—that some people refer to a new 'thumb culture'." (Joyce 2000) A Japanese schoolgirl's "thumb moved around the keyboard with the lightning dexterity of Midori playing a violin concerto. 'We call it thumb culture,' said Yumiko Hayashi, my translator. 'It's really frightening sometimes being on the subway and watching all these people talking on cell phones with their thumbs.'" (Friedman 2000) What has already been experienced in Japan around the year 2000, soon started to appear in Western countries. It is this culture of thumbs which defines the meaning of mobile phones for society.

We start this volume with a section beginning with macro-level discussions about the role of the mobile phone. Hans Geser launches the first section by considering the potentially subversive and regressive impact of mobile telephony—re-connecting the individual with a smaller, tighter social world, one which is perhaps solipsistic in its concentration on small individual social networks, oblivious to the larger institutional society surrounding it. Geser argues that the mobile phone achieves this both as an empowering technology, putting communicative power into the hands of the individual, and as a consequence of its mobility, which removes communication across society from stable and formal institutionalised channels into a de-centralised, individualised network. This freedom from the institutionalised tyranny of place and time that Geser identifies as a radical force is one which he argues points towards an almost 'anti-evolutionary' trend backwards from the homogenised culture of the many to a heterogeneous culture of the individual.

The freedom from place and time offered by the mobile phone is developed further in Jonathan Donner's chapter on how the mobile phone is effecting social change in developing countries. Donner's is the first of three chapters in this volume that provide regional focus from around the world for social and ethnographical studies into changes caused by the mobile phone. In Donner's study of Rwandan users, the mobile phone is an expensive and treasured item, used in the main by small individual businessmen and women, where it has the power to expand the horizons of their business and open up their workplace and work schedule, allowing them to organise their work effectively in a way previously unthinkable. In one case documented by Donner, a small restaurateur is able to develop, via the mobile phone, the kind of simple 'just-in-time' stock control management and delivery techniques that large corporations spend millions on IT systems and consultancy to replicate at their scale. At either end of the scale, the business impact of the technology is simple, and is experienced by both Donner's Rwandan restaurateur and large multinational corporations alike. The technology provides a freedom to move through time and space and stay connected to the business, to make decisions for the business, and to run the business according to an ever-changing micro-schedule.

From negotiating individual businesses we move to negotiating the business of being individual in Larrissa Hjorth's study of mobile phone personalisation in an Australian sample group. Hjorth sees the sending of text (SMS) and picture (MMS) messages as crucial to the maintenance of personal social connections. At the centre of this activity is the mobile phone itself, both as a machine for sending messages, and as an artefact that displays a message about the individual users via the personalisation choices they have made. By choosing screensavers, ringtones and faceplates for their phone, Hjorth documents how the users in her study are able to manage the display of their own identity (a fetishisation of the object discussed further in this volume in Leopoldina Fortunati's chapter). Hjorth sees this personalisation as a performative act, after Judith Butler's definition, which proves that gender and identity are not innate but are constantly practised, rehearsed and expressed in everyday life. In the case of the mobile phone, personalisation is therefore seen as an extension of this performative acting of gender and identity, the phone taking on the practised identity of the individual and, through its broadcast of these individual identities via faceplates and ringtones, disseminating this into the immediate social environment of the user.

Genevieve Bell develops these themes of identity management further to look across Asian societies to see how the mobile phone is used to maintain individual identities and social roles within families and tight-knit social groupings. Bell documents how the technological advances of the mobile phone enable new ways of navigating the often complex social structure of Asian society. Rigid hierarchies in such cultures can be more easily deferred to when the name of the caller is displayed to the user before a call is taken. Amongst other things, Bell reveals how one Korean user uses five different ringtones to differentiate five different social groups. This enables the user to prepare the right formal greeting to use before accepting the call, ensuring that she does not offend whoever is calling her. This is an interesting development of the use of ringtones—a movement away from the ringtone identifying the individual owner to the ringtone identifying the social group of the caller—which points to the complex way in which similar technological developments have been utilised for quite different social tasks in cultures across the globe. Bell also discusses how the mobile phone is used specifically to negotiate social interaction between family members, not only in maintaining hierarchies but also in providing a sense of security. Mobile phones are bought for children so that they can be used to communicate with them, but also as a form of *fort/da* game that parents perform with their children, whereby the phone provides a constant umbilical link spooled out from parent to child that the parent is able to use to reassure them of their child's safety and security.

The next two chapters look at these tight familial interactions in more detail. Leslie Haddon builds on his growing body of research into telephony usage by considering what specific problems emerge as sites of tension between groups of users. Haddon uncovers how miscommunication between generations can transfer into mobile phone usage. These communication problems, argues Haddon, stem from fixed-line telephony and are exacerbated by mobile phones. In particular, Haddon discusses how the frustration we often feel when dealing with voicemail and answering machines increases with mobile telephony where there is less chance of the receiving party being genuinely 'out' and unavailable.

Familiar issues about price emerge as motivating factors in conflicts, and the negotiation of the cost of mobile phone calls between family members—specifically parents and children—is a theme returned to in Richard Harper's chapter. Here Harper sees the negotiations around price not as something specific to mobile phones but as an example of a general theme of discussion that the parent has with the child as part of their efforts to prepare them for entering a larger social world than the family. Almost comically, one father in Harper's study refers to his annoyance that his children have stolen his sausages from his fridge. It is not the fact that the sausages have been eaten that annoys the father—he would hardly deny his children food—but the theft is indicative of his children's lack of economic awareness. Harper sees conversations between parents and children like these—about missing sausages, and also about the cost of mobile phone bills—as symbolic, as they are not intended to limit the child's consumption, but more to open a discussion that may make them more aware of the economic and social consequences of their actions. Negotiating phone bills within families is, therefore, a method some parents use to try to prepare their children for a time when they will have to take responsibility for their actions. The management of the mobile phone becomes an activity where moral and ethical codes are discussed with the children.

In the second section, we move away from the macro focus that began section one and begin to focus more tightly on small social groups and the individual, and we begin to approach the subject from a more philosophical angle rather than a sociological one. Continuing on from the focus on the family in Haddon and Harper's chapters, Jane Vincent considers the emotional range of the usage of the mobile phone to maintain relationships between family and friends. As well as the positive emotional associations users had with their mobile phones, Vincent identifies alarming feelings of panic and anxiety amongst users that seem to indicate that the growing reliance we place upon the mobile phone as a device for social connectivity comes with a price when the device is absent. This emotional attachment to the mobile phone is a consequence, Vincent argues, of the investment we have made in our handsets. As well as being personalised—as previously discussed in section one—these devices become the repositories of our memories and social connections in the phone numbers, photos and messages that they store. The phone becomes an icon of 'me, my mobile and my identity' (see Hulme and Truch in this volume), something that embodies our social and emotional life rather than just merely enabling it.

Jane Vincent also identifies the growing problem of managing a private emotional life via what is essentially a device designed for use in public environments.

This is expanded in Joachim Höflich's chapter, which goes on to develop an understanding of the dynamic between these private personal and public social spaces. Höflich sees the phone as an 'indiscreet' technology, one which leaks the personal into the public in a way that mirrors a growing cultural trend across all communications media—for example, as in the growing trend for intrusive reality television such as *Big Brother*. Höflich points out the conflict of this dual public/private role of the mobile phone. Social networks sustained by mobile phones are intensely private—there is no public directory of mobile phone numbers — and yet the contents of the conversations within these private social networks are often performed in very public spaces. Höflich takes a European perspective within his study, detailing data from his research that shows where there are distinct cultural differences between sometimes close neighbouring countries in what is perceived to be permissible and what is not in public mobile phone usage. What is clear is that concepts of public and private space regarding mobile phone usage do no travel well—behaviour accepted in the Nordic countries is not in more Mediterranean countries, and vice-versa. It is clear that the mobile phone redefines the sense of personal and public space, whilst also reflecting what may perhaps be more deeply rooted national cultural and social behaviours.

These concepts of social spaces return in Michael Hulme and Anna Truch's chapter on 'Interspace', in which a new field in between the established ones of home, work and social lives is developed. Hulme and Truch argue that the mobility of the device allows what has previously been a transitory space to become a social field in its own right. Following on from spontaneous comments from the subjects in their study, they define this space as increasingly important. Throughout the present volume, the way in which the mobile phone stretches boundaries of social time and space is returned to. In this chapter this stretching opens up a whole new territory, which becomes a place of negotiation that exists in the travels the individual subject makes between the more formalised spaces. Echoing comments made by Hans Geser in the first chapter, Hulme and Truch define this space as one of transition between established, more formalised fields; one of overlapping fields—in interspace the individual is juggling roles from a variety of social fields, creating a subjective habitus, to borrow from Bourdieu, managing many social identities via the device. The strategies needed to manage this new social space are complex, but we can find evidence in previous chapters of how the very technology that created this space can also provide tools to manage it (Genevieve Bell's Korean subject using ringtones to manage her many identities comes to mind). Again, the phone amplifies multiple social identities for the user as well as providing a means to manage them.

Leopoldina Fortunati has lead the academic field in recent years in her research into this transformative personal effect of the mobile phone. In her chapter in this volume she specifically focuses on how we come to associate ourselves so tightly with the device that it becomes a fetishised technological artefact. Looking at the design of the mobile phone (something Laura Watts discusses in her later chapter), Fortunati discusses how the mobile phone becomes fetishised because of our investment into it of our complex emotional feelings (as discussed by Jane Vincent in this volume). Fortunati sees the mobile phone, distinct from other technologies, as being the most able to be fetishised through the senses, through fashion, through the synaesthetic properties that we can design into it, until it almost disappears as a technological artefact, becoming 'a more fashionable and seductive object, somewhere between accessory and jewel'.

Kristóf Nyíri then neatly encapsulates a number of the threads throughout sections one and two, proposing that mobile communication is actually a retrogressive step, returning us to a more immediate, unalienated form of communication that relies heavily on the visual and the oral via MMS messages and voice calls. Again echoing the chapter by Hans Geser, Nyíri argues that the phone re-establishes a sense of personal, micro-social community that is in direct contrast to the more formalised, structured organisation that has been prevalent in modernist thinking. This is a 'new-old age' in which the mobile phone 'promises to re-establish, within the life of post-modern society, some of the features formerly enjoyed by genuine local communities'.

We close the second, wholly academically focused section of the book with James Katz's summation of current research trends and his forecasts of the future research trends which seem to be emerging. Katz has been a leading light in the development of research into the social impact of mobile phones for a number of years, and it is fitting that he closes this section with predictions of where the research area is headed next.

The third section of the book provides a variety of perspectives both from and on the mobile phone industry. As mobile saturation increases, operators find it harder and harder to differentiate themselves in the marketplace. Two chapters discuss this aspect in particular. Initially, Raimund Schmolze discusses the many problems faced by mobile operators in trying to develop and market the products that a divergent, segmented customer base requires. Operators have had to develop strategies as quickly as the industry has developed, and in recent years have found themselves increasingly moving away from their core market of voice service provision to becoming anything from fashion brands to putative multimedia companies. The variety of skills needed to manage these tasks has seen operators stretched to their limits, and from an industry perspective Schmolze discusses how this challenges operators both now and in the future. From the consumer's perspective, Peter Gross and Stefan Bertschi discuss how a customer navigates such a 'multi-option' society. Bewildered by choices—not just in service level and provision but in the way these products are coded with brands that suggest identities and cultural behaviour—how is a consumer to relate to such a plurality of options?

From one of the industry's governing bodies—the International Telecommunication Union (ITU)—Lara Srivastava examines the mania that has accompanied the exponential rise in mobile phone usage, arguing that a whole new set of mobile manners have emerged that are in use in different cultures around the world. Srivastava's perspective on mobile culture allows us to approach recent industry developments from an academic standpoint, as does Nicola Döring and Alex Gundolf's chapter on the development of 'moblogs' or mobile weblogs. Pointing to the convergence of mobile and Internet technology, 'moblogs' provide a means for users to archive their lives via photos that can be taken via a mobile phone and viewed via the Internet. Nokia have named their product to provide this service 'lifeblog', and it is this uncensored publication of everyday life that Döring and Gundolf investigate, from subjects as mundane as a user capturing his waking state everyday, to as personally and globally historic as the moblog by a US soldier in Iraq. What we are seeing in the 'moblog' is how organically some product development is in the mobile world—the early moblogging software came not from operators, handset or software manufacturers but from the social software community that thrives on the Internet. It is precisely this level of organic, spontaneous product development that occurs as a by-product of networked communities that many companies seek—and often fail—to emulate. Laura Watts offers us a (partially fictionalised) ethnographic account of how this is being attempted within the mobile handset design industry.

Finally, we close the third section of the volume with two strikingly divergent views from senior industry figures on where the future of the mobile industry lies. Paul Golding points to a technologically-led future where the convergence and increased performance of mobile phone hardware and software, coupled with the continuing miniaturisation of the components, will lead to more reliance upon the phone in everyday life and also the disappearance of the technology as artefact—as suggested by Leopoldina Fortunati earlier. Nick Foggin, however, is more circumspect in his predictions, suggesting that existing data products have been a draw on precious resources for operators, neither generating revenues nor serving the needs of the consumers they are supposedly developed for. Foggin closes by suggesting that it is time we accept (as Jane Vincent suggests in her chapter) that it is the positive reinforcement of person-to-person communication in which the mobile phone excels, not as a one-size-fits-all super-computer in our pockets.

We conclude the book with the project that initiated both this volume and the one-day symposium at the London Science Museum in 2004 that many of these chapters come from. Peter Glotz and Stefan Bertschi have managed a Delphi study involving a collection of industry and academic experts that investigates opinions across all aspects of social and cultural developments concerning mobile phones. Whilst it draws some conclusions, opinions are clearly divided. What is clear is that whilst the future development of both the industry and academic study are unpredictable, the almost tyrannical hold the mobile phone has on our lives now is far too tight for it to be loosened and ebb away.

Finally, before letting the reader explore the cornucopia of meanings of mobile phones for society, the editors should like to thank all of those who helped to realise this book. They are too many to be listed here—amongst them are the many contributors and all others who know that we are grateful for their support. The research project 'Thumb Culture' was carried out in cooperation with and funded by T-Mobile International. Without their initiative the present volume would not exist. With transcript in Bielefeld, Germany we are glad having found a particularly suitable publisher for our volume. Karin Werner and Gero Wierichs made it a pleasure to bring our vision into the present shape. Now we hope that the reader has as much fun and valuable insights reading this book as we had bringing it to life.

References

Friedman, Thomas L. (2000), 'Brave New World', *The New York Times*, 22 September.

Joyce, Colin (2000), 'Japanese give thumbs-up to silent mobiles', *The Daily Telegraph*, 7 August.

Section One—Cultural Identities

Is the cell phone undermining the social order? Understanding mobile technology from a sociological perspective

HANS GESER

Introduction

Since its invention in 1876, the telephone has interested very few sociologists because it is too exclusively connected with the very lowest level of social life: the level of bilateral interaction. The Internet arouses much more interest because it is a far more universal technology and able to support multilateral relationships of all kinds; resulting in virtual groups, communities and organizations, as well as trans-societal networks, on a local, regional as well as on a global scale.

Within the scant theorizing available we find extremely contradictory positions. On the one hand, the phone is seen as a medium of organization. It enables the real-time integration of highly complex organizations as well as myriad coordination processes within cities that could not be realized on the basis of face-to-face interaction. As a substitute, people would have to adopt the role of moving messengers most of the time (e.g. Lasen 2002: 20, 26; Townsend 2000).

On the other hand, German sociologist Hans Paul Bahrdt considers the phone to be a "medium of disorganization" which produces anarchy by enabling everybody to reach everybody else directly, without observing formalized channels of communication (Bahrdt 1958). Such disruptive effects are especially pronounced in model bureaucracies that allow only vertical (not diagonal) communicative flows. Evidently, the phone is "regressive", at least in the sense that it supports the oldest mode of verbal exchange: oral communication. In this way it reduces the usage of letters or other written documents (which future historians could use for reconstructing our present time) and in addition enables even illiterates to engage in trans-spatial communication.

In this chapter, it is maintained that this "regressive" and "subversive" impact of landline phones is very much amplified and generalized by mobile phone devices, because they empower informal micro-social networks to communicate much more efficiently beyond any institutional control.

When visiting Paris in summer 2004, after many years of absence, the author was suddenly struck by seeing so few bistro guests reading newspapers, and so many engaged in mobile phone conversation. This raises the question as to whether the cell phone has a generalized capacity (or even, an effect) to direct the free-time resources of individuals to the sphere of personal interaction: thus shielding them from new acquaintances in their environment as well as from messages originating in the larger world.

Four regressive impacts on social and societal structures

Looking into the fascinating history of communications media, it is remarkable how much emphasis has been given to the development and implementation of various "one-to-many" media with the capacity to empower centralized and formalized organizations: for example, the printing press, radio and TV. All these one-to-many media share the fact that they invade the private sphere of individuals with propaganda, commercials or other messages that serve the interest of enterprises, governments, political parties or other collective entities that are not usually part of daily life. As a stationary device, the landline phone also supports supra-individual institutions by connecting locally fixed offices and by forcing individuals to be at a certain place and to use such institutionally provided intermediaries for entering into mutual communication.

By contrast, current digital technologies have given rise to various innovations with at least some capacity for slowing down or even reversing this long-term trend. Thus, the Internet certainly empowers individuals by providing everybody with identical technical capacities for engaging in any kind of bilateral or multilateral interaction, for researching information, or for publishing his or her personal views on a worldwide scale—and all of this at a minimum of cost and effort, without any spatial restrictions.

Similarly, the mobile phone empowers and enlarges the sphere of micro-social interaction by making individuals free to reach each other under any circumstances and without the need to conform to institutional norms that demand a presence in a specific place (and a relationship with others present at this same location). The seeds are therefore sown for a long-term countertrend that may lead to a major shift from supra-individual collectives (like bureaucratic organizations) based on stable locations and depersonalized formal rules to decentralized networks based on ongoing inter-individual interaction.

Looking at the usage patterns of cell phones shown by children and friends, and studying the still scarce empirical research findings on this same topic, the author increasingly has the impression that, apart from diverting attention from mass media, there are several other aspects in which the cell phone works as an "antievolutionary device" by promoting the retrogression to more simple, "pre-modern" patterns of social life.

In at least four different ways, the mobile phone seems to undermine or even reverse long-term trends of societal development thought to be irreversible, at least since the inception of the industrial revolution and the rise of larger bureaucratic organizations. This falsifies well-established macro-sociological theories hitherto used to model the development of modern societies:

1) by increasing the pervasiveness of primary, particularistic social bonds,
2) by reducing the need for time-based scheduling and coordination,
3) by undermining institutional boundary controls and replacing location-based with person-based communicative systems,
4) by providing support for anachronistic "pervasive roles".

The new pervasiveness of primary social bonds

Despite its technical capacity for making any individuals immediately accessible to each other, the landline phone has nevertheless contributed to strengthening ties among people already familiar with each other (e.g. in the neighbourhood or community), while its contribution to larger social networking has been rather modest (Lasen 2002: 25).

Cell phones can even more effectively be used to shield oneself from wider surroundings by escaping into the narrower realm of highly familiar, predictable and self-controlled social relationships with close kin or friends (Fortunati 2000; Portes 1998). Such tendencies are supported by the fact that, in contrast to fixed phone numbers, which are usually publicized in phone books, cell phone numbers are usually only communicated to a narrow circle of self-selected friends and acquaintances. In this way, no calls from unpredictable new sources (including insurance salespeople, telephone survey institutions etc.) need to be feared (Ling 2000).

Mobile phones may therefore support tendencies towards closure rather than towards the opening up to new acquaintances. This function is highlighted by the empirical finding that in Finland, ownership of mobile phones is most frequent among members of two or three-person households (Puro 2002: 20), not among single people. In Italy, usage is highest among individuals who maintain close contact with their kin (Fortunati 2002: 56). Similarly, Koreans have been found to use the cell phone much more for strengthening existing social ties than for initiating new ties (Park 2003). Finally, a Japanese study shows that one of the major functions of web phones is to get into contact with nearby friends (Miyata et. al. 2003).[1]

As Fox vividly describes, the cell phone can function as a powerful tool for re-establishing the fluid, casual modes of informal communication typical to traditional communal life. In this way it counteracts the loss of communalistic social integration caused by traditional media, as well as the depersonalization of modern urban life (Fox 2001).

> "[...] this for me is the essential thing about mobile phones: they enable the type of (virtual) communication and interaction that characterizes pre-modernity: people who never move far, live in small towns and villages near each other, everybody knows where everybody else is etc. But being virtual, this kind of communication is no longer bound to any single locality, as was the case in pre-modern times." (Roos 2001)

While the intrusion of strangers can be reduced, circles of established friendships can be deepened because a higher density of communication within such circles can be maintained, irrespective of time and place (Ling 2000).

Given their capacity to retain primary social relationships over distance, the use of cell phones can be matched by regressive psychological tendencies: e.g. with the need to cushion the traumatic experiences of foreign environments by remaining tightly connected to loved ones at home. In this way, the mobile can function as a "pacifier for adults" that reduces feelings of loneliness and vulnerability in any place and at any time. A similar metaphor conceptualizes the cell phone as an "umbilical cord", making social emancipation processes more gradual and less traumatic by allowing parents and children to retain a permanent channel of communication during periods of spatial distance (Palen/Salzman/Youngs 2001; Ling 2004: 48).

Given the constant availability of external communication partners (as sources of opinion and advice), individuals may easily unlearn the ability to rely on their own judgment, memory and reflection. They therefore regress to a state of infantile dependency on a consistently narrow circle of "significant others"—even in cases where these people might be 10,000 miles away (Plant 2001: 62). As a consequence, individuals may become less prone to develop certain "social competencies": e.g. the ability to react adaptively to unpredictable encounters, participate in conversations about unforeseen topics, form quick impressions

1. The broad relevance of such "regressive" modes of usage is vividly illustrated by the results of the pan-European EURESCOM study of 1999, where almost 85 per cent of younger users (aged 14-24) shared the opinion that "a mobile telephone helps one to stay in steady contact with family and friends." (Ling 2004: 60)

and judgments about new acquaintances, or learn quickly how to conform in new "collocal" gatherings and groups (Fortunati 2000).

While the fixed phone has promoted the diffusion of universal linguistic expressions (like "Hello", "Pronto", etc.), the cell phone seems to support the Balkanization of language into numerous particularistic subcultures characterized by a highly informal style of expression (Ling 2004: 145ff.). Given such an empowerment of informal language, schools may have increasing difficulties imposing formal writing styles on individuals who permanently use a very different jargon when writing their SMS (or when chatting on the web).

The decline of time-based scheduling and coordination

Continuous campfire sites established more than 500,000 years ago testify to the skills of emerging hominids to reach agreement about convening at the same place at a specific hour (or day). Since then, evolutionary advances of human societies have been closely associated with an increasing capacity to use timekeeping for purposes of social coordination.

Since the early 13th century, artificial clocks have increasingly replaced natural indicators (e.g. the position of the sun, moon or stars): thereby making coordination more precise and independent of geographical location (Landes 1983; Ling 2004: 64). Since the 17th century, philosophers have used the clock as a paradigm for modelling a universe where everything that occurs is strictly determined in advance, and since the 18th century, *"the clock, not the steam engine is the key machine of our industrial age"* (Mumford 1963: 14). The life of contemporary individuals is increasingly permeated by time regulations forced upon them by formal institutions: by the time-tables of railways and buses, by the opening hours of shops, the scheduling of school classes, or the rigid daily, weekly and yearly oscillations of work hours and leisure time.

Under conventional technological conditions, preplanning was inevitable because people had no means of communicating at later points in time (especially if they were already on the move). Taking this perspective, it is evident that cell phones reduce the need for temporal preplanning, insofar as rearrangements can be made at any moment, even very shortly before an agreed time. A new, more fluid culture of informal social interaction therefore can emerge, one which is less based on ex-ante agreements, but more on current ad hoc coordination according to short-term changes in circumstances, opportunities, or subjective preferences and moods (Ling/Yttri 1999; Ling 2004: 69ff.).

"The old schedule of minutes, hours, days, and weeks becomes shattered into a constant stream of negotiations, reconfigurations, and rescheduling. One can be interrupted or interrupt friends and colleagues at any time. Individuals living in this phone space can never let it go, because it is their primary link to the temporally, spatially fragmented network of friends and colleagues they have constructed for themselves." (Townsend 2000)

Such social settings are "real-time systems" where everything happening is conditioned by *current* situations, while the impact of the past (effected through rules and schedules) and of the future (impinging in the form of planning activities) declines (Townsend 2000; Plant 2001: 64). Transnational empirical studies have shown that such contributions to the coordination of everyday activities are universally recognized as one of the most outstanding advantages of new technology. Rich Ling judges them to be "the greatest social consequence" of mobile telephony (Ling 2004: 58f.).

The extremely high penetration rate of the mobile in Italy seems to be associated with the spontaneous, disorganized lifestyle that has always reigned among most of the country's population (Fortunati 2002: 55). To the degree that this deregulation takes place, there is a growing discrepancy between the sphere of informal, interpersonal relationships and the realm of formal organizations and institutions (where time scheduling is relentlessly maintained). As a consequence, there are more tensions at the interface of these two discrepant worlds: e.g. when public transport timetables limit the spontaneity of intra-urban movement, or when schools and work organizations experience growing difficulties in imposing norms of punctuality on children and youths no longer accustomed to scheduling their daily life (Ling 2004: 77f.).[2]

The Deregulation of Institutional Boundary Controls and the Shift from Location-Based to Person-Based Social Systems

In the view of Spencer, Parsons, Luhmann and many other reputable theorists, the major defining characteristic of modern society is its outstanding degree of differentiation along functional (instead of ethnic or stratified) lines. In other words: the net of social reality is woven by complementary relationships between highly autonomous institutional orders and other functional subsystems, each cultivating its own distinctive views, values and norms. A closer look reveals that such autonomy is heavily based on spatial segregation. By insulating social systems from their general social environment, the preconditions have been created for subjecting them to processes of systematic (e.g. technological and organizational) development and specialization.

2. Similarly, there is a growing gap between small groups (especially pairs) where ad hoc coordination by cell phone can be fully effective, and larger groupings that must still rely on more conventional, time-based pre-scheduling modes (Ling 2004: 77).

Modern economic systems are therefore anchored in industrial organizations that have separated work processes from their traditional embedment in family households or other institutional settings. Modern medicine, for example, would be unthinkable without hospitals where patients are spatially concentrated for systematic diagnosis and treatment (Foucault 1963).

While designed for talking at a distance, landline phones have paradoxically facilitated dense aggregations of people in space, for example by supporting communication within large-sized firms (Townsend 2000). Similarly, the fixed phone had a stabilizing impact on location-based social orders because it created communicative connections between stationary, supra-individual systems (e.g. offices or households) rather than individual members. Thus, it still fundamentally belongs to the historical era of "place-to-place networks". Just as people had to *go somewhere* to meet someone, they also had to *phone somewhere* in order to communicate with a specific person (Wellman 2001).

By contrast, cell phones undermine these traditional orders by creating direct links between particular individuals: irrespective of their institutional role and location. They tend to weaken the control of all formal institutions over their members' behaviour. This is because they provide the opportunity for all members to reduce or interrupt their formal role involvements by engaging in alternative role behaviour and wholly private interactions anywhere and anytime: e.g. during office hours, school lessons or military duties, and when driving a car or piloting a plane. Schools therefore come under pressure to allow pupils to use cell phones, because their parents are eager to keep in touch with them at any time, whenever needed (Mathews 2001).

Under such new circumstances, centralized institutional control of system boundaries is more difficult to maintain, because it is no longer achieved as a simple correlate of physical walls or spatial distances, but has to be actively upheld by constant controlling procedures (e.g. by preventing employees from using mobile phones for private purposes).

Cell phones undermine the basic notion that physical and communicative isolation are tightly correlated, so that measures on the "hardware" level of physical allocation and transportation are no longer sufficient to produce parallel effects in the loftier "software" sphere of interpersonal communication. They introduce an element of entropy into all social groups and institutions anchored in places or territories, because they permeate them with communicative relationships that transcend system boundaries in highly heterogeneous and unpredictable ways (Agre 2001).

Homes, churches or school buildings will of course continue to symbolize the unity of families, parishes or schools as organizations and institutions. However, they may become "empty shells" without much determining influence on what is "really going on" on the level of social communication and cooperation.

SUPPORT FOR THE SURVIVAL (OR RE-ESTABLISHMENT) OF ANACHRONISTIC "PERVASIVE ROLES"

Cell phones can be instrumental in preserving diffuse, pervasive roles which demand that the individual is available almost all the time, because such encompassing availability can be upheld even when people are highly mobile and involved in other activities. In this way, mothers can use mobile phones as "umbilical cords" to their children, so that they are in contact with them the whole day even when they are at work or travelling. Paradoxically, the cell phone could make it easier to perpetuate (rather than to eliminate) traditional forms of labour division between the genders, because mothers are still available as traditional "caregivers" even while working (Ling 2004: 63). The husbands of successful "remote mothers" may feel it more legitimate to evade family duties.[3] Similarly, traditional family doctors can be available to their patients whenever needed, even if attending a dinner party or at some other private location. Male business owners can also preserve a traditional patriarchal leadership role, which demands their availability around the clock. This can inhibit processes of organizational differentiation because these businesspeople remain "on duty" all the time instead of delegating responsibility to subordinates.

In general, the cell phone can give new impetus to the old-fashioned idea that individuals "belong" exclusively to particular groups, communities or organizations—to which they have to be committed unconditionally for limitless hours. This idea clashes totally with all of the recent societal developments that have provided a secure basis for individual autonomy: for the individual capacity of everyone to maintain a secure private sphere as well as to divide his or her commitment to several segregated roles.

Empirical studies indicate that the needs to increase "safety" and "security" are the most prominent motives for adopting cell phones (Ling 2004: 35ff.). This implies that most users are ready to tolerate the loss of personal freedom inevitably associated with such gains in social involvement and personal protection. The freedoms gained by being able to connect to anybody from anywhere at any time is therefore at least partially offset by the increasing obligation to answer incoming calls and to "keep in touch" with kin and friends who expect to be con-

3. Consequently, the cell phone may enable women to retain the traditional "social administrator" role they have taken on by being the ones usually answering the fixed phone at home (Ling 2004: 63).

tacted (Bachen 2001). In addition, a whole gamut of newly emerging reciprocity norms have to be observed: by responding promptly with an equivalent message that must not be standardized (such as a canned joke), but produced ad hoc for the specific occasion (Ling 2004: 153). In fact:

"one higher order consequence of wireless communication is that it makes us more responsible, for both our own actions and those of people for whom we have assumed responsibility. In effect, we become more subject to social control". (Katz 1999: 17)

In contrast to many earlier negative visions of an emerging "surveillance society" (Marx), it is less likely to be some sort of "Big Brother" wishing to trace our whereabouts than it is our own "little brother", sister, parent or child. In other words: the Orwellian visions of "totalitarian control" emanating from unlimited governmental and mass media power have given way to a sort of "neo-communitarian" control emerging from a denser horizontal cohesion of informal groupings facilitated by the ubiquity of mobile digital communication.

Some preliminary conclusions

To view the mobile phone as a transformative factor of contemporary society means adopting Georg Simmel's view that even the largest societal structures and institutions are determined from below. This means they emerge from the numerous tiny, inter-individual interactions ("Wechselwirkungen") not subject to encompassing planning and control. While *conventional mass media (and fixed phones)* have primarily supported centralized, formalized organizations, households and other supra-individual systems, *cell phones* increase the reach and capacity of decentralized, informal systems based on inter-individual interactions. In this way mobile phones decelerate or even reverse long-term evolutionary trends of human society: trends toward stable, depersonalized, formalized, complex and predictable supra-individual institutions.

Firstly, the cell phone is prone to increase the pervasiveness of the most intimate personal relationships in individual life. Anywhere and anytime, we can evade unfamiliar contacts in public places, bridge time gaps of loneliness and avoid reliance on our own judgement by contacting our loved ones at home. This increases the extent to which social life is filled out with the most simple of relationships: bilateral interaction. It offers an easy escape route from unfamiliar public encounters and from more complex multilateral situations, thus limiting the possibilities for acquiring more demanding "social competencies".

Secondly, a decline in time-based scheduling and the re-emergence of spontaneous, unpredictable patterns of social life is likely.

Long-term evolutionary trends toward planning, scheduling and temporal discipline come to a halt, giving way to spontaneous, ad-hoc coordination according to current whims and circumstances. Social life therefore becomes more unpredictable and more complex forms of social cooperation may become more difficult to create and maintain.

Thirdly, in a very general way, mobile phones undermine the traditional mechanisms that have secured segregation between different social systems. Instead, each individual is now burdened with the task of regulating the boundaries between different social relationships, groupings, organizations or institutions.

Fourthly, cell phones support the maintenance of highly pervasive social roles that bind individuals wholly into particular groups, communities or occupational functions. This diminishes their capacity for keeping a separate private life or maintaining any other commitments.

In all these four aspects, a kind of "disintermediation" takes place: in the sense that the mediating contribution of supra-individual institutions is no longer required for realizing and coordinating informal interactions, because such informal interactions can be initiated and maintained by direct interpersonal communication. This is most vividly illustrated by the declining relevance of objective time as a medium of interactive coordination:

> "In a sense, mobile telephones allow us to cut out the 'middleman'. Rather than relying on a secondary system—which may not necessarily be synchronized—mobile telephony allows for direct interaction." (Ling 2004: 70)

Another disintermediation effect is seen in the case of adolescents who have no further need to meet in public places in order to decide about common endeavours because such decisions can easily made directly from home. This again encourages a social life that is exclusively taking place inside homes—thereby reducing the relevance of public localities and events altogether (Ling 2004: 102).

To quote the famous terminology of Habermas, this would imply that the recognized "colonization of the everyday life-world by formalized systems" would give way to a countervailing trend in which the life-world will increasingly encroach on systemic institutions. This can be seen, for example, in the way that schoolchildren cannot be prevented from reading and writing SMS messages during class, or that even religious services are nowadays interrupted by mobile calls.

By facilitating highly informal, spontaneous modes of social cooperation, the cell phone promotes collectively acting networks that operate on the very lowest level of organization. This involves actors that remain opaque and incalculable because they do not manifest themselves in terms of explicit formal organization. The problematic downside of these developments can be seen vividly in the case of clandestine terrorist groups that use the cell phone for remote detonations, or in the case of highly "chaotic" anti-globalisation movements that act without leadership and explicit planning because they constantly re-specify their collective actions by means of mobile communication (Klein 2000).

Given its affinity with informal, non-institutional social spheres, the cell phone may be most useful for more marginal population groups (e.g. children, adolescents, migrants, the jobless or retirees) not integrated into work roles or other stationary institutions.

In our own societies, it seems that the unrestricted public usage of mobile phones is more suited to lower-class culture than to middle- and higher-class settings. Studies show that the intrusive effects of cell phone calls are much better tolerated in proletarian restaurants than in higher-class dining rooms (Mars/Nicod 1984; Ling 1997). From a worldwide perspective, the cell phone may be particularly popular with populations used to living in a sub-institutional world of social informality, by people who have never been much affected by the standards of Western formal bureaucracies and the tyranny of time-based regulations.

The "digital divide" separating high and low user groups is therefore of a much different kind than that associated with the PC and the World Wide Web (Ling 2004: 15). Considering its affinity with lower-class culture, the cell phone could well become a "negative status symbol" in the future: so that its explicit *non-use* or even *conspicuous absence* would increasingly become an indicator of positive social distinction.

References

Agre, Philip E. (2001), 'Changing Places: Contexts of Awareness in Computing', *Human-Computer Interaction*, 16 (2-3), http://dlis.gseis.ucla.edu/people/pagre/hci.html (14 July 2005).

Bachen, Christina (2001), 'The Family in the Networked Society: A Summary of Research on the American Family', Santa Clara University, CA: Center for Science, Technology and Society, http://sts.scu.edu/nexus/Issue1-1/Bachen_TheNetworkedFamily.asp (14 July 2005).

Bahrdt, Hans Paul (1958), *Industriebürokratie*, Stuttgart: Enke.

Fortunati, Leopoldina (2000), 'The Mobile Phone: New Social Categories and Relations', Presented at 'Sosiale Konsekvenser av Mobiltelefoni Seminar', Oslo, 16 June.

Fortunati, Leopoldina (2002), 'Italy: Stereotypes, true and false', In: Katz, James E./Aakhus, Mark A. (Eds.), *Perpetual Contact. Mobile Communication, Private Talk, Public Performance*, Cambridge: Cambridge University Press, 42-62.

Foucault, Michel (1963), *La naissance de la clinique*, Paris: Edition Page.

Fox, Kate (2001), 'Evolution, Alienation and Gossip. The role of mobile telecommunications in the 21st century', Oxford: Social Issues Research Center, http://www.sirc.org/publik/gossip.shtml (14 July 2005).

Katz, James E. (1999), *Connections. Social and Cultural Studies of the Telephone in American Life*, New Brunswick, NJ: Transaction Publishers.

Klein, Naomi (2000), 'The Vision Thing', *The Nation*, 10 July, http://www.commondreams.org/views/062300-103.htm (14 July 2005).

Landes, David S. (1983), *Revolution in Time: Clocks and the Making of the Modern World*, Cambridge, Mass.: Belknap Press.

Lasen, Amparo (2002), *The Social Shaping of Fixed and Mobile Networks: A Historical Comparison*, University of Surrey: DWRC, http: //www.surrey.ac.uk/dwrc/Publications/HistComp.pdf (14 July 2005).

Ling, Rich (2000), 'Direct and Mediated Interaction in the Maintenance of Social Relationships', In: Sloane, Andy and van Rijn, Felix (Eds.), *Home Informatics and Telematics: Information, Technology and Society*, Boston: Kluwer, 61-86.

Ling, Rich/Yttri, Brigitte (1999), *'Nobody Sits at Home and Waits for the Telephone to Ring': Micro and Hyper-Coordination through the Use of the Mobile Telephone*. Telenor Forskning og Utvikling, FoU Rapport 30.

Ling, Rich (2004), *The Mobile Connection. The Cell Phone's Impact on Society*, San Francisco: Morgan Kaufmann.

Mars, Gerald/Nicod, Michael (1984), *The World of Waiters*, London: George Allen & Unwin.

Marx, Gary (1988), *Undercover. Surveillance in America*, Berkeley: University of California Press.

Mathews, Joe (2001), 'Cell Phones on Campus Advocated', *Los Angeles Times*, 30 September.

Miyata, Kakuko et al. (2003), 'The Mobile-izing Japanese: Connecting to the Internet by PC and Webphone in Yamanashi', Presented at the conference 'Front Stage/Back Stage and the Renegotiation of the Social Sphere', Grimstad, Norway, 22-24 June.

Mumford, Lewis (1963), *Technics and Civilization*, San Diego: Harvest Books.

Palen, Leysia/Salzman, Marilyn/Youngs, Ed (2001), 'Going Wireless: Behavior & Practice of New Mobile Phone Users', Boulder CO, http://www.cs.colorado.edu/~palen/Papers/cscwPalen.pdf (14 July 2005).

Park, Woong Ki (2003), 'Mobile Phone Addiction: A case study of Korean college students', Presented at the conference 'Front Stage/Back Stage and the Renegotiation of the Social Sphere', Grimstad, Norway, 22-24 June.

Plant, Sadie (2001), *On the mobile. The effects of mobile telephones on social and individual life*, commissioned by Motorola, http://www.motorola.com/mot/doc/0/234_MotDoc.pdf (14 July 2005).

Portes, Alejandro (1998), 'Social Capital: its origins and applications in modern sociology', *Annual Review of Sociology*, 24, 1-24.

Puro, Jukka-Pekka (2002), 'Finland: a mobile culture', In: Katz, James E./Aakhus, Mark A. (Eds.), *Perpetual Contact. Mobile Communication, Private Talk, Public Performance*, Cambridge: Cambridge University Press, 19-29.

Roos, Jeja Pekka (2001), 'Post Modernity and Mobile Communications', ESA Helsinki Conference, August, http://www.valt.helsinki.fi/staff/jproos/mobilezation.htm (14 July 2005).

Townsend, Anthony M. (2000), 'Life in the Real-Time City: Mobile Telephones and Urban Metabolism', *Journal of Urban Technology*, (7) 2, 85-104, http://urban.blogs.com/research/JUT-LifeRealTime.pdf (14 July 2005).

Wellman, Barry (2001), 'Physical Place and Cyber Place. The Rise of Personalized Networking', *International Journal of Urban and Regional Research*, 25, http://www.chass.utoronto.ca/~wellman/publications/individualism/ijurr3a1.htm (14 July 2005).

The social and economic implications of mobile telephony in Rwanda: An ownership/access typology

JONATHAN DONNER

Introduction

This chapter will explore the social and economic implications of the rapid adoption of mobile telephony in Sub-Saharan Africa, drawing particularly on examples from Rwanda. It will contrast the experiences of three groups of people: those who own a telephone, those who rely on public telephones, and those without access to any telephone at all. While some universal patterns of mobile use are evident, the exercise will also highlight ways in which mobile adoption has different implications in an environment of limited landline availability.

One overarching theme of telecommunications in Africa is the persistent scarcity of telephones of any kind. The International Telecommunication Union (ITU 2004a) estimates that in 2003 across Europe there were 96.3 telephone subscribers—fixed and mobile combined—per 100 people. In the Americas, there were 66.6 subscribers per 100. In Africa, there were 8.7 per 100. Africa's telephone subscribers are concentrated in cities, and in the relatively more prosperous nations on the continent, particularly South Africa and Botswana.

Despite this scarcity, a second theme is the rapid increase of mobile telephone users in the region. Africa is the world's fastest growing mobile market (ITU 2004b). By 2003, 67 percent of the total telephone subscriptions in Africa were mobile lines, compared to 50 percent in the Americas and 58 percent in Europe (ITU 2004b). Landline penetration in the region continues to grow, but slowly. Meanwhile, from Senegal to Somalia, mobile providers are adding base stations and customers as quickly as possible.

These dual themes of overall telephone scarcity and increasing mobile use provide the rationale for this chapter's typology. 'Private phone owners', 'public phone users' and 'telephone non-users' are categories that will remain salient in Africa for years to come. However, rapid mobile adoption is changing the composition of the groups: new *mobile-only* owners are joining the ranks of the phone-owners, once the domain of only the most prosperous households. Meanwhile, mobile-based payphones are extending the reach of shared connectivity, allowing more frequent use of phones among those who cannot afford or access a telephone subscription of their own.

Rwanda suffered through a devastating civil war and genocide in 1994. Relative stability has returned to the country, but poverty remains the everyday reality for many. Though Kigali is a vibrant small city, most of Rwanda's eight million inhabitants live in rural areas and rely on agriculture for their livelihoods (CIA 2004). Thus, Rwanda's experiences with both urban and rural telecommunications challenges make it illustrative for the region. Rwanda's mobile provider, MTN Rwanda Cell, began offering GSM service in 1998. By 2003, Rwanda had 1.6 mobile subscriptions per 100 people compared with 0.28 landlines (ITU 2004b). Coverage now extends to all of Rwanda's major cities and commercial centers, though parts of the countryside remain without a signal.

This brief review will draw on the results of a series of studies conducted in Rwanda, as well as on references to recent studies and initiatives from elsewhere in Sub-Saharan Africa. The participants in the Rwanda studies are micro-entrepreneurs—owners of small businesses, generally with fewer than 5 employees, which are critical to urban economies in the developing world (Mead & Leidholm 1998; Santos 1979). The initial study was a Q-sort (prioritization) exercise, in which 31 micro-entrepreneurs articulated their perspectives on mobile use (Donner 2003). A broader survey in Kigali focused on the list of recent calls stored on user's phones to assess "whom micro-entrepreneurs call, and why" (Donner 2004a; 2005a). Most recently, we conducted open-ended interviews on topics ranging from business-specific uses to social coordination (Donner 2005b).

Private phone owners

We start with what remains the smallest of the three groups in the typology: those individuals (or households) who own their own telephone. In the days before the widespread use of mobiles, membership of this group was easy to discern; only the most prosperous Rwandan households had the income, bank accounts, credit, status, proximity, and/or political clout to get a landline installed (Panos 2004). Now, there are two paths to private phone ownership: landline purchase (still reserved for the most prosperous) and mobile handset purchase (open to a wider range of Rwandan society).

Mobile and landline owners

Many fortunate households with landlines were among the first to purchase mobiles. Landline-owning households still represent a disproportionately large share of Rwanda's mobile users, since nearly every wealthy Rwandan now owns a mobile. In many ways, the trajectory of mobile adoption resembles that found in Europe and the United States, as the technology was adopted first by business, professional, and government elites before making its way into broader domestic/personal use (Katz 1999). These prosperous households welcomed the mobile in the same way their counterparts in Europe did—as an additional *mobile* telephone line which could complement and extend the reach of landlines at home and at work. As elsewhere, purchasing decisions for this group mix instrumental and intrinsic dimensions. Though certainly convenient, mobiles are also symbol of affluence and a source of comfort and security (Donner 2003).

The mobile is not simply a complement to the landline for those who possess both. It is a competitor for the same calls (Hamilton 2003). Since MTN Rwanda Cell's international rates have consistently been lower than those of the landline provider, RwandaTel, some households purchase mobiles to save on international calls. This rate competition will benefit all telecommunications consumers in the country in the long run by putting downward pressure on prices. Some users are 'cutting the cord' altogether. We interviewed a few former landline owners; some had cancelled their lines, others decided not to renew a line when they moved.

New mobile-only owners

There is now a second, larger group of telephone owners in Rwanda—those who for the first time in their lives find they can afford and purchase a telephone subscription of their own (Gamos 2003). Members of this group never had a 'cord to cut'; they are the mobile-only users. Driving a mobile boom in the developing world that is moving beyond the most prosperous homes, this group represents a growing cadre of users worldwide. For these users, the mobiles provide benefits of basic connectivity offered by the telephone (Pool 1977), plus the mobility, security, and status/display benefits more unique to the mobile.

Complementary attributes of mobile telephony fuel this increased adoption. At the network/infrastructure level, the addition of a mobile base station in an urban neighborhood or rural village can change the availability of telecommunications services literally overnight, at a lower cost per potential household. At the pricing/service level, inexpensive and used handsets are becoming plentiful. Most importantly, the introduction of pre-pay plans has been critical for expanding mobile use in Africa (Minges 1999; Oestmann 2003), since many would-be owners lack bank accounts, access to credit, and even mail service to support contract accounts. By contrast, pre-pay cards allow users to recharge their phones whenever they have a little bit of money on hand, and to carefully meter their own expenditures. The vast majority of Rwanda's mobile users rely on pre-pay cards. The economic and social benefits of telephone ownership for this group of new users are discussed below.

Economic benefits

Many of the micro-entrepreneurs we interviewed described significant changes in the productivity of their businesses. Here are three examples.

- Innocent is a baker. His operation is small; most days, he and his employee cook samosas over an open flame in his home. Two years ago, he purchased his mobile, which has allowed him to coordinate more easily with his regular customers. He no longer spends a good part of his day traveling to customer's shops to see what their order might be. Instead, he calls ahead and arranges to bring the proper amount of baked goods. In addition, Innocent estimates that 30 percent of his customers are now from outside Kigali—every one of which is able to contact Innocent only because he has his mobile.
- Afsa, a hair braider, moved to Kigali as an orphan after losing her family in the 1994 genocide. She learned braiding from a woman who provided lodging in exchange for her work, but she did not receive much money from this arrangement. At the recommendation of her customers, and having seen how much success others were having with their mobiles, Afsa saved for months and purchased a mobile of her own. Now, Afsa's customers can give her number to people who like their braids, and her business is growing by word of mouth. Thanks to referrals, and the ease with which she can schedule braiding sessions with regular customers, her business has tripled—from four clients a week to twelve. Now, she lives on her own, is saving money, and is planning to open her own salon. As she puts it, "When I got the mobile, I began to see braiding as a business—as work—and could see a future."
- Annette runs a small restaurant near the airport, which serves Ugandan food. (She is Ugandan). Lately, since she purchased her mobile, her lunchtime customers have gotten in the habit of calling her each day, to order in advance. She explains: "It's always on time and easier for them. Not like first reaching here and ordering and so forth. No sooner do they park than we put food on the dining table,

> since we are aware of what they'll have." Others, later in the lunch hour, will call ahead to make sure she hasn't yet run out of food.

These stories of increased productivity are not limited to the urban areas. One owner of a dairy store in Kigali explained that many of his suppliers "up-county" had purchased mobiles and would contact him when milk was available for purchase. Rural farmers, ranchers, and fishermen are using mobiles, particularly text messages, to stay in touch with markets, cut travel costs, gain price knowledge, and reduce the bargaining power of middlemen (King 2004).

Most of these productivity gains come from the ability to rapidly exchange information between people who are beyond convenient travel distance, even if the distance is just a matter of a kilometer or two. In many cases, a landline could provide the same benefit (Aronson 1971), but other benefits are unique to mobiles, particularly to the fact that the mobile travels with the person instead of being tied to a location. For a self-employed tailor like Speciose, having a mobile means she can finally take lunch away from her sewing machine without risking the loss of a client. As has been the case in other regions mobiles give the self-employed greater flexibility and reachability (Aspden & Katz 1994).

Social benefits

While the economic benefits are important to this group, they are not the only story. Roughly 70 percent of calls made and received by the micro-entrepreneurs we interviewed were with family or friends, rather than with business contacts (Donner 2005a). When a married couple uses the mobile to arrange to share a taxi ride home after work, or a woman uses the mobile to talk to a family member about a sick relative, or when Annette's customers call her restaurant to see if lunch is still being served, the mobile is allowing new users the same power to coordinate everyday life from a distance that people in high-teledensity countries may take for granted, whether via conventional telephones (Cherry 1977) or via mobiles (Ling & Haddon 2003).

One way to understand the social impacts of the mobile is to consider how mobile use may change a user's network of communication partners. The Kigali surveys looked at micro-entrepreneurs' call logs; asking users "who did you talk to?" and "what did you talk about?" We also asked respondents when they met each call partner, and to estimate whether the amount of overall contact with each of these call partners had increased, decreased, or stayed the same since getting the mobile. Thus, we could identify which kinds of contacts were new to the user's social network. We found little evidence that users are meeting new family members or friends because they have the mobile—they are, instead, talking more frequently with the family and friends they already have. New customers, on the other hand, are very much a feature of the networks sampled on the call logs. Indeed, the highest concentration of new customers was found among those who had only a mobile line, versus those who had a mobile line and a fixed line (Donner 2004a). As sociologists have observed with the landline in other settings (Ball 1968; Thorngren 1977), mobiles are increasing the frequency of contact with existing friends and family, both locally and among geographically distant partners.

As the convenience of the mobile in everyday life has become apparent, some families with the wherewithal to do so have begun purchasing multiple handsets. For example, one interview respondent described frequent conversations between him and his wife—both on mobiles—about what time he would be coming home from work that day. Another respondent spoke of his four year old son, who would borrow his mother's mobile to tell his dad he missed him. These stories seem familiar to us—as they should. The preceding paragraphs have presented examples of how mobiles are being used in familiar ways, for familiar purposes. However, at least three other factors illustrate ways in which the use of mobiles in resource-poor (and connection-poor) settings is different than that in more prosperous settings.

Firstly, the mobile helps maintain family relationships at a distance, in the form of the diaspora (Paragas 2004). International or long-distance internal relocation in search of economic opportunities has become central to the economies of many nations. In Rwanda, we met Ugandans like Annette, the restaurant owner, who were in Rwanda for economic opportunities and met Rwandans with family in Uganda, Burundi, and South Africa. In each case the mobiles helped people feel closer, even when hundreds of miles apart. Annette, for example, can regularly call her mother, check on the money she has sent back, and check on her daughter, who is still in school in Uganda. Each individual call Annette makes to her mother and daughter may be about family matters, but the overall effect may also be economic. Without an affordable and reliable way to be in touch, Annette might not feel comfortable staying in Kigali with the thriving restaurant.

Secondly, a powerful technique to maximize the mobile's benefits while minimizing costs is 'beeping' (Donner 2005b; Oestmann 2003). Beeping occurs when an individual places a call to a mobile subscriber, and then hangs up before the call is complete. The resulting "missed call" message on the mobile's call log is *usually* a signal requesting the mobile owner to call back. However, as the practice has spread it has diversified. If the beeper and the beepee have arranged the beep in advance, it can mean "pick me up now" or "I've arrived safely" or anything else that they can think of. For Fred the dairy vendor, a beep from his supplier meant "there's milk now—send the truck".

Meanwhile, the lucky few Rwandan youths with mobiles have taken to beeping each other as a virtually free way to say "I'm thinking of you" (it is even cheaper than texting). There is no instrumental content to these messages; instead, the beeps represent a form of "phatic" communication (Malinowski 1923) where messages are used to signal the existence of a relationship or open communication channel (Haddon 2000; Ling 2004; Thurlow & Brown 2003).

Since beeping allows many more users to maintain a mobile subscription than would otherwise be able to do so, Kigali, Nairobi, Kampala, and other African cities are awash with beeps (Borzello 2001; Mutahi 2002). Thanks to prepay cards and the calling-party-pays structure, a mobile owner must pay only the basic monthly access charge of a few dollars a month to keep his phone able to receive incoming calls. If he or she can "beep" other phone owners and convince them to pay for the call, the user's monthly expenditures can be quote low. Of course, this leads to a complex battle of wills as to who will pay, though generally the wealthier person is expected to pay (Donner 2005b). Beeping also provides a vehicle for one interaction between users of public telephones and mobile owners. Non-mobile owners can use public payphones to 'beep' their friends, families, and business partners who do own mobiles, transferring the cost of the call to city dwellers (Oestmann 2003).

Finally, there is the issue of mobile theft. Theft is a worldwide problem (Katz 2004), but can be especially damaging in settings like Rwanda, when the mobile might be the most expensive object a user owns, representing months of savings. Petty thieves will snatch the unattended mobile, or slash a handbag to free the mobile likely to be inside. Many of our interview subjects said they had been the victim of mobile theft. One jeweler we spoke with has had three mobiles stolen—one by a customer, right out of his store! Options to recover the mobiles are few; Angel, the arts and crafts saleswoman, had to rent a new mobile immediately (while saving to get a new one) after her mobile was stolen. Afsa the hair braider has an 'emergency fund' set aside specifically in case hers is stolen. Such emergency funds and immediate rentals indicate how, for individuals who had lived without their own telephones for years, the mobile has become an essential part of everyday life. Rangeria, an auto mechanic, explained "I always get frustrated when I don't have my phone because I am used to it. And it disappoints those that do usually talk to me on my mobile". Reminiscent of Wurtzel and Turner's (1977) findings about "missing the telephone" another respondent compared a household without a mobile to a "home without water".

Public phone users

Though it is tempting to focus the chapter on the excitement surrounding the new mobile owners, the great majority of households in Rwanda and elsewhere in Sub-Saharan Africa do not own a mobile or a landline. There are two interrelated barriers to mobile ownership. The first, quite simply, is money; even with prepay cards, inexpensive handsets, and the beeping strategies to reduce the cost of call, many Rwandans cannot afford mobiles or the airtime to support them. The second is access to a mobile signal; MTN is moving to cover as much of the nation as possible, and Rwanda's small size and dense population mean it will eventually end up with a higher proportion of its landscape covered then Chad or Mali or the Congo, but currently the nation is not 100 percent covered. The twin barriers to mobile ownership—cost and signal availability—clearly interact to privilege the urban areas over the rural ones. Indeed, mobiles may not be much better than fixed lines as a solution to connect many rural households (Panos 2004).

That said, recent data from London's Gamos Group (2003) suggests that though phone ownership in Sub-Saharan Africa is rare, phone utilization is not. Based on surveys in Botswana, Uganda, and Ghana, Gamos reports that roughly 75 percent of respondents living in rural areas with low levels of phone availability nevertheless reported using a phone at least once in the last three months, often traveling a significant distance to do so. The proportion of regular telephone users was even higher in the urban areas.

The recent introduction of mobile-based public phones and telecenters is good news for these regular users. In many areas, both rural and urban, public fixed-wireless payphones are springing up. These payphones provide GSM-based access in places where a conventional landline might not be practical or profitable to install (Oestmann 2003), and add additional lines in neighborhoods with long queues for existing public phones. Indeed, South Africa's three mobile providers are required as part of their license agreement to provide equipment for thousands of fixed-wireless shops, which entrepreneurs run as franchised, individual businesses (Reck & Wood 2003). Sometimes, the public phone is simply a mobile handset; Bangladesh's Grameen Village Phone is famous for developing a financial and technological model to empower thousands of women entrepreneurs to act as "phone ladies" for a village (Richardson, Ramirez & Haq 2000); Grameen Phone is replicating the model in Uganda, in collaboration with MTN (USAID 2004).

Users of public payphones don't enjoy the same flexibility to receive calls as mobile owners, but the shared-phone model will be an important aspect of telephone service for the years to come. Indeed, even a single phone or shared mobile line in a village can increase the linkages between rural residents and their mobile-owning families in urban areas (Gamos 2003), and can improve the ability of farmers in villages to receive the best prices for their goods (Eggleston, Jensen & Zeckhauser 2002; Saunders, Warford & Wellenieus 1994).

Telephone non-users

What of the rest? If Gamos's (2003) estimates are correct, roughly 25 percent of citizens in Ghana, Botswana, and Uganda (and possibly Rwanda) do not regularly use telephones at all, either because they live out of easy travel distance to a phone, or because they choose not to make any calls. One could argue that these households benefit indirectly from recent improvements to connectivity among non-governmental and governmental service organizations that serve them, particularly in rural areas. For example, the software firm Voxiva and Columbia University are working with the US Centers for Disease Control and the Rwandan Government to develop a system that uses mobile telephones and internet connections to connect rural health clinics with central hospitals and government offices. The resulting nationwide information system will support Rwanda's efforts to dramatically scale-up the treatment of HIV/AIDS with antiretroviral drugs (Casas & LaJoie 2003; Donner 2004b; Nyaruhirira et al. 2004). Similar efforts are underway in South Africa—using text messages to coordinate patient care (Lindow 2004)—and in Uganda, where wireless-enabled PDAs put up-to-date information in the hands of rural caregivers (Phipps, Sanguidi & Woolway 2003).

For the most part, however, the encouraging developments in mobile ownership and the expansion of public phone availability must be presented with a caveat: that the split between rural and urban levels of mobile use is the latest wrinkle in an ongoing challenge for rural connectivity in resource-poor settings (Andrew & Petkov 2003; Hudson 1984; Panos 2004; Saunders et al. 1994). Mobiles are extending connectivity to populations on the urban periphery and even to some rural areas where landlines were unprofitable, but for the foreseeable future, GSM signals are unlikely to cover every village on the continent. The digital divide (Norris 2001) remains an important policy issue for Africa, even at the level of basic voice connectivity. Like a village without electricity or a paved road, a village without a mobile signal may be ill-equipped to participate in the interconnected formal economy.

Where market forces encourage neither the landline provider nor a mobile provider to provide connectivity at a reasonable cost, a number of other approaches are available to increase coverage and reduce the costs of use. Though a full review of these approaches is beyond the scope of this chapter, these include regulatory levers, such as

South Africa's phone shop requirement, flexible franchise models for rural GSM service (Engvall & Hesselmark 2004), and the pursuit of alternative satellite or WiFi/WiMAX technologies to support rural/remote connectivity (O'Neill 2003). These solutions require skillful collaboration between and integration with existing services so as to best balance the needs of all stakeholders. But by looking beyond where mobiles are working to where they are not, we can underscore that mobiles are but one part of an evolving telecommunications landscape that is the result of complex interactions between technologies, regulatory frameworks, geography, and user demand.

Conclusion

Despite challenges in serving remote areas, mobile ownership clearly provides significant economic and social opportunities to millions of individual users throughout Sub-Saharan Africa. Much of this value comes from the fact that many residents in cities like Kigali now have significantly greater access to basic voice telephony. Annette's restaurant thrives because her customers have mobiles; Celestine, the plumber, has the numbers of his three main contractors programmed on his mobile; Yousef the taxi driver is happy because both he and his wife can stay in touch during the day. Each story is a reflection of Metcalfe's law (Gilder 2000), illustrating how a network's value grows as a function of the square of the number of terminals; as more Rwandans become mobile owners, existing mobile and landline users benefit as well.

When the proportion of telephone users in a city triples in five years, there are significant changes to both the social and economic networks permeating the city. Townsend (2000) argues that mobiles are "rewriting the spatial and temporal constraints of all manner of human communications—whether for work, family, or recreation and entertainment [...] speed[ing] up the metabolism of urban systems, increasing capacity and efficiency." The acceleration Townsend observed is certainly evident in Kigali. Indeed, it is possible that the effect he describes is even more pronounced in this city, where mobiles are often their owner's only telephones. The productivity gains are palpable. Rangeria, a self-employed auto mechanic, told us: "Before, when I wanted a spare part, I was supposed to go to pick it up. But now I just call from where I am, and they bring it to me. Before, I would waste a lot of time." Indeed, Rangeria often now engages in *four* telephone conversations to fix a car: one for the appointment, one to tell the customer what the cost will be, one to the supplier to get the parts, and one to tell the customer the car is ready. Every call eliminates or streamlines a trip.

As with the economic benefits, the usefulness of the mobile in social relations may be even stronger among this population of new mobile users. People who before could arrange a talk once a month with far-flung relatives can do so more frequently. Families can coordinate their daily lives more effectively than previously possible. But we must be careful about whether we attribute this power to the mobile handset/network in particular. When we ask Kigali's residents what they perceive to be the benefits of their mobiles, they might mention increased social status, or security, or constant contact and increased mobility (Donner 2003), but, particularly if they are new mobile-only users, they may also mention the simple value of their new capacity to make and receive calls when they desire—as we have seen with landline users (Dimmick, Sikand & Patterson 1994; Pool 1977).

At one level, the similarities in observed patterns of mobile use generally support Katz and Aakhus's (2002) theory of a universal '*Apparatgeist*' (common patterns) of mobile use. The micro-coordination of the lunchtime call to the restaurant, the long-distance call to the loved one, and even the teenager's sending of an "I'm thinking of you" beep each represent similar kinds of behaviors to what we would see in parts of the world with higher teledensities. But by looking at the mobile's implications for three kinds of individuals (those who now own a phone, those who access a public phone, and those who can not access any phone), we can focus on the critical distinction between the few who now have their own telephone and the many who do not. That distinction used to represent a clear line between the elite and the rest of the nation, but no longer.

There are two distinct transitions underway between the three groups: as new public phones are installed, some people who previously could *not make calls at all* are now able to *place calls, from time to time*. Meanwhile, new mobile owners, who previously had to rely on public phones, now can *make and receive calls, whenever they want*. It remains a rich area for future research to further explore the magnitude and meaning of these two transitions, particularly the one between public phone use and private phone ownership. The interviews with micro-entrepreneurs suggest that the difference is fundamental—a critical change rather than a mild difference in degree of reachability or convenience. There are 1.5 billion mobile subscribers on the planet, already more than there are landlines (ITU 2004b). Thus, many of the next billion mobile owners in China, India, Africa, and throughout the developing world may have experiences more like the new mobile owners in Rwanda—their first and only phone will be the mobile.

It is probably too early to determine what the long-term impacts of mobile telephone use on the region will be. Are mobile owners and payphone users in Rwanda happier? Wealthier? Healthier? Most evidence is still anecdotal. Though we are likely to see increased urban economic activity, and increased urban-rural contacts from the mobile, it remains an open question whether the productivity gains we observed at the firm level will translate into increased levels of national prosperity. For now the key observable implication of mobile use seems to be social and economic amplification, as Townsend's metaphor of a 'speeding up' urban metabolism suggests. A reframing of the role of mobiles around amplification rather than transformation would have special significance for analysis in Africa, since doing so might highlight the ways in which mobile use is interrelated with the continent's distinct social, political, and economic structures.

Nevertheless, Rwandans are quite optimistic about the potential of mobiles to improve their lives, and express this optimism by voting with their pocketbooks, buying and using mobiles almost whenever possible. By focusing on the distinct experiences of three phone-user categories, this chapter has helped illustrate both the benefits and the challenges associated with the spread of mobile telephony in Rwanda and beyond. Even as we are pleased to see how so many Rwandans are benefiting from mobiles, it is worth paying attention to the other, still larger categories of public phone users and non-users in the country, and, to continue to work on the issues of connectivity, access, inclusion, and broad-based development that are important to them.

References

Andrew, T. N. & Petkov, D. (2003), 'The need for a systems thinking approach to the planning of rural telecommunications infrastructure', *Telecommunications Policy*, 27 (1-2), 75-93.

Aronson, S. H. (1971), 'The sociology of the telephone', *International Journal of Comparative Sociology*, 12 (3), 153-167.

Aspden, P. & Katz, J. (1994), *Mobility and communications: Analytical trends and conceptual models* (No. OTA N3-16040.0), Washington, DC: US Congress, Office of Technology Assessment.

Ball, D. W. (1968), 'Toward a sociology of telephones and telephoners', In: M. Truzzi (Ed.), *Sociology and everyday life*, Englewood Cliffs, NJ: Prentice-Hall.

Borzello, A. (2001), 'Uganda's "beeping" nuisance', Retrieved 29 October, 2004, from http://news.bbc.co.uk/1/hi/world/africa/1132926. stm.

Casas, C. & LaJoie, W. (2003), 'Voxiva: Peru', Retrieved September 30, 2004, from http://www.bus.umich.edu/BottomOfThePyramid/Voxiva.pdf.

Cherry, C. (1977), 'The telephone system: Creator of mobility and social change', In: I. de Sola Pool (Ed.), *The social impact of the telephone*, Cambridge, MA: MIT Press, 112-126.

CIA (2004), 'World factbook—Rwanda', Retrieved 20 Dec, 2004, from http://www.cia.gov/cia/publications/factbook/geos/rw.html.

Dimmick, J., Sikand, J. & Patterson, S. J. (1994), 'The gratifications of the household telephone: Sociability, instrumentality and reassurance', *Communication Research*, 21 (5), 643-663.

Donner, J. (2003), 'What mobile phones mean to Rwandan entrepreneurs', In: K. Nyíri (Ed.), *Mobile democracy: Essays on society, self and politics*, Vienna: Passagen Verlag, 393-410.

Donner, J. (2004a), 'How mobiles change microentrepreneurs' social networks: Enabling and amplifying network contacts in Kigali, Rwanda', Paper presented at the 'Mobile Communication and Social Change: 2004 International Conference on Mobile Communication', October 17-18, Seoul, Korea.

Donner, J. (2004b), 'Innovative approaches to public health information systems in developing countries: An example from Rwanda', Paper presented at the conference 'Mobile Technology and Health: Benefits and Risks', June 7-8, Department of Economics, Society, and Geography, University of Udine, Italy.

Donner, J. (2005a), 'The mobile behaviors of Kigali's microentrepreneurs: Whom they call ... And why', In: K. Nyiri (Ed.), *A sense of place*, Vienna: Passagen Verlag.

Donner, J. (2005b), 'What can be said with a missed call? Beeping via mobile phones in sub-Saharan Africa', Paper presented at the Conference on Communications in the 21st Century: Seeing, Understanding, Learning in the Mobile Age, April 28-30, Budapest.

Eggleston, K., Jensen, R. & Zeckhauser, R. (2002), 'Information and telecommunication technologies, markets, and economic development', In: G. Kirkman, P. Cornelius, J. Sachs & K. Schwab (Eds.), *The global information technology report 2001-2002: Readiness for the networked world*, New York: Oxford University Press.

Engvall, A. & Hesselmark, O. (2004), 'Profitable universal service providers', October, Retrieved January 27, 2005, from http://www.eldis.org/fulltext/profitable.pdf.

Gamos (2003), 'Innovative demand models for telecommunications services', Retrieved December 23, 2004, from http://www.telafrica.org/pdfs/FinalReport.pdf.

Gilder, G. (2000), *Telecosm: How infinite bandwidth will revolutionize our world*, New York: Free Press.

Haddon, L. (2000), 'The social consequences of mobile technology: Framing questions', Paper presented at the 'Sosiale Konsekvenser av Mobiltelefoni Seminar', Oslo.

Hamilton, J. (2003), 'Are main lines and mobile phones substitutes or complements? Evidence from Africa', *Telecommunications Policy*, 27, 109-133.

Hudson, H. E. (1984), *When telephones reach the village: The role of telecommunications in rural development,* Norwood, NJ: Ablex.

ITU (2004a), *African telecommunication indicators 2004,* Geneva: International Telecommunication Union.

ITU (2004b), 'Online statistics', Retrieved December 20, 2004, from http://www.itu.int/ITU-D/ict/statistics/.

Katz, J. E. (1999), *Connections: Social and cultural studies of the telephone in American life,* New Brunswick, NJ: Transaction Publishers.

Katz, J. E. (2004), 'Mobile phones in educational settings', Paper presented at the conference 'The Global and the Local in Mobile Communication', Budapest, Hungary.

Katz, J. E. & Aakhus, M. (2002), 'Conclusion: Making meaning of mobiles—a theory of *Apparatgeist*', In: J. E. Katz & M. Aakhus (Eds.), *Perpetual contact: Mobile communication, private talk, public performance,* Cambridge, UK: Cambridge University Press, 301-318.

King, B. M. (2004), 'Text messaging empowers Kenyan farmers', Retrieved 2 December, 2004, from http://www.interaction.org/ict/success_text_Kenya.html.

Lindow, M. (2004), 'How SMS could save your life', Retrieved November 23, 2004, from http://www.wired.com/news/medtech/0,1286,65585,00.html.

Ling, R. (2004), *The mobile connection: The cell phone's impact on society,* San Francisco: Morgan Kaufmann.

Ling, R. & Haddon, L. (2003), 'Mobile telephony, mobility, and the coordination of everyday life', In: J. E. Katz (Ed.), *Machines that become us: The social context of personal communication technology,* New Brunswick, NJ: Transaction Publishers, 245-265.

Malinowski, B. (1923), 'The problem of meaning in primitive languages', In: C. K. Ogden & I. A. Richards (Eds.), *In the meaning of meaning: A study of the influence of language upon thought and of the science of symbolism,* London: K. Paul, Trench, Trubner & Co., 296-336.

Mead, D. C. & Leidholm, C. (1998), 'The dynamics of micro and small enterprises in developing countries', *World Development,* 26 (1), 61-74.

Minges, M. (1999), 'Mobile cellular communications in the southern African region', *Telecommunications Policy,* 23 (7-8), 585-593.

Mutahi, W. (2002), *How to be a Kenyan,* Nairobi, Kenya: Kenway Publications.

Norris, P. (2001), *Digital divide: Civic engagement, information poverty, and the internet worldwide,* New York: Cambridge University Press.

Nyaruhirira, I., Munyakazi, L., Donner, J., Ruxin, J., Schocken, C., Ellis, D. et al. (2004), 'Technology supports rapid scale-up of Rwanda's HIV/AIDS care and treatment programs', Paper presented at the AIDS 2004: XV International Conference, Bangkok, Thailand.

Oestmann, S. (2003), 'Mobile operators: Their contribution to universal service and public access', Retrieved 29 October, 2004, from http://rru.worldbank.org/Documents/PapersLinks/Mobile_operators.pdf.

O'Neill, P. D. (2003), 'The "poor man's mobile telephone": Access *versus* possession to control the information gap in India', *Contemporary South Asia*, 12 (1), 85-102.

Panos (2004), *Completing the revolution: The challenge of rural telephony in Africa* (No. 48), London: The Panos Institute.

Paragas, F. (2004), 'Migrant mobiles: Cellular telephony, transnational spaces, and the Filipino diaspora', Paper presented at the conference 'The Global and the Local in Mobile Communication', Budapest, Hungary.

Phipps, K., Sanguidi, G. & Woolway, S. (2003), 'What works: HealthNet Uganda's evolution from NGO to sustainable enterprise: Portable healthcare service delivery to Uganda's rural areas', Retrieved September 29, 2004, from http://www.digitaldividend.org/pdf/health net.pdf.

Pool, I. d. S. (Ed.) (1977), *The social impact of the telephone*, Cambridge, MA: MIT Press.

Reck, J. & Wood, B. (2003), *What works: Vodacom's community services phone shops*, Seattle: World Resources Institute.

Richardson, D., Ramirez, R. & Haq, M. (2000), 'Grameen telecom's village phone programme in rural Bangladesh: A multi-media case study', Retrieved July 6, 2004, from http://www.telecommons.com/village phone/contents.html.

Santos, M. (1979), *The shared space: The two circuits of the urban economy in underdeveloped countries*, New York: Methuen.

Saunders, R. J., Warford, J. J. & Wellenieus, B. (1994), *Telecommunications and economic development*, 2 ed., Baltimore, MD: Johns Hopkins University Press.

Thorngren, B. (1977), 'Silent actors: Communication networks for development', In: I. de Sola Pool (Ed.), *The social impact of the telephone*, Cambridge, MA: MIT Press, 374-385.

Thurlow, C. & Brown, A. (2003), 'Generation txt? The sociolinguistics of young people's text-messaging', *Discourse Analysis Online*, 1 (1).

Townsend, A. M. (2000), 'Life in the real-time city: Mobile telephones and urban metabolism', *Journal of Urban Technology*, 7 (2), 85-104.

USAID (2004), 'Using cellular phones in Uganda for rural income generation and more', Spring/Summer, Retrieved November 23, 2004, from http://www.dot-com-alliance.org/newsletter/print_article.php ?article_id=36.

Wurtzel, A. H. & Turner, C. (1977), 'What missing the telephone means', *Journal of Communication*, 27 (2), 48-57.

Postal presence:
A case study of mobile customisation and gender in Melbourne

LARISSA HJORTH

Introduction

The dissemination and appropriation of global technologies is far from homogeneous. This is clearly evident in the status and significance of the mobile phone in contemporary culture. Indeed, the mobile phone is symbolic of globalisation and the increasing inclination towards mobility and so-called immediacy. In first world contexts, a line can be drawn between two types of public performance—one is the romantic flâneur that laments the demise of an imagined public, the other is what Robert Luke calls the "phoneur" in which the phone is almost surgically attached to the individual (Luke cited in Morley 2003). The former expresses great disdain when a mobile phone "goes off" in their public space, the latter desperately clutches their phone. However, most of us live somewhere in between the flâneur and phoneur modes. The mobile phone is not just a functional technology; it is a maker of certain kinds of status and cultural capital. What polyphonic ringtone or customised phone strap we attach connects us to a process of identification and identity formation.

As a vehicle arguably furthering the collapse between work and leisure distinctions, the mobile phone is a clear extension of what Raymond Williams dubbed "mobile privatisation" (1974) whereby one can be physically and geographically still within the home and yet, simultaneously be electronically transported to other places.[1] With the mo-

1. Mobile privatization needs to be contextualised in terms of specific socio-economic and cultural factors. For example, in the case of Japan, Kenichi Fujimoto (2005) has argued for a distinctively Japanese form of mobile privatisation in the concept of '*nagara* mobilism' ('*nagara*' inferring 'while-doing-something-else'). *Nagara* mobilism is a key

bile phone, the domestic comes out of the private sphere and deploys itself, with much contestation, in the so-called public sphere. But, like domesticated technologies (Morley 2003), this process is far from simple and ever completed, as each specific site locates and adapts to this cultural artefact. We domesticate domesticating technologies (i.e. TV, phone) as much as they domesticate us. If domesticating technologies are underscored by new modes of "mobile privatisation" then they are fraught with feelings of paradox, contradiction and duplicity of what it means to experience and imagine "home" (Bell 2005). I argue that the humanising "personalising" force of customisation (i.e. making the technology "friendly") that is particularly apparent within customisation is an important phenomenon attendant to the rise of mediated communication whereby the user demonstrates agency subject to local nuances. Customisation operates on both personal and social levels as integral to the appropriation of a technology into a cultural artefact. Customisation is, just as any implementation of a domestic technology, never complete and always on-going (Ling 2004; Silverstone and Haddon 1996). Domestication may have moved out of the home—whilst notions of place are subject to flows and mobility—but we may find that the local and the domestic are only a phone call away...

The dynamic interaction between globalisation and practices of locality are no more apparent than in the debates surrounding mobile telephony and its dissemination and appropriation at the level of the local. This is particularly evident in the Asia-Pacific region that houses the four technological tigers and yet bears witness to diverse penetration rates and "user" performance. Mobile telephony is both everywhere and nowhere; or, to take Heidegger's state of "undistance" (*entfernen*), the abolishment of distance also, paradoxically, destroys nearness (Arnold 2003a: 236). As Michael Arnold notes in his study on mobile telephony in Melbourne, the phenomenology of the mobile phone is best understood as "janus-faced" whereby seemingly paradoxical concepts and practices are continuously at play—being here and there, local and global, private and yet public, free and yet always on a leash (Arnold 2003a). In Melbourne we can see the dominance of SMSing and burgeoning MMSing is best encapsulated by continuing a tradition founded in the role of the postcard; a type of postal presence/presents metaphor that highlights changing relations between visual and textual, public and private, individual and social formations.[2]

characteristic of Japanese mobile phone (*keitai*) practices and the associated politics of co-presence.

2. See Esther Milne's (2004) study on the endurance of telepresent forms of "post" from 18th and 19th century letter writing genres such as visiting cards to contemporary email practices. Milne, like Margaret Morse (1998), highlights that intimacy has always involved processes of mediation. The "exchange" notion—underscoring postcard tradi-

Locating the mobile—The role of customisation and SMSing/MMSing practices in Melbourne

In Melbourne, one is confronted by images of being mobile. From the plethora of printed matter deploying intertextual means through such TV programs as *Australian Idol* and *Big Brother* to the cacophony of mobile ads and chat services flooding late night TV and weekly magazines and daily newspapers, one could be mistaken for thinking that everyone is "connected". On the streets one is greeted by the autistic behaviour of one-side conversations as people walk, bike, catch public transport and drive. Supermarkets and video stores are fecund with mobile users asking their invisible friend/partner about appropriate choices. In particular, the popularity of SMSing—and now MMSing—is undeniable. Is it just the case of a severe case of what Ling dubs as "micro-coordinating" of everyday practices whereby being "anywhere" and "everywhere"—demonstrating the underlying logic of co-presence (Morse 1998) in new forms of mobile privatisation—is the mantra for these urbanities?

As part of the Asia-Pacific, with obvious influences from techno-savvy places such as Tokyo and Seoul but without the full implementation of 3G (third generation) technologies, the usage of mobile phones in Melbourne is marked by various differences in terms of class, age, gender and ethnicity. In a multicultural city such as Melbourne, Sanrio (makers of the Japanese white cat, *Hello Kitty*) products can easily be found among the various forms of customisation.[3] In such a place, customising one's mobile phones (or the choice not to) is a decisive form of representation—both as an extension of one's identity and as a form of identification to certain forms of cultural capital. From quirky polyphonic ringtones, to mobiles dressed to the nines in a cornucopia of cute Asian merchandise, Melbourne is an example of a city with ubiquitous mobile consumption and customisation. Whilst not as conspicuous as places such as Tokyo, Melbourne mobile users are customising—from cute dolls hanging from the device to dialect-specific phonetic SMSing—to demonstrate the importance of customisation to signify types of lifestyle. However, much of the customising—as noted by the sample survey—tended towards internal forms from screensavers to particularising SMS.[4] As Gerard Goggin notes in his

tions—is pertinent to discussion of mobile telephonic practices replicating earlier social rituals (Taylor and Harper 2002).

3. Brian McVeigh has defined this Japanese form of cute (*kawaii*) character customisation as "technocute" whereby users appropriate *kawaii* characters to make "warm" or "friendly" the coldness of new technology (2000).

4. This internalised mode of customisation is just as much part of an exchange and participation in forms of cultural capital and individualisation as the "external" customi-

study of the usage of SMS (Goggin 2004), and as seen in the work of Anita Wilhelm, Marc Davis (and the Garage Cinema Research) Nancy Van House (2004), and Mizuko Ito and Daisuke Okabe (2003) on MMSing (particularly the function of camera phones), this is an burgeoning area of expression that needs to be understood as not just a remediated (composition of older and new technologies, Bolter and Grusin 1999) form of expression and exchange but also a media/genre in its own right.

In the case of Melbourne, the second largest city in Australia and notably constituted by a multicultural demographic, the mobile phone is a dominant form of everyday practice. The practices and experiences of mobile telephony are divergent and ubiquitous, marked by different factors such as ethnicity, age, gender, class and sexuality. As a city part of the Asia-Pacific region, one can find many appropriations of customisation practices (such as cute characters and other fashion accessories) for the phone. The streets are filled with a cacophony of polyphonic ringtones as users traverse the city with phone in hand. With 3G technologies set to sweep the Australian market, dominant practices such as SMS will be challenged by the burgeoning of content-driven applications and services—most notably the relatively new emerging mobile gaming market. Due to economic restraints, the cheaper options of SMSing (rather than MMSing) and instant messaging are the main forms of usage, marked notably by gendered inflections. But whilst cost may have been the initial main motivation for opting for SMS over voice calling, now it is a dominant form of expression that is preferred by many Melbournians as the chosen form of intimacy and co-presence.

With four main service providers—Telstra (the largest), Hutchison (Orange, 3), Optus and Vodafone—all vying for the Australian market, there seems innumerable amounts of choice.[5] However, this choice is underscored by what James Fergusson (a specialist in new market trends in the Asia-Pacific region working for the third largest information research company in the world, TNS global) sees as a market still in need of service providers offering content and applications to niche demographics. In an interview with Fergusson, I inquired about the role of customisation—that is the hanging of characters from the phone, face plates, personalised screensavers and ringtones—and whether it was just a fleeting trend (Hjorth 2004). He believed that

sation. This shift towards internal customisation could be seen as part of the general trend towards 3G mobile technologies whereby presence migrates from a noun to a verb (Joichi Ito 2005) and context becomes pivotal in negotiating content.

5. Australia has many service providers apart from the aforementioned—such as AAPT and Virgin mobile to name but a few. For details on the various providers see: http://toolkit.gov.au/mobile.csp.html (19 January 2005).

users' customisation of phones was a way of completing what the service providers had overlooked—the need for specific applications for particular niche groups. This is particularly the case in the introduction of 3G mobile phones such as Hutchison's 3 whereby the phones are crammed with applications not necessarily relevant for users. Fergusson believed Hutchison 3's hybridisation of 2G and 3G technologies—the first example of 3G in Australia—has resulted in much confusion on the behalf of consumers as to what exactly constitutes "3G" technology and whether it has any relevance in facilitating everyday practices.

Telstra (once known as Telecom when it was a Government service and had a market monopoly) was set to adopt the "Blackberry" phone—successful in UK and US markets—but the launch subsequently fell through. Now Telstra has signed with NTT DoCoMo to take up *i-mode*, six years after it was implemented in Japan in 1999.[6] According to Telstra press releases, it is believed that one in twenty Australians will have i-mode in the next 3 years. Already established 3G content service providers include Optus Zoo and Vodafone Live. According to Fergusson, for 3G technologies to take off in Australia, the carriers and device manufacturers need to consider niche applications for corresponding demographics. Fergusson argues that currently 3G devices available in Australia are gimmicky—jam-packed with various applications most users will only use once or twice. The applications that are important, Fergusson notes, are those that make a difference to people's lives. Fergusson sees that the relatively poor picture quality and resolution of MMS applications and camera phones has seen them mainly adopted by youth markets rather than work-related users. Unlike markets such as Japan and South Korea where government infrastructure and financial support helped to fully implement 3G technologies, Australia's take-up has been much slower, uneven and cautious.

Pixoleur—The art of being mobile: A case study of a sample group

Much of the advertising for mobile phones in Australia—from service providers such as Optus, 3, Vodafone and Telstra to device manufacturers such as Sony Ericsson, Nokia, Siemens, Motorola, LG and Samsung—reiterates the importance of being connected both literally and

6. For critiques of DoCoMo's i-mode as not "mobile with Internet" but, rather, mimicking the closed architecture of Minitel see Harmeet Sawhney (2004). Also see the comprehensive anthology by Mizuko Ito et al. (2005) that focuses on the social and cultural dimensions of the rise of Japanese mobile media—"*keitai* IT revolution"—from pagers to contemporary configurations of i-mode.

metaphorically. In the advertising media on TV and in printed matter we see the significance of the phone as a status symbol (corresponding with types of cultural capital) and increasingly this identification is marked by the choices offered to users for customising and personalising the device. More and more, different device providers are selling types of identity and status—from prestigious Nokia designer phones (such as models 7260 and 7280) to Motorola's fun play on the currency of Japanese popular culture in Australia. Once a market dominated by Nokia, the Australian market is now awash with various brands and associated consumer stereotypes. Of the twenty people surveyed, only three had Nokia phones; the rest of the respondents had brands such as Siemens, LG and Samsung.

In a sample survey I conducted in Melbourne in November 2004 with twenty students, administrators and staff—both male and female ranging from 20-50 years old—from the University of Melbourne I found that the role of the mobile phone as a predominately personal device was deeply interwoven in attempts to articulate modes of intimacy whilst trying to negotiate co-presence. Isolating the survey to one university entailed that only certain types of cultural capital (tastes and values) were occupative with all respondents being attached to tertiary education. Of the twenty surveyed I conducted follow-up in-depth interviews with six users to gain a sense of the symbolic role of the phone and the gendered function of customisation. I asked users about the role of the mobile phone in their everyday rituals and social relations and how customisation operated to personalise the device.

When asked to provide adjectives to describe their relationships to mobile phones, some of the responses were: easy-going, casual, evolving, distanced, frustrating, resistant, obsessive, attentive, fun, easy, takes over my life, happy, sad and pathetic. Many saw the mobile phone as beneficial in maintaining relationships, especially in terms of being available anytime for friends and organising meetings. One respondent was ambivalent towards the medium, acknowledging its ability to establish intimacy with new people but creating distance with already existing friends.

Whilst still not immersed in the world of 3G mobility, Melbourne has a burgeoning industry for convergent mobile media aimed at socialising—especially to establish new relationships through the non-evasive mode of mobile net telephony. Dating services, chat lines and after-production customising services (downloading specialised ringtones and screensaver animations) fill the TV airwaves (after 10pm) and tabloid newspapers and magazines. When people are not actually customising and SMSing or MMSing, they are perpetually bombarded by a plethora of usage possibilities. However, in the sample survey, very few respondents used such services, arguing that mobiles were more important in reinforcing already existing relations rather than establishing new relationships. In terms of customising services such as downloading screensavers, only two out of twenty had used the downloading services; many preferred to either use their own images (mostly taken by camera phones) or choose from the images provided with the phone. Images used included places visited, Asian animations of cute characters, Betty Boop, the user's name and a flower. Some had tried the downloading services but had found them unsatisfying, too costly and often frustrating to use. Whereas most (70 percent) selected ringtones and screensavers supplied with the phone, many claimed that they would do their own customisation if the phone had the capabilities (i.e. camera phone, Bluetooth).

Gender featured predominantly in discussions about customisation, with female respondents tending to be more decisive and opinionated about their selections, often downloading different screensavers and ringtones rather than using the generic (and unsatisfying) ones supplied by the manufacturer. In turn, female respondents spoke about the ways in which people judged others by the types of mobile phone used and such features as ringtones. Key features for ringtones were factors such as being 'distinctive but not annoying'. As one female respondent noted:

> "I have chosen Betty Boop (screensaver, face plate and doll hanging from the phone) because she is a bit of a role model of mine—she operates like a type of avatar or alter ego. There are some physical similarities such as we both have black curly hair. My ringtone is one of the Nokia ringtones supplied with the phone. It was chosen because it suits another alter ego of mine—so I felt it correspond with that identity; it's like playing dress-ups."

When asked about whether she saw customisation as an extension of the user's personality/identity she replied, 'I think so because I think you get judged by your ringtone when you are in public. When you hear someone's ringtone that is the same as yours you expect to find your doppelganger... It (customising) does become a fashion thing that you do get judged on'.

Here we are reminded of the work by poststructuralist Judith Butler on the performative elements of gender—that is, rather than gender being innate it is continuously practiced and informed by social and self-regulatory practices (Butler 1990). The performative element of customisation—from customising the phone to customising text messages—was acknowledged by most of the female respondents. Whilst both male and female respondents predominantly used the mobile phone to contact friends (rather than family or work colleagues), many of the female respondents preferred SMS as a means of communication with over half of the female respondents preferring SMSing—more than 80 percent compared to 20 percent preferring voice calling. Both male and female respondents claimed that at least 80 percent of their friends had mobiles; the only respondent (female) who did not SMS used her mobile to mainly contact family and only 10 percent of her friends had mobiles.

It would be easy to surmise that the rationale for using SMSing over voice calling and MMSing would be the cost factor; and whilst this was acknowledged, it was not the only reason. One male respondent stated, 'Most of my communication is SMS because it is cheaper. But I don't like telephone conversations; I think they are often misleading—there is not enough eye contact or body language to determine what they are really saying. So hence I prefer SMSing.' The same respondent noted a difference in his frequency of contact with the acquisition of a mobile only one year ago. He noted, 'probably in a space of a week I keep in contact with just over a dozen people. It's very important—particularly with people I am close to—that I can communicate with them immediately when necessary. The mobile does reinforce relationships. I would take calls/messages from people at 2am; it is very unlikely that I would with the landline.'

For one female respondent, SMSing was a new form of expression that she saw as an 'art form'.[7] In combining the spoken with the written, she viewed SMS as a very particular mode of communication that was assuring and not confronting (as is face-to-face). She stated:

"I see texting as a new form of expression; it's not necessarily destroying (English language) but a borrowing and reappropriation—not the same as. It has a lot to do with compression, speed, and efficiency. The main form of writing I do is texting; I do see it as an art form. I enjoy making a funny message; and I appreciate receiving ones where the sender has put in time and thought by personalising and individualising it... A text message is like a book, each sentence can be compressed to become a chapter... I spend time editing texts... Often the initial original message is quite different from the one I end up sending; for example, if I am sending a long text message that goes over into two messages I will edit into one message. This is not because of the cost but more about the flow of the message; often it gets sent as two separate messages that hinders the message and its intentions. Recently I got a message from someone who sent six messages in a row; they were obviously familiar with texting! She wasn't concise, it was literally as if she were talking!"

Here the respondent identifies the role of customisation, especially inside the phone through modes such as SMS, to signify a type of cultural capital, performativity and self-presentation. As the respondent described her process creating an SMS, there was nothing immediate about it. The editing and regulatory process was, as she stated, not just

7. See Gerard Goggin's (2004) discussion of SMS as a new emerging—and yet remediated—genre.

a matter of cost. Rather, it was about a type of conversion into a different genre utilising the language (vernacular) of the user. It was about flow and individualisation, not just efficiency and speed. Like all media and genres, SMS comes with often unspoken conventions and etiquette marked by cultural and social capital. As the female respondent conveys the story of her friend's long-winded messages—who overlooked the medium's convention of word compression and conservation—we can see the importance of acknowledging and adapting the conventions (such as compression and the politics of co-presence) in the experience or, to borrow from Marshall McLuhan, "massaging" of the medium (1964). Here, the medium's message/massage is a type of hybridising of phonetics, vernacular, spoken and visual that was identified by many of the surveyed female users. When the above female respondent was asked about whether SMS was in the vein of a type of hallmark genre—whereby the generic and the personal is negotiated—she answered, 'yes, it is a compressed form of writing and it does make you revalue words. Although it can be instant, it can also be very deliberate and premeditated.' There goes the cliché about co-present immediacy and mobile phones… well, in this case, at least!

Another female respondent spoke of the gender divide in terms of male users opting towards predictive text and a more direct conveying of data rather than as an expressive form of communication. Often certain terms were used between specific people to create a type of intimacy in the text that would be lost on the outsider. One male respondent played with the predictive function that converted his name "brian" as "asian"; he now uses "asian" as his sign name with specific friends. Another female respondent commented:

> "I'm not big on smiling faces; it's too generic. You want people to read the text like you would hear it—incorporating both the written and the spoken. When I read a text I read it in their voice. I try to make it a bit more personalised. Sometimes I put the generic kiss thing; I like when people make strange faces or symbols. I don't like when people use predictive text; I never use that (predictive text tends to choose wrongly)… For example, "go" becomes "in". I notice with my male texters there tends to a usage of "in" when I think they mean, "go". I don't like it because I like people's personalities to come across, to express their sense of humour."

The so-called divide between those that have mobiles and those that do not was broached with the respondents, but female respondents believed there was a difference and male respondents did not. The gendering of attitudes was also noted in the respondent's comments about mobile etiquette in public. Whilst James Fergusson believed that Australia was relatively unfazed by public mobile performance in comparison to the US or Japan, the female respondents felt otherwise. Although both male and female respondents tended not to put the phone on silent mode they tended to lower the volume of the ringtone, and if they answered a call they spoke briefly and quietly. Of the respondents, only a handful of female respondents put their mobile on silent mode and many did not initiate phone calls unless it was imperative. The key experience identified by most respondents was a type of "self-consciousness". One female respondent stated:

"I think the correct mobile etiquette in public is brief and discrete. I use silence mode more when I am in private, rather than public, places. I usually don't have my phone on a loud ring mainly out of respect for other people's personal spaces. I don't think it should be banned; you should just act as you would normally—not talking loudly and making it brief... I don't think it is frowned upon to use your mobile in public but people do seem weary and self-conscious to use mobiles in public because—unless you're an extrovert—it is quite a self-conscious process as everyone can hear what you are saying and find out quite a bit about you (i.e. where you are going, where you have been)."

The gendering of mobile behaviour was noted by most respondents, however most noted the influence of age and class in the equation. One male respondent stated, 'I don't know the difference. It seems as if women take more phone calls and text messages than men. That's something I have just noticed but I don't know if it's true.' Another female respondent stated:

"I do think gender has a role. I could agree with the myth that males use more voice calls and tend to be more to the point in their text messaging. I suppose young females text a lot, males tend to be more familiar with the games on the phone, whilst females don't care about the games. If I were to generalise I would say that males use the calling phone function more often, females send and receive more SMS. However, I do think it is subjective—it depends on the person."

The respondents noted the function of the mobile as a type of souvenir, caching of moments or electronic diary, similar to what the postcard once signified. Many stored SMS and MMS that had personal significance. One female respondent stated:

"Yes, I do use my mobile as a form of electronic diary. But it's not quite stable because you can delete it; I know it's not that safe but because it is easy—it's with me all the time. I do use it as a way of remembering events and certain messages people have sent to me are kept for sentimental reasons. But I am aware that they could all just go very quickly and I wouldn't have a way of retrieving them."

Another respondent, this time male, stated that he kept specific messages from each one of his close pool of frequent contacts. He said, 'I don't remember people's phone numbers anymore. I have no idea, no recognition of people's numbers anymore. If I don't have my mobile with me I couldn't communicate with anyone via a landline.' When asked how he determines which messages to save and which to delete he responded, 'If someone has text me about a dozen times I will always communicate with them via one of the saved SMS. I always use one to reply to, not necessarily the most recent one. I choose carefully which ones I save and which ones I delete.'

Issues such as age, class and ethnicity underscored the role of gender to define modes of mobile telephony in Melbourne. In this sample study I have sought to uncover some of the ways mobile customisation is signifying different forms of self-presentation, representation and identification. Within the dominance of SMS as the main form of communicating, we can see the ways in which individuals are personalising and customising the mode. As aptly identified by one respondent, SMS can be seen as a type of art form—a remediated media borrowing from the likes of postcards (especially in terms of MMS) and yet having its own conventions. Whilst SMS may be immediate it can also be deliberate and premeditated; to use the metaphor discussed by one respondent, if SMS were a book, each sentence would be a chapter. As noted by many of the respondents, SMS and MMS are not about a simple form of information dissemination or organising (Ling's "micro-coordination", 2004), most (predominantly the female) respondents commented on the importance of SMS/MMS to be reassuring, to be about a type of co-presence not unlike the postcard's 'wish you were here' status. However, in the context of SMS phonetic textuality, 'wish you were hear' might be more apt!

Conclusion—Wish you were hear

The Asia-Pacific region is marked by diverse penetration rates and modes of mobile telephony performativity (Bell 2004; Katz and Aakhus 2002; Plant 2001). In areas of high penetration-rates one can notice exponentially large usage of after-production customisation. In 3G centres such as Tokyo and Seoul one notices a cornucopia of mobile phone fashioning inside and outside the phone as users attempt to personalise the device—operating as both a site for self-identification and cultural capital for on lookers. In contrast to such data-savvy locations, 3G is yet to be fully implemented into Melbournians everyday life. No respondents had 3G mobile phones—only two out of twenty respondents in the survey had camera phones (although many stated that they were "upgrading" soon to camera phones) and only six had part MMS functions.

Whilst from the outset, Melbournians seem less embroiled in the cute character customisation frenzy as seen in such places as Tokyo and Taipei, however this is not to say that less customisation is occurring. Rather, much of the personalising and customising of mobile phones is through the (internalised) genre and conventions of SMSing. The play with the vernacular, colloquial and dialect through phonetic textuality is as vast as the city is multicultural. Here, through implicit modes of SMS customising individuals can denote types of similarities and differences that extend beyond gender, class, age and ethnic stereotypes. Having said that, the fact that females do SMS more than males (and do so in more inventive ways) speaks about a type of relationship to orality and communication that extends the mobile phone from purely a functional technology to a tool for sociality and a discourse for remediated forms of expression. Welcome to the art of "being hear"...

References

Arnold, M. (2003a), 'On the phenomenology of technology; the "Janus-faces" of mobile phones', *Information and Organization*, 13, 231-256.

Arnold, M. and M. Klugman (2003b), *Mobile phone uptake: a review of the literature and a framework for research*, Heidelberg, Vic.: Heidelberg Press.

Beck, U. and E. Beck-Gernsheim (2002), *Individualisation*, London: Sage.

Bell, G. (2004), *Satu Keluarga, Satu Komputer*, [One home, one computer]: Cultural Accounts of ICTs in South and Southeast Asia. Design Issues.

Bell, G. (2005), This volume.

Butler, J. (1990), *Gender Trouble*, London: Routledge.

Bolter, J. and R. Grusin (1999), *Remediation: Understanding New Media*, Cambridge, MA: MIT Press.

Bourdieu, P. (1984 [1979]), *Distinction: A Social Critique of the Judgement of Taste*, translated by Richard Nice, Cambridge, MA: Harvard University Press.

Castells, M. (2001), *The Internet Galaxy*, Oxford: Oxford University Press.

du Gay, P. et al. (1997), *Doing Cultural Studies: The story of the Sony Walkman*, London: Sage.

Fujimoto, K. (2005), 'The Third-Stage Paradigm: Territory Machine from the Girls' Pager Revolution to Mobile Aesthetics', In: M. Ito, D. Okabe and M. Matsuda (Eds.), *Personal, Portable, Pedestrian: Mobile Phones in Japanese Life*, Cambridge, MA: MIT Press, 77-102.

Goggin, G. (2004), 'Mobile Text', *M/C—Media and Culture Journal*, 7 (1), http://journal.media-culture.org.au/(10 January 2004).

Haddon, L. (1997), *Empirical Research on the Domestic Phone: A Literature Review*, Brighton: University of Sussex Press.

Hebdige, D. (1979), *Subculture, the meaning of style*, London: Methuen.

Hjorth, L. (2004), Interview with James Fergusson, unpublished (2 December).

Ito, J. (2005), 'The Creative Commons: intellectual property and public broadcasting—opportunities for common sense and public good', Presented as part of the Alfred Deakin innovation lecture series, held at the Melbourne Town Hall, 8 May.

Ito, M. and D. Okabe (2003), 'Camera phones changing the definition of picture-worthy', *Japan Media Review*, http://www.ojr.org/japan/wireless/1062208524.php (10 June 2004).

Katz, J. E. and M. Aakhus (Eds.) (2002), *Perpetual Contact: mobile communication, private talk, public performance*, Cambridge: Cambridge University Press.

Lévi Strauss, C. (1972 [1966]), *The savage mind*, London: Weidenfeld and Nicolson.

Ling, R. (2004), *The mobile connection*, San Francisco: Morgan Kaufmann.

López, J. (2003), *Society and its metaphors*, New York: Continuum.

McLuhan, M. (1964), *Understanding Media*, New York: Mentor.

McVeigh, B. (2000), 'How Hello Kitty Commodifies the Cute, Cool and Camp: "Consumutopia" versus "Control" in Japan', *Journal of Material Culture*, 5 (2), 291-312.

Milne, E. (2004), 'Magic bits of Paste-board', *M/C—Media and Culture Journal*, 7 (1), http://journal.media-culture.org.au/ (10 December 2004).

Morley, D. (2001), *Home Territories: Media, Mobility and Identity*, London: Routledge.

Morley, D. (2003), 'What's "home" got to do with it?' *European Journal of Cultural Studies*, 6 (4), 435-458.

Morse, M. (1998), *Virtualities: television, media art, and cyberculture*, Bloomington: Indiana University Press.

Plant, S. (2001), *On the mobile. The effects of mobile telephones on social and individual life*, http://www.motorola.com/mot/doc/0/234_MotDoc.pdf (10 December 2003).

Sawhney, H. (2004), 'Mobile Communication: New Technologies and Old Archetypes', Presented at the 'Mobile Communication and Social Change Conference', October, organized by Shin Dong Kim, Seoul, South Korea.

Silverstone, R. and L. Haddon (1996), 'Design and domestication of information and communication technologies: Technical change and everyday life', In: R. Silverstone and R. Mansell (Eds.), *Communication by Design: The Politics of Information and Communication Technologies*, Oxford: Oxford University Press.

Taylor, A. and R. Harper (2002), 'Age-old Practices in the "new World": A Study of Gift-giving between Teenage Mobile Phone Users', Presented at 'Changing Our World, Changing Ourselves' (SIGCHI Conference on Human Factors in Computing Systems, Minneapolis), 439-46.

Telstra website, http://www.telstra.com (10 November 2004).

Wajcman, J. and J. Beaton (Eds.) (2004), 'The Impact of the Mobile Telephone in Australia: Social Science Research Opportunities (A Discussion Paper)', Presented at 'The Australian Mobile Telecommunications Association Conference', September.

Wilhelm A., Y. Takhteyev, R. Sarvas, N. Van House and M. Davis (2004), 'Photo Annotation on a Camera Phone', Presented at CHI2004, 24-29 April, Vienna, Austria.

Williams, R. (1974), *Television: Technology and Cultural Form*, London: Fontana.

The age of the thumb: A cultural reading of mobile technologies from Asia

GENEVIEVE BELL

Introduction[1]

The People's Republic of China is currently the world's largest market for cell phones. Indeed cell phones are now such a commodity, that some fashionable Chinese women wear them as jewelry, on chains around their necks. One young professional I interviewed joked that China is now in a new age, the age of the thumb [*muzhi shi dai*]. She was referring not only to the remarkable text message traffic in China—an estimated 100 million messages per day for the more than 340 million cell phone subscribers in that country—but also to the growing sense that mobile technology is ushering in a new era in Chinese history and culture, as well as a new place for China on the world technology stage. Chinese cell phone users account for slightly less than one third of the world's total number of phone users. It is not unimaginable at this point that the next big thing in cell phones might happen in

1. This chapter started as a talk at the Institute of Design's annual 'about, with, for' conference in 2002 and I am grateful for the organizers for their insistence. The text was fleshed out in discussions with Nina Wakeford, Malene Skaeved, Paul Silverstein, Victor Margolin, Nicola Green, Julian Orr, Katrina Jungnickel, Jim Mason, Joseph Jofish Kaye, Larissa Hjorth, Eric Paulos, Diane Bell, Bettina Ngweno, Mimi Ito and Danah Boyd. The chapter has benefited from the close readings of Paul Dourish, and I am grateful for his suggestions and patience. Original research materials for this chapter were gathered and organized by Ellie Blue, Katrina Jungnickel and Joshua Rohrbach, and additional materials were shared with me by many friends, colleagues and fellow travelers and I thank them all. I also thank the various organizations within Intel that continue to support this kind of research and have found value in its results, along with my colleagues in Peoples and Practices Research and Intel Research.

China, rather than Europe or the US. In fact, one of the most popular services on phones in China right now bears witness to that potential. China Mobile—the largest of the Chinese mobile providers—is currently offering a novella in serial form on its cellular handsets. This approach is possible because of the ideographic nature of Chinese characters. Most cell phones offer text messages of somewhere between 160 to 240 spaces in length. In English and other languages with non-character based scripts, these spaces are taken up with letters; hence the need for smart abbreviations and short words. Even with these textual plays, texting in English is limited. Chinese, however, is a character based language, and as such, each of the 160 to 240 slots in a message can be filled with a character, or word. Thus a far richer messaging experience is possible, extending to novellas by installment—the cell phone becomes a literary device, in way, almost unimaginable in the West.

The Asian cell phone market has seen rapid and remarkable growth in the late 1990s and early twenty-first century, defying analysts' expectations. Indeed, it is the case that in many Asian countries, most recently India, the number of cell phones in circulation has eclipsed the number of domestic landlines, and the rate of adoption of cellular technology far outpaces fixed line deployment. In fact, in Singapore, there are more cell phones than citizens. These rapid rates of adoption also reflect an interesting constellation of factors: existing patterns of high (albeit localized) social mobility outside of the home; strong government regulation mandating national, or pan-national standards; poor existing terrestrial telephony, high rates of urbanization and very good national cell coverage; and competitive and strategic calling plans and pricing policies. The impact of calling plans and pricing policies should not be underestimated. As of 2003, in most of India and China, consumers do not pay for incoming calls. In India in 2002, although Bombay, Bangalore and Calcutta did not charge for incoming calls, Delhi's local mobile companies do, and as a result there was a marked absence of cell phone use as compared to the other cities. Indeed, Asia, as a region, bears a stronger resemblance to Europe than the United States: there is a single standard (GSM) which means that cell phones can operate across many geographies; metered local phone calling is still the norm, though in many places consumers pay only for outgoing calls which means that phones are left switched on all the time; prepaid phone cards and calling plans are typical; text messaging (SMS) is extremely popular; and phones are common across most age groups. But there is more going on that this set of facts and figures might suggest.

For the last three years, I have been running a research project to critically interrogate the ways in which cultural practices are shaping people's relationships to new information and communication technologies (ICTs) in urban Asia.[2] This project was shaped by the work of George Marcus, and his theoretical interventions: "This mode of constructing the multi-sited space of research involves tracing the circulation through different contexts of a manifestly material object of study (at least as initially conceived), such as commodities, gifts, money, works of art and intellectual property" (Marcus 1998: 91). It also owes much to the contemporary literature on consumption, consumer and material culture, in particular the work of Appaduri (1988; 2001) and Miller (2001). The multi-sited ethnographic research followed information and communication technologies through seven different sites of production, consumption and resistance, encompassing urban life in India, China, Malaysia, Singapore, Korea, Indonesia and Australia.[3] In the one hundred households I visited from 2002 to 2003, I relied on a range of ethnographic methods, including participant observation, semi-structured interviews, 'deep hanging-out', and genealogies of ICTs.

Throughout this research, I was repeatedly struck by the ways in which people were appropriating cell phones, inscribing local cultural practices, solving local problems, and re-charting social relationships fractured by colonial and post-colonial geographic separations.[4] These appropriations and usages provide some useful interruptions to our assumptions about technology in emerging markets, and as such, are worth rehearsing here. There has been a lot of good work focusing on usage models of cell phones in particular (mostly Western) geographies (Brown et al. 2001; Crabtree et al. 2003; Ling 2004; Taylor and Harper 2002) and some good surveys across multiple locations (Katz and Aakhus 2002; Berry et al. 2003; Harper 2005), here I am interested in documenting some broader cross-cultural understandings of cellular technology, and in so doing, suggest a different vantage from which to consider mobile phones. I am particularly interested in the ways in which cell phones are being deployed, consumed, regulated, rejected, and naturalized in urban Asia.

2. I am grateful here for the assistance of Debashis Chaudhuri, Adam Yuet Chau, Eunyun Park and Katrina Jungnickel throughout this project.

3. These sites represented a diversity of governmental structures, geo-political and colonial histories, policies re: ICTs, family and social organization, religions and the role of women within the home. We visited 19 cities: India—Pune, Hyderabad, Chandigarh; Malaysia—KL, Ipoh, Penang; Singapore; Indonesia—Jakarta, Pekanbaru, Surabaya; PRC—Shanghai, Guangzhou, Xiamen; Korea—Seoul, Pusan, Daejon; Australia—Newcastle, Melbourne, Adelaide.

4. Bill Maurer's recent work on globalization also informs this examination by calling attention to the importance of such things as historical and cultural forces (including kinship relationships) on the circulations of goods (2000a; 2005).

Cultures of mobility in Asia

In America, a great deal of social activity, intimacy and affect goes on within the home. Within certain demographics, the locus of social activity is entirely domesticated. However, outside of the US, there is a great deal more slippage between the notion of social activity and the appropriate site that such an activity might take place. There are range of sites through which people transit and linger and a variety of ways by which such sites are connected, and disconnected, from the home. This sort of social mobility can be critical to understanding the ways in which mobile devices have been adopted and used. I would argue that pre-existing patterns of social mobility outside of the home play an enormous role in the up-take of mobile devices and the uses to which such devices are put. Here I am suggesting that 'mobility' is inflected through a profoundly cultural lens—what it means to be 'mobile' (or away from home) has distinct cultural meaning. To put it another way, the construction of 'home' and 'public' and the relationships between them also impacts the adoption and use of mobile devices. Social mobility also implies a certain notion of geography, where distances can be collapsed or negotiated. Some forms of social mobility are very local, (i.e.: the *danwei* as organizing principal for Chinese workers in the 1950s-1980s); others imply wider networks and spaces (i.e.: the American 'road warrior'). Social mobility also recalls the particulars of history and geo-politics.[5] It is into these different cultures of mobility that cell phones have been deployed, consumed and sometimes resisted.

Cell phones were present in almost every household we visited. As such, they represent an important part of the constellation of ICTs within daily life, but cell phones are a very different sort of ICT than computers. In Asia, phones are also performing multiple cultural functions; they operate within a range of cultural and symbolic registers. They are more than just technologies; they are sites of cultural production. For rather than validating the centrality of the United States as a center of innovation, technology production and consumption, a closer examination of cell phones in Asia, even in its emerging economies, suggests a very different, albeit complicated, vision. Indeed my recent experience suggests, that in many ways when it comes to technology uptake, the US is more the anomaly than the rule. Technology uptake

---

5. For instance, until the last ten years, most of China operated under a system of government that actively discouraged mobility beyond well-defined and heavily policed boundaries; certain sites were off-limit and social activities and social circles were prescribed. Indeed, the legacy of the *hukou* [residency papers] system is such that cell phones are the only sorts of phones some Chinese citizens can obtain.

and distributions are mapping an unexpectedly new terrain of haves and have-nots, suggesting not only new centers of innovation and demand, but also, to borrow the vernacular of the wireless industry, new 'dead zones.'

In this chapter, I want to chart some of this terrain, using particular features of this new landscape to highlight critical divergent paths for technology's adoption and use. These new paths provide remarkable perspective on the cultural work of technology—that is, to see the ways in which technology is linked to different cultural narratives and forms of material and cultural production, beyond the well rehearsed tropes of modernity, progress and even revolution. In looking across all of my research material and field sites, I have been struck by some surprising similarities in the ways people imagine and actively use cell phones. In this chapter, I identify four different ways in which phones function as cultural, rather than technological objects—as objects for communication, as manifestations of information, as a form of identity politic, and as sites of anxiety and control.

We talk every day: Cell phones as a communication tool

Cell phones sometimes augment existing fixed land line infrastructure, sometimes replace them, sometimes provide access where none has existed previously, and sometimes the service providers offer new rates and pricing packages. In Indonesia, where there is still greater mosque density than tele-density, there are three times as many mobile phones as fixed lines. In China and India, there are now more cell phone subscribers than there are fixed land lines. In Australia, Korea, Singapore and Malaysia, more than 80 percent of the population owns a cell phone, meaning that almost all citizens have some form of access to one. It seems safe to say that cell phones are pervasive in middle class, urban Asian homes and as such they are embedded in daily life and culture (Ito 2004; Hjorth 2003b; Robison and Goodman 1996). In the former British colonies of India, Singapore, Malaysia and Australia, people talk about *mobile phones*—the experience of mobility is the modifier. In Singapore and Malaysia, people also talk about *hand phones*; in China, *Shouji* [hand-machine]—how the phone is carried is the relevant modifier in these contexts. In Indonesia, the label *hand phone* has been shortened to the initials *HP* and then re-interpreted through a more *Bahasa* sound to *ha-pe*. More recently, in Australia, people have started to refer to their mobile phones as *my phone*, distinguished from *my home phone*, where the home is now the differentiating modifier. The cell phone nomenclature bears striking witness to colonial histories, contemporary capitalisms, multi-national agendas and understandings of technology (and the body). But, no matter what they are called, in the Asian homes in which I spent time cell phones most obviously functioned as communication tools, resembling in many ways their fixed line antecedents.

When reflecting on their own cell phone habits, people described remarkably similar experiences: activities such as talk, chatter, gabbing, gossip, family business, and socializing. Sunia, a new thirty-something mother in Hyderabad, was quite clear about what she did with the shared family cell phone: 'I like to keep in touch. I know exactly what everyone is doing, all the details.'[6] She called her mother every day, sometimes more than once; she communicated with her siblings and cousins and kept up with her friends from high school, university and work. She joked with me that she could spend hours on the phone every day and frequently did. For other men and women, it was less about needing to know everything about everyone than it was about this notion of 'staying in touch' or 'keeping in touch.' I think it is safe to say that much of this represents a form of light weight social interaction or what Prøitz (2005), in her richly detailed accounts of young Norwegian romance via cell phones, calls 'intimate discourse'—a kind of intermediated togetherness where the social-ness of the interaction was more important than the time that it took.

Organizing co-presence appears to be another function of cell phones. Variously described as micro-location work or the last fifty meter problem (Ling 2004), cell phones in Europe and the US are often used to co-ordinate the finer points of physical interactions. In Asia it appears to be no different. Angeline is a member of a large extended Chinese family in Penang, Malaysia. In her early 30s, she has a five year old son who is tended by his mother's mother and his mother's father's mother at the family's terrace (or link) home. Angeline uses her phone to co-ordinate day care as well as family time. She recalls with rueful laughter that the cell phone has changed the way her family gets around: 'Sometimes when we are all in the mall, I am on the first floor, and my mother is on the 4th floor. And she calls to say, where are you? Ten years ago we would have gone looking for each other but now we just call.' In other households, people told similar stories and recalled similar strategies for managing family and social interactions beyond the home. In Korea, this has been taken one step further. Mr. Lee is forty nine years old; he is married with two teenage kids. When I visited his family in their remodeled flat in Pusan in 2003, he had recently enabled location tracking functions on his daughter's cell

6. Households have been compensated for their participation, and have been guaranteed privacy. Thus throughout this chapter material drawn from interviews and household visits is disguised through pseudonyms.

phone—he remarked, 'I know where my daughter is within a radius of 500 meters. I bought her a phone because she was back later and I was concerned with her safety.'

Mr. Lee is also not alone in his decision to purchase a cell phone for his teenage daughter. Children entering high school, or a time consuming after-school academic academy, often prompted parents that I interviewed to acquire cell phones. Parents talked a lot about ensuring their children's safety, and providing a communication channel in the case of emergencies. Richard and Jasmine, parents of teenage kids in Penang, recalling buying a cell phone for their two kids; 'we got it more for security than anything. It was for the kids, so that we can find them,' they say. Parents also acquired phones for themselves so that their kids could track them down. As one Indian father of teenage boys put it to me, 'technology has developed in this house because of my wife's insistence.' His wife says that 'I have a mobile phone for my son only. He is supposed to call me when he gets home, because I am still at work. I worry about him.' Not only are parents acquiring phones for themselves and their children for safety and security reasons, this same logic is applied to the purchase of cell phones for aging relatives. 'My daughter bought me my first cell phone five years ago, we talk on it every day, but mostly I do all the phoning, because she is too busy. She says to me, I am too busy. What is it? What is it?,' recounts another Penang resident, a retired sales woman in her early 60s. Apparently it is possible to have a phone but not always have the desire to use it.

People also used cell phones for business and work-related activities. In some households I visited, particularly in Indonesia, it was standard practice to maintain two cell phones—one for work, the other for home and social life. This seems to hint at a strong demarcation between public and private lives. In other cases, dual phones were maintained for domestic and international travel—one aid worker we spoke to had three hand-sets and four SIM cards to accommodate a travel schedule that included Australia, the United States, Afghanistan and parts of Europe. For the most part, however, it was more likely that people blended domestic and business lives. For some this lead to inevitable tensions—a journalist who claims that the stories follow him home. Others have developed strategies for maintaining some barriers. One forty-something Australian consultant we interviewed talked about assigning his wife and co-parent of his three young children a distinctive ringtone: 'For Ginny, there is a certain ring tone and I can pick it up immediately. As soon as it sounds—bingo—I know it is Ginny. The only time I take a call in meetings is Ginny [...] I only answer it for her.'

Most Koreans we interviewed used a similar, albeit elaborated, strategy, applying it to all the contacts in their address books. In Pusan in 2003, Mr. Lee told us that he relied on his cell phone for everything. At that time he estimated that he had more than 500 entries in his phone's address book. This prodigious number of entries (one of the highest we encountered in any Asian country) was organized into eight folders—family, business clients, business support, company, friends, relatives, *dong a ris* [semi-official circles of friends or shared communities] and his bowling club. Each folder was assigned its own ringtone. Younger people in Korea use similar methods to organize and regulate their social contacts: Sun-Hye also lives in Pusan, with her parents and older sister. At twenty, she is still at university and has a busy social life. She described her phone: 'currently I have five different bell tones for five designated groups; family, girls, boys, dong a ris and junior/ senior classmates.' All of these organizational methods owe some of their structure to the nature of the Korean language and its use of formal and informal predicates and pronouns. In order to avoid giving offense, one uses formal pronouns for those more senior to you (by rank, age, birth order, career, or university graduation)—cell phones help in that process, by making sure that you always know who is calling and how to respond. Communication here is not just about the exchange of words, but of the right form of those words.[7]

The high density of cell phone users in many Asian cities, and in some Asian countries (including Singapore, Australia and Korea with adoption rates over 85 percent), has created the possibilities of cellular platforms providing more than just a means of communication. In addition to this function as a communication tool, resembling in many ways their fixed line cousins, cell phones also seemed to function as a site for, and a source of, situationally relevant information production and consumption—that is the use of text messaging or SMS, and the various forms of media or information enhanced messaging (MMS). Unlike the United States where SMS has yet to see real adoption, almost all of the Asian countries I visited have remarkably high SMS traffic. In Singapore, there are an estimated 75 million messages sent a month from 4.3 million phones; in Korea, it is estimated that more than 100 million messages are sent per day, from 12 million cell phones.

In most of the households I visited, personal SMS was a regular part of people's daily usage of their phones—rates, contents and contexts varied considerably by age, occupation, life stage and gender. This fact is clearly recognized by service providers. One of Australia's leading providers advertises 'SMS your mates for FREE, 9pm to midnight', while Malaysia-based Maxis offers prizes and glory for speeding texting. In China, where texting is a complicated matter of negotiating a QWERTY keyboard phone-pad input through *pinyin* to Mandarin, SMS

7. Kim (2002) describes Korean cell phone practices as reflecting hierarchical authoritarianism (2002: 68), crony collectivism (2002: 69), personalism (ibid) and "appointment reciprocity" (2002: 71). This produces a constellation in which social interaction is incredibly important and is a measure of one's social network.

traffic is always high. Chinese consumers are using SMS to communicate all manner of information outside formal channels; it is probably not surprising then that the Chinese government recently announced that they were monitoring all SMS traffic in China. As one young Shanghai entrepreneur put it to me, 'my friends send me garbage messages, jokes, proverbs, silly sayings. The hottest topic is sex, because we cannot talk openly about it. Second to sex is politics.' He and his friends have many such messages saved on their phones (Taylor and Harper 2002). I am shown some: 'Christmas is arriving, so the Shanghai municipal government is cleaning up the streets and they have decided to get rid of ugly retarded men like you, so go hide. Don't tell anyone I told you.' Or, 'What's happiness? Happiness is a thankful heart, a healthy body, a good job, someone who loves you, a group of friends you can trust. When you get this, you will have everything.' Or, 'Good friends are like underwear; even if you fall very badly and rise spectacularly, it will always wrap around you. Very good friends are like condoms, always thinking of your safety. Best friends are like Viagra when you cannot find your strength to raise your head, they will help. Happy New Year.' The richness of these messages, irregardless of the value of their content, again points to the remarkable ways in which Mandarin lends itself to the SMS domain like no other language. Many of China's largest portals offer web to phone services, allowing you to input messages on a larger keyboard and send them to a phone, or giving you pre-entered messages to circulate and share.

In China, it might be all about contraband content, but in Singapore and Malaysia, at least when it comes to SMS, it is sometimes just about speed. Both countries regularly host speed SMS championships and a Singaporean woman recently took the crown for the fastest text messenger in the world, entering 26 words in 43.24 seconds. While this kind of record breaking speed was not something that most people I spoke with aspired to, they certainly did talk about the comparative ease of SMS as a way of sharing information. Denny, a Surabaya business man in his early 30s remarked that his wife used SMS when she wants to avoid confrontations: 'She uses SMS if she doesn't want to shout at me. So rather than calling and asking when I will come home, she sends SMS saying, "I am hungry, bring me food."' Ratnasari, a mother of five young children who lives with her husband in a suburb on the outskirts of Kuala Lumpur offers a slightly different take. An IT professional in her mid-thirties, she has a busy life, between full time employment and all the obligations of her children's education. She relies on her mobile phone to co-ordinate child-care with her mother who lives next door, Koran lessons, after school activities and meals, as well as to take care of various professional obligations. 'We use SMS, we don't play with it. The thing about SMS is that if you cannot call them, especially at night, you can send a message. And it is so much cheaper than calling. You don't have to talk longer, you just send a message.' By contrast, Phil and Susan, a recently married Australian couple talked about using SMS to rally members of the Church group —'we used SMS to contact people. It is very immediate because you can do it on a Saturday night, and catch people's attention.' That SMS can both grab attention ('Come to church in the morning') and be low band width ('I have sent the presentation') speak to the wide range of ways in which the mobile platform itself is integrated into people's lives—cell phones are pagers, notice boards, answering machines, fridge front doors, and bedside tables.

There are also barriers to adoption of SMS and these came up frequently too. In her early 20s, Gloria lives and works as a secretary in Xiamen. She is a heavy cell phone user, by her own account, but really does not like SMS. She says, 'Mostly I just call. I am too lazy for short messages. I don't like to send messages because I think you can spend too much time putting in one letter. My thumbs move too slowly.' I heard this refrain over and over again in China, in particular, but the issue of access to SMS was also one for older people, where arthritis made the size of the keypad difficult to manage, or the font and screen size were hard to manage for those with fading eye sight or bi-focals. The mother of a Korean teenager tells me that she perseveres with SMS, despite the difficulties, for her son: 'I have to do this so that my son will not think that I am uncool. He gets so excited and boasts to his friends when he gets a text message from me. I guess not many mothers can do it.'

Wickets while you wait: Cell phones are for information

The use of the mobile phone as an information platform does owe much to the rapid uptake of personal SMS and many of the early services and applications offered rely on that format, or things that evoke that format.[8] Information services send stock, weather and sport updates. Sports information is a good example—both information push and pull models exist. Some information push models consist of simple text notifications, others are more sophisticated. One Australian mobile carrier offers cricket updates—*Wickets while you wait*—as a streaming video service on its 3G platform. In Malaysia during the 2002 soccer World Cup when consumers were encouraged to use their cell phones

8. Various Malaysian political parties used SMS to rally voters during the 2004 election cycle, sending out more than 50,000 messages daily to party faithful. Not much against a backdrop of more than eight billion messages sent per month in Malaysia, but perhaps a harbinger of an interesting trend and certainly a sharp contrast from the last big information push.

to obtain up-to-the-minute soccer scores by accessing proto-internet services. For many of the people we interviewed this was their first attempt to use their phone to get up-to-the-minute information and the experience was often frustrating.

For many service providers moving consumers into these new information spaces is a challenge. In Korea, for a nominal fee, you can get SMS notifications of all credit card charges allowing for immediate verification of the charges. One young career woman in Seoul uses her phone as an extension of her wallet—paying for coffee in cafes, donating money to charities, and paying for things on the web. She says, by way of explanation, 'I am a communication freak. I feel nervous when I don't have access to a phone and email. I have been like this ever since I was a little girl.' JungEyn is not the only one using her phone for a wider and wider range of information practices. The mobile nature of cell phones creates the new opportunities for location-based services —everyone in Singapore jokes about the impossibility of hailing a taxi without a cell phone. Standing on Orchard Road one night in a sudden tropical down pour, I discovered just how true this was. Most public locations in Singapore now have some kind of code which you send in a SMS message to a taxi company who dispatches a taxi to your location—simple, but effective. Airports seem to be a favorite cellular enhanced location in Asia. Singapore's Changai International Airport provides interactive gaming stations for SMS users, cell phone and laptop recharging stations and real time flight information updates if you notify the airport you are present through an SMS message. Sydney's Kingsford Smith Airport responds to text requests for flight arrival and departure information.

Perhaps one of the most provocative information services provided on cell phones can be found in Malaysia. Maxis, Malaysia's largest provider, which offers a range of services targeted to different demographics. For Malaysia's substantial Muslim population, a cell phone can function as a *qiblah* or direction arrow pointing to Mecca. For an additional charge, you can also receive regular reminders of *salat* or prayer time customized to your location in Malaysia. This set of services is very popular in Malaysia (and indeed in other Muslim nations around the world). Information here is of a religious or ritual nature, yet is stored on a device frequently linked to ideas of modernity and progress (Bell 2004a). This tension seems less in Malaysia where the notion of a modern Muslim nation is common currency but again serves to highlight the different sorts of cultural work that cell phones are performing in Asia.

Sites of anxiety and control

Pick up any newspaper in urban Asia, and you can read a story about new technologies—many times these stories worry at great length about the negative effects of the internet, mobile phones and computers on society at large. Cell phones have been blamed for everything from the rise in divorce rates in India, to teenage suicides, political unrest and government overthrow. In 2003, cell phones were fast becoming an indispensable item for middle class urbanites living in Indonesia—whilst they represented a kind of new economy, or simply a new-found wealth, they also signaled a new vulnerability. Several people I interviewed worried about what it meant to be seen carrying a cell phone, and they had good cause. In Jakarta, the 'Red Axe Gang' targeted drivers stopped at red lights, talking on their cell phones. Whilst brandishing an axe menacingly, they would say 'your hand phone, or your windshield.' The logic here is simple: the most valuable thing in the car is the cell phone—it yields money on the black market and can be easily resold. It is also faster and cheaper to replace your cell phone than your windshield. Whilst never so well organized elsewhere, newspapers in India, China and Malaysia all reported on similar acts, one dubbing them 'lifestyle crimes.' As cell phones have become increasingly pervasive technologies, they have also become sites of anxiety and control, both on the part of individual users and of larger social institutions.

Over the last decade, social and governmental institutions across Asia have grappled with how to regulate cell phones, both as an industry and also as potential sites of social unrest or disruption. The Chinese government, which has maintained increasing tight control over digital media, is known to monitor all SMS traffic—a remarkable technical feat when you consider that Chinese subscribers sent more than 220 billion text messages a year, or more than half the world's text messages. In July of 2004, the government announced new regulations that effectively allows mobile service providers to police and even filter (i.e. censor) SMS content. Although designed to control the spread of pornography and 'fraudulent' content, many commentators believe that this move should be read against other government policies tightening control over the spread of electronic information (Lim 2004). The Indian government has asked mobile operators and service providers to develop and deploy technology to facilitate the monitoring and interception of SMS (Shahin 2002). In Singapore, ongoing debates about how national censorship regulations and practices impact text messaging transpire against the backdrop of new services like 'Hanky Pranky'—which offers consumers pre-recorded prank voice messages and SMS to send to their friends—and the 2001 decision by the Islamic Religious Council of Singapore (MUIS), the Sharia Court and the Registry of

Muslim Marriages that divorce via SMS was unacceptable. Although the rationale for cell phone purchases is the safety and well-being of one's children (see above), school officials in many countries have banned phones on school property as they served as a distraction to students.

Information services on mobile platforms are also subject to forms of governmental and social regulation, oversight and control. In Malaysia, the National Fatwa Council, a group of Islamic scholars appointment by the Kind, have recently barred Malaysia's Muslim population from participating in prize winning competitions and lotteries via SMS. Until February 2005, China Mobile and other mobile service providers have offered their customers the lunar almanac via SMS. However, in a surprise move, coming only a week before the Year of the Rooster began, the State Administration of Radio, Film and Television banned "any advertisements that harm young minds or violate regulations" through the promotion of superstition—this included 'birthday decoding', and 'new year fortune telling' text messages and phone services (The Age 2005). Shares in China Mobile and Sina took an immediate beating on the market as it became clear that much of their revenue stream was derived from these very popular and culturally grounded services.[9]

Of course, government regulation is just one dimension of the ways in which cell phones exist within cultural dynamics of anxiety and control. In Jakarta, a number of people commented on the utility of cell phones during periods of political instability to achieve personal safety. One remarkable tech-savvy sixty-something resident told me that her cell phone was vital—'it is easy access to everyone. When things happen in Jakarta, we use SMS. We say "be careful, don't go that way." We used it a lot during the "sweepings" [the riots of 1996].' Here phones kept people safe. Elsewhere phones are seen to put people in danger. In several households I visited in Malaysia, parents worried that mobile phone ownership put their children at risk of petty crime and street violence. Australian researchers recently published a study suggesting that phone ownership among young people often produces higher rates of debt (La Trobe University 2004); and over the last couple of years, Australian newspapers have carried warnings about the dangers of driving and talking, or driving and texting, comparing it unfavorably

9. According to a class-action lawsuit filed in United States District Court, Southern District of New York in February 2005, a substantial part of Sina Mobile (and presumably other mobile services providers in China) revenue stream came from 'fortune-telling' horoscopes, but this fact was not well known (Alexander O'Riordan, Individually and On Behalf of All Others Similarly Situated [Platiff] vs. Sina Corporation, Wang Yan and Charles Guowei Chao [Defendants]. Class Action Complaint, in United States District Court, Southern District of New York, February 18, 2005).

with drink driving—something that has surprising social stigma in Australia.[10] In China, CDMA technology was launched in 2003 with an ad campaign that showed consumers holding bunches of grapes to their heads, as if they were a cell phone. The message was simple—our technology is clean, green and good for you—concerns about the negative health impacts of cell phone technology clearly resonates here. In southern China, I encountered young people having their cell phones blessed in Buddhist temples in part to neutralize any negativity the object might exude—here health and well-being take on a broader set of meanings.

In the pages of the popular press in India, debates have waged for several years now about the ways in which mobile phones are leading to a breakdown of traditional courtship patterns.[11] Late in 2002, the cover of *India Today*, one of India's largest circulating news magazines, proclaimed that it was "Love in the time of SMS", suggesting among other things that SMS stood for "some more sex" and that cell phones were the new Viagra (Vasudev 2002). Interestingly in this piece and several following pieces, much was made of the fact that women, in particular, were taking advantage of this medium to explore their sexuality, thwart their family's plans, or circumvent their husband's control (Shahin 2002)—here the anxiety seems to be about female sexuality. Of course, these articles also raise issue about phone etiquette—about when it is appropriate to text or not. Larger questions about phone etiquette still seem in flux. Some spaces in urban Asia have tried to put themselves off limits to cell phones—several churches in Seoul have installed cell site dampeners to discourage parishioners from using their phones during services. In China and India, sending text messages on important ritual holidays like *Chinese New Year* or *Diwali* is prevalent but still viewed as somewhat less caring than calling or sending cards.

Thinking of sons: Phones say something about who we are

Mr. Woo's clam shell phone is decorated with a wooden dangle, hanging on a black thread. On the coffee table, his wife's phone has a matching ornament. In Korean, her reads, 'Mother, I love you', his

10. Drunk dialing is apparently sufficiently prevalent in Australia that at least one mobile service provider offers a phone lock to preclude phone calls within a particular time window.

11. Researchers have explored the link between new technologies and sex and sexuality in a number of Asian countries (Berry et al. 2003; Ellwood-Clayton 2003; 2005).

'Father, I love you.' They were gifts to the phone's owners from their teenage daughter before she went away on a long school trip. In addition to their more obvious cultural functions as communication and information tools, cell phones also say something about who their owners are. Cell phones operate as forms of intimate computing (Bell 2004b)—they are carried close to our bodies, are embedded into our daily lives, become an extension of ourselves and our personalities, our social relationships and larger cultural contexts. There are lots of ways to customize phones: dangles, ringtones, covers, buttons, lanyards, face plates, services, carry cases, numbers.

At its most basic level, consumers can augment their cell phones with a range of charms, amulets and kitsch that hang from a small eyelet frequently located near the top of the phone case. Some of these charms have deep seated cultural resonances—*bok* pouches and golden pigs in Korea, zodiac animals and jade in China (Hjorth 2003a). The next level of after-market addition comes with new face plates. There is an astonishing cottage industry of face plates, with everything from fashion labels, brand names, sports franchises, actors, musicians, icons and cartoon characters available in face plate sized incarnations. In the Coex Mall in Seoul, this kind of customization is taken one step further with stalls offering custom illustrations painted onto your phone while you wait. In a mall in a small Malaysian city, on a floor mostly dedicated to selling technology, I came across a shop front selling all manner of face plates: Disney charters, Britney Spears, Manchester United, colorful dragons. Hanging next to Winnie-the-Pooh were two face plates. One bore the face of Osama bin-Laden surrounded by the kind of halo one associates with older paintings of saints. On it, in yellow plastic Arabic script is the phrase, 'Give me your sons and I will make them martyrs.' Hanging right next to this, in a matching pink Hello Kitty wrapper, was a face plate depicting the first plane crashing into the World Trade Center buildings in New York—this face plate bore the date stamp of 11 September 2001. These are shocking artifacts but speak powerfully about the ways in which cell phones and their decorative function as a kind of extended body politic.

Phones can also manifest all forms of familial and social relationships, as well as aspirations. In Korea, there seems to be a well developed set of practices of setting screen IDs, wall paper and messages to appear when phones are first opened or switched on. One Pusan teenager translated her screen ID as 'this is not a commoner's phone, please close the phone and go away.' The words floated over a cartoon empress fanning herself. Another older boy in the same city had hacked his parents' phones so that their screens displayed a photo of him and his older brother with the words 'thinking of sons' written over it. Yet another young girl, this time in Daejon, sharing a cell phone with her mother, had set the screen to read 'please God, let me be top of the school.' These quite private messages are a revelation; teenagers are using cell phones to express their own identities but also to re-inscribe their relationships with their parents.

Although the dominant model of cell phone ownership seems to be at an individual level. It was also the case amongst many of the households that we visited that people shared cell phones—they were jointly used by parents and children, siblings, spouses, members of an extended household. These models of 'ownership' clearly violate some Western expectations about privacy, but they map onto extant cultural patterns around sharing and notions of social solidarity beyond the individual (Bell 2004b). In Malaysia, where phones are banned in school, it was quite common for teenagers to share phones with one or both of their parents. Benazir, a Malaysian teenager, shares a phone with her mother—she has it on weekends, and always carries it with her after school classes so that her family can track her down, but her mother uses it the rest of the time to arrange her own complex social life and the phone rings for both regularly. Again, this constitution of phone ownership speaks to larger social relationships and cultural practices.

In more than one household, choices about new phone purchases were driven by pragmatic concerns, like the brands of existing phones in the household—strategic purchase decisions make it possible to share parts, and batteries. Disposal of older phones represents an interesting set of social practices: older phones moved from husbands to wives, children to aging parents, or parents to younger children. Older phones also circulated outside of the home. In Indonesia, those living in Jakarta will send their aging phones to relatives in the outlying islands and smaller cities; in India, where second-hand cell phones have been a dominant part of the market, available handsets have often had prior lives in Hong Kong, Taiwan, and Singapore. It was also not uncommon for people to sell or trade-in cell phones and it was almost unheard of to throw one out, though many were damaged beyond repair in the comings and goings of daily life. Still this circulation and re-circulation of technology echoes older social, kin, political and geographic relationships (Maurer 2000b).

For many older people I interviewed, phones also said something about their age and relative abilities. In Korea, several men and women in their 60s, 70s and 80s described a rich and complicated pattern of cell phone usage for socializing, keeping in touch with family and friends, business contacts and university contacts. Unlike other age contemporaries I interviewed in Australia, China and Indonesia, the Korean seniors not only made and received calls, but also relied on SMS as a form of communication.[12] This was possible because there

12. At least one household in Australia also reported being unable to text message because of arthritis.

was a widely available hack that allowed consumers to increase the font size on their cell phone screens, empowering those with bi-focals or other eye-sight impediments to read the screen. Seemingly, this incredibly simple little detail—an unreadable small font—keeps the full functionality of cell phones out of the hands of many users. In China, knowledge of *pinyin*—the Romanized version of Mandarin and principle input method for cell phones—is also restricted to younger Chinese.

Phone form factors and after-market customizations are not the only ways in which phones are personalized, or linked to very particular sorts of identities and identity politics. When purchasing my own cell phone in Shanghai in 2003, I was told by the sales assistant that there were no phones in the store; it was a very Monty Python moment, because to my naive eye, the store seemed full of phones. As it quickly became clear, however, the problem was less the availability of phones, than the availability of a phone number that I could give others and that others would call. In China, and the Chinese Diaspora, where numbers are read as symbols with varying degrees of auspicious or inauspiciousness, phone numbers taken on new significance—not only are some numbers more auspicious (or lucky) than others, but certain sequences of numbers sound like auspicious phrases in Mandarin or Cantonese. The word '8' is particular lucky as it resembles the word, in both Mandarin and Cantonese for 'getting rich', though groups of the number '3' are also lucky.[13] The word '4', by stark contrast sounds very similar to 'death' in Mandarin. Number sequences too have alternate readings—'168' in Mandarin sounds like 'a road to prosperity.' Not surprisingly then, cell phone vendors display their available numbers outside their stores, and many consumers make decisions about cell phone purchases based on the phone number as much as the brand of handset. In Beijing in November of 2004, a man paid US$215,000 for the ultimate in lucky cell phone numbers: 133 3333 3333. In the pages of the *Strait Times*, Singapore's major daily, it was common in 2002 (and I suspect even today), to advertise services with an eye to these numeric practices. I have a full page ad from August 2002 that reads '$88—StarHub and SCV have come together—discover why it's double happiness in any language before these offers end.' Not only did the ad play on notions of marriage, but all the prices quoted on the page ended in eight.

13. In Sichuan province in 2003, a land-line number (8888-8888) was auctioned off for nearly US$290,000 to a local airline. In Vietnam, where the number nine is considered luckiest, the cell phone number 098 888 8888 was auctioned off for VN$1.91m in 2004.

So what is a cell phone?

Cell phones are obviously pieces of technology; arguably they seem to be more communication than information technologies, but they are technologies nonetheless (Abowd et al. 2005). They are also, in and of themselves, mobile objects, crossing boundaries within and beyond the home with comparative ease. They are completely open to commodification and profound personalization, and they maintain relative ease-of-use. Cell phones are also becoming ubiquitous forms of computational technology and as such are sites of interesting technical, design and social experiments (Hooker and Rabe 2000; Höök 2004). As technical platforms, they are also undergoing transformations, upgrades and feature expansions; the business models by which they are defused and the strategies by which profits are made are similarly undergoing transformations, regulations and de-regulations.

However, for as much as cell phones are pieces of technology, they are also constellations of social and cultural practice. In June 2002, Malaysian newsstands carried the latest issue of *Mobile Stuff*—a magazine geared toward Malaysia's growing population of cell phone subscribers. On the cover, two young Malay men in clothing that suggests more LA hood and less KL suburbs, hold out their cell phones to the camera beneath the banner headline "Real Men Use SMS." Six months later, billboards in Shanghai carried the image of a woman's shapely calves and ankles, bound with black patent leather ankle straps; positioned beneath one strap is her cell phone. Beyond their utility as a technology of information exchange, cell phones it appears have inserted themselves into the cultural fabric of societies across the world. Even small children prize cell phone ownership and there is a burgeoning industry for up-to-date cell phone replica toys for children. At least one Singaporean parent complained that his son had more up-to-date 'phones' than he did. Clearly, cell phones, and their various accoutrements, have become key symbolic markers and objects of fetish for the Asian 'new rich'—as such they can be read as markers of modernity, success, wealth, social standing, class and filial piety.

Of course not everyone in urban Asia has embraced cellular technology. Several Indonesian families talked about not having the 'culture of *hape*', of not being ready for it. Others talked about cell phones as prisons, or constant interruptions. In Korea, a couple in their early 30s identified themselves as 'machine idiots' by way of explanation of their failure to adopt cell phone technology. An Indian small business owner said to me, 'my mobile phone makes me mobile, but less efficient. When we had just one phone, and no phone in the factory, and none in the office at all, I felt more efficient. I have to plan everything out well. Now I am less efficient. If I forget something, I can just call. I am the worst. I spend more money, I am always available, I get nothing done.' In Australia, there seemed to be interesting gendered resistances to technology, with young mothers deliberately 'forgetting' to take their cell phones with them to the grocery store while their partners remained at home on child-duty. The language used to describe these resistances was interesting too—one married thirty-something woman described herself as a rebel for steadfastly refusing to adopt a cell phone; another, in her early sixties, declared that cell phones were not 'umbilical cords' and that she could do without it.

The very nature of these resistances however, strongly reinforces the notion that cell phones are as much cultural objects as technology objects (Özcan and Koçak 2003). As one Indonesian commentator put it in the op-ed pages of *The Jakarta Post* —"They are not just objects and technology; but also a system of ideas—of family, of intimacy, emergency and work" (Yanuar 2002). In urban Asia, at least, these cell phones, rather than facilitating an idealized universal communication, actually contribute to the re-inscription of local particularity and cultural difference as dimensions of a larger political economy of value. Here I have been tracing certain circulations of an ICT across multiple Asian urban geographies, and how they disrupt globalization discourse. This chapter offers a very different set of vantage points on how technologies are naturalized, and suggests new research questions and challenges using ethnographic methodologies and theoretical vantage points.

References

Abowd, G. et al. (2005), 'The Smart Phone', *IEEE Pervasive Computing*, 8 (2).

Agar, J. (2003), *Constant Touch: A global history of the mobile phone*, Cambridge: Icon.

The Age (2005), 'China launches astrology crackdown', *The Age*, 31 January, http://www.theage.com.au/articles/2005/01/31/1107020303300.html (14 July 2005).

Appadurai, A. (Ed.) (1988), *The Social Life of Things: Commodities in Cultural Perspective*, Cambridge: Cambridge University Press.

Appadurai, A. (2001), *Globalization*, Durham, NC: Duke University Press.

Bell, G. (2004a), 'Fieldnotes: Auspicous Computing?' *IEEE Internet Computing*, 8 (2).

Bell, G. (2004b), 'Fieldnotes: Intimate Computing?' *IEEE Internet Computing*, 8 (6).

Berry, C., Martin, F. and Yue, A. (2003), *Mobile Cultures: New Media in Queer Asia*, Durham, NC: Duke University Press.

Brown, B., Harper, R. and Green, N. (Eds.) (2001), *Wireless World*, London: Springer.

Crabtree, J., Nathan, M., and Roberts, S. (2003), *MobileUK: mobile phones and everyday life,* London: ISociety.

Ellwood-Clayton, B. (2003), 'Virtual strangers: Young love and texting in the Filipino archipelago of cyberspace', In: K. Nyiri (Ed.), *Mobile Democracy: Essays on Society, Self and Politics,* Vienna: Passagen Verlag.

Ellwood-Clayton, B. (2005), 'Desire and loathing in the cyber Philipines', In: R. Harper (Ed.), *The Inside Text: Social Perspectives on SMS in the Mobile Age,* London: Springer.

Fischer, C. (1992), *America Calling: A social history of the Telephone to 1940,* Berkeley: University of California Press.

Harper, R. (Ed.) (2005), *The Inside Text: Social Perspectives on SMS in the Mobile Age,* London: Springer.

Hjorth, L. (2003a), 'Pop and ma', In: C. Berry, F. Martin and A. Yue (Eds.), *Mobile Cultures,* Durham, NC: Duke University Press.

Hjorth, L. (2003b), 'Kawaii@keitai', In: M. McLelland and N. Gottlieb (Eds.), *Japan Cybercultures,* London: Routledge.

Hooker, B. and Raby, F. (2000), *Project #26765 FLIRT: Flexible Information and Recreation for Mobile Users,* London: Art Books International.

Höök, K. (Ed.) (2004), *Mobile Life: The Mobile Services Project,* Kista: Swedish Institute of Computer Science, http://www.sics.se/humle/projects/moblife/mobilelife.pdf (14 July 2005).

La Trobe University (2004), *Mobiles: massive Money Monsters,* Research Bulletin, March, http://www.latrobe.edu.au/bulletin/assets/downloads/2004/bulletin_maro4.pdf (14 July 2005).

Ito, M. (2004), 'A new set of Social Rules for a newly Wireless Society', *Japan Media Review,* March.

Katz, J. and Aakhus, M. (2002), *Perpetual Contact: Mobile Communication, private talk, public performance,* Cambridge: Cambridge University Press.

Kim, S. D. (2002), 'Korea: personal meanings', In: J. Katz and M. Aakhus (Eds.), *Perpetual Contact: Mobile Communication, private talk, public performance,* Cambridge: Cambridge University Press, 63-79.

Levinson, P. (2004), *Cellphone: The Story of the World's Most Mobile Medium and How It Has Transformed Everything!* New York: Palgrave McMillan.

Lim, L. (2004), 'China to censor text messages', *BBC Online News,* 2 July, http://news.bbc.co.uk/2/hi/asia-pacific/3859403.stm (14 July 2005).

Ling, R. (2004), *The Mobile Connection: The Cell Phone's Impact on Society,* San Francisco: Morgan Kaufmann.

Marcus, G. (1995), 'Ethnography in/of the World System: The Emergence of Multi-Sited Ethnography', *Annual Review of Anthropology,* 24, 95-117.

Maurer, B. (2000a), *Recharting the Caribbean: Land, Law and Citizenship in the British Virgin Islands,* Ann Arbor: University of Michigan Press.

Maurer, B. (2000b), 'A fish story: rethinking globalization on Virgin Gorda, British Virgin Islands', *American Ethnologist,* 27 (3), 670-701.

Maurer, B. (2005), *Mutual Life, Limited: Islamic Banking, Alternate Currencies, Lateral Reason,* Princeton, NJ: Princeton University Press.

Miller, D. (1998), *Material Cultures: Why some things matter,* Chicago: University of Chicago Press.

Özcan, Y.Z. and Koçak, A. (2003), 'Research Note: a need or a status symbol. Use of Cellular Telephones in Turkey', *European Journal of Communications,* 18 (2), 241-254.

Prøitz, L. (2005), 'Intimacy Fiction: Intimate Discourses in Mobile Telephony Communication Amongst Young Norwegian People', In: K. Nyiri (Ed.), *A Sense of Place: The Global and the Local in Mobile Communication,* Vienna: Passagen Verlag.

Robison, R. and Goodman, D.S.G., (Eds.) (1996), *The New Rich in Asia: Mobile Phones, McDonald's and Middle-class Revolution,* London: Routledge.

Shahin, S. (2002), 'India's love affair with high-tech flirting', *Asia Times Online,* 8 November, http://www.atimes.com/atimes/south_asia/DK08Df02.html (14 July 2005).

Taylor, A. and Harper, R. (2002), 'Age-old practices in the 'new world': A study of gift-giving between Teenage mobile phone users', In: *CHI 2002,* Minneapolis USA.

Vasudev, S. (2002), 'Love in the Time of SMS', *India Today,* 14 October.

Yanuar, N. (2002), 'Addiction to mobile phones amid neo-liberalism', *The Jakarta Post,* 12 August.

Communication problems

LESLIE HADDON

Communication problems as issues to be managed

Understanding people's use of telecommunications, their take up of new innovations and the social consequences of this can sometimes be enhanced by considering people's communication problems. Such problems can sometimes be experienced at an individual level, as in the amount of spam some people receive over the Internet. However, the main emphasis of this chapter is on problems experienced in relation to other people, especially in relation to other household members. This is because many of the examples given emerged from the domestication framework of analysis. Through empirical studies, this focused mainly on the household as a unit of analysis, although this could now be expanded to consider interactions with other social network members (Haddon 2003a; 2004).

The second point to note is that talking about 'problems' is a shorthand. Sometimes people might regard something more as minor irritant, even if they then develop strategies to deal with it. To return to the above example, deleting a few spam messages sometimes falls into this category. At the other extreme there can be real tensions and interactions between people around something explicitly perceived as a problem, such as telecoms bills—as we shall see below. And sometimes some aspect of communications is just a matter to be dealt with rather than a source of interpersonal confrontation, such as the wish to avoid surveillance by other household members and enjoy some privacy when contacting others—as we shall also see below. So when talking about communications problems, issues to be handled may sometimes be a more accurate description, conceptualising the user as communications manager.

In the rest of the chapter we first set the scene by looking at some research conducted in the 1990s on problems relating to the fixed-telephone line. This leads us to the question of how things are different now, a decade later, when we have far more communications options, and our communications repertoire has become more complex

(Haddon 2003b). Three different ways in which communications problems can be affected by these new options are then outlined. In the conclusion we return to the opening theme of why this is relevant for understanding communications behaviour, take up of new options and their social consequences.

Framework and fixed line research in the early 1990s

British qualitative research from the early 90s looking at the domestication of ICTs in general considered how people managed their relationship to the fixed telephone line (Haddon and Silverstone 1993; 1995; 1996). In other words, rather than focusing just on the number and the nature of the calls that people make, these studies explored the types of communications or situations that counted as 'problems' for them, and charted the type of strategies people develop for dealing with these. This sometimes included efforts to control communications, both outgoing and incoming (Haddon 1994).

One of the chief reasons for wanting to control outgoing calls was, as might be expected, the cost of calls. However, there were other problems, such as when some household members blocked the phone line with their own calls at a time when others in the home want to make or receive calls of their own. Years later, using the Internet on the single phone line could raise similar issues. The main problem from incoming calls was that they could sometimes by disruptive, if they were received during 'quality' family time together, dinner time, relaxing time after work, or times when people were otherwise busy, e.g. getting children for school, preparing meals. Finally, there were some issues around the desire for privacy when making calls, the desire to avoid the surveillance of other household members, which was especially important for teenagers.

These problems, tensions or issues led to various interactions with other household members, e.g. negotiating rules and understandings about making calls, perhaps trying to persuade others to ration calls. They could also lead to discussions with wider family, friends and colleagues, trying to persuade them to call at some times rather than others. And they could lead to other strategies. In the case of outgoing calls this might involve getting children to pay for some of their calls. In the case of incoming calls it could entail blocking incoming calls at certain times (e.g. unplugging the phone line, turning down the sound of the ringer), not answering the ringing phone or getting other people to answer the phone (to say, often falsely, that they were not available). In the case of privacy, this might mean going to another room, phoning when other household members were not around or going as far as to make some calls from outside of the home, including from public phone boxes. This reason for using public phone boxes was also found in French research (Carmagnat 1995).

A subsequent 5-country European quantitative study[1] aimed to explore the scale of such problems as well as the degree to which different types of strategy were used (Haddon 1998a). To give a flavour of its findings, here is a summary of the data for the five countries combined. In households with multiple members, 24 percent of the interviewees received complaints about the cost of the calls they made, but that figure is perhaps understandably over double that for 14-17 year olds.[2] Regarding strategies to control outgoing calls, 64 percent used cheaper tariffs, 64 percent rationed their own use, and 42 percent tried to limit the calls of other household members. The scale of the strategies indicates the extent to which telecoms costs are an issue in households, one shaping telecoms usage. Meanwhile, the attempts specifically to limit others and the complaints figures provide some sense of the interaction going on in households and the potential tensions that exist.

Regarding incoming calls, a substantial minority of respondents (37 percent) found these to be disruptive at least some of the time. When we look at the different control strategies used, 22 percent of users blocked phone calls as least some of the time, 22 percent had not answered the ringing phone, 29 percent had got someone else to answer and 32 percent had persuaded others to redirect calls to other times. While all of these strategies tended to be used occasionally rather than often, disruptive calls are clearly an issue for many people—which they try to do something about.

Finally, turning to the question of privacy, 39 percent used the strategy of phoning from another room, 30 percent phoned when nobody was home and 18 percent had phoned from outside the home, all the figures being higher for younger age groups. Privacy, too, is clearly an issue, and a significant number of people develop ways to manage it.

That was the 1990s. The more contemporary question is what happens when we now have many more communication options—the mobile phone and Internet as the obvious major examples? We must remember that there are on-going innovations and developments in relation to these technologies, such as the rise of texting after the mobile had already started to become a mass market, and changing tariff structures for both mobile and fixed lines. One set of questions one can ask about this expanding communications repertoire concerns the relationships between old and new elements. For example, elsewhere there

1. This covered, France, Germany, Italy, Spain and the UK (Haddon 1998). The published chapter is in Italian, but an English version of this can be downloaded from http://members.aol.com/leshaddon/Date.html.

2. This rose to as high as 65 percent for this age group in the UK.

has been an attempt to explore the circumstances in which new means of communication replace or complement older ones. This involved asking about the continuities between old and new, as in general we know that much of what people do with new communication technologies builds upon past practices (Jouet 2000). One can also ask how we accommodate new options and in general manage a more complex repertoire. For example, how do we choose which media to use when we want to communicate? (Haddon 2003; Haddon and Vincent 2004)

However, the point of this chapter is that in addition to these types of inquiry we can pose the question about relationships between communications options in a different way: how do new communications options relate to old communications problems. Three possibilities will be considered here:

1. Where new options are perceived as providing solutions to old problems.
2. Where new options shift the issue to be managed and alter the negotiations between household members.
3. Where new communications options can themselves give rise to new problems and new things to be managed.

Solving old problems

If we take the example of disruptive calls (for some people at certain times) we saw how even by the 1990s people had already developed a range of coping strategies. Yet even by this stage the innovation of the answering machine had provided yet one more option, one more solution to the problem. Despite being sold as a device to take calls when people were out of the home, the answering machine was also in practice widely used for filtering calls. Once again, referring back to the European study, if we take the combined figures for the five countries concerned, 18 percent often used the answering machine for filtering calls, 32 percent doing this occasionally. At a later stage Caller ID provided a related filtering option. This reminds us that we need to consider not only totally new communications channels when considering the repertoire of options, but also related innovations in terms of new devices or services.

We noted earlier that in the 1990s privacy was sometimes sufficiently important, for some more than others, that people were developing a range of strategies to manage this. Even by the mid-1990s European research, when the mobile phone was still not so widespread, 14 percent of interviewees were already acknowledging that the mobile phone was sometimes used precisely because it enabled such privacy (Haddon 1998). Indeed subsequent research specifically on youth showed how the mobile phone enabled young people to avoid parental monitoring of their calls (Ling and Helmersen 2000; Ling 2004).

The same point could be made in relation to other 'problems' identified in the 1990s. For example, the mobile phone and later broadband offered more than one line, both helping to overcome the problem of one household member blocking the single household line with their calls. In some households parents getting children to pay for their own pre-paid cards for their mobile was one way of avoiding arguments about the cost of the calls they made (Ling and Helmersen 2000).

While the above examples are used to illustrate the main point, that new elements in the repertoire can offer solutions to older problems, this is inevitably also a simplification. Let us return to the example of the answering machine. They themselves could constitute a new 'problem', or at least an irritation, for callers who did not like to deal with them.[3] Sometimes the knowledge that filtering was an option could create the suspicion that the people being called were hiding behind their machines, and could lead to verbal attempts to persuade them to pick up the phone. Conversely, other callers learnt to expect answering machines at the end of the line, and were at ease with asynchronous communication. Sometimes they even preferred this, phoning a fixed line when they anticipate the person will be out—and occasionally they were surprised and unprepared when the person called was unexpectedly present. In other words, while a new option may address an old problem at one level, it can in turn lead to a whole new set of interactions, issues or strategies.

Shifting problems

In addition to solving old problems, new options also transform the issue to be managed. For example, in the 1990s, we saw how there was evidence of some concern, or at least wariness, about the potential or actual size of phone bills, with examples of parents especially trying to ration children's use of the phone. A recent British small-scale study (Haddon and Vincent 2004) suggested that this underlining concern with telecoms costs was still present. However, UK tariff options are far different now, with a host of mobile phone and even fixed-line tariff packages offering flat-rate tariffs, either for certain times of day or all day. Therefore some households in that study have moved to flat-rate fixed line calls. This meant that the question of rationing was no longer

3. In the 1996 European survey, 55 percent of people were annoyed when they encountered an answering machine. At that time, 36 percent said they immediately hung up, 12 percent listened and then hung up, 44 percent left a message and 7 percent said that their response depended on the circumstances (Haddon 1998b).

so relevant, if there were no extra costs incurred in making additional calls. However, there were still efforts to persuade children, for example, to use the fixed line in the first place rather than other channels such as the mobile phone, since the latter could incur further costs per call. Or if the tariff was such that flat-rate billing applied to the fixed line or mobile after a certain time, then children (and adults) were sometimes persuade to steer their calls to those times when call were regarded as being effectively 'free'.

Moreover, some of the discussion about how best to keep down telecommunications costs arose not only when particular calls were made or, more often, when bills arrived but also when negotiating which operator and tariff arrangement to have in the first place or deciding whether to change these. To summarise, the problem of telecommunications costs may still be present, it has not necessarily disappeared, but the details of its management and the nature of the search for solutions can change.

New problems, new strategies

New communications options can also give rise to new problems, new things to be managed. A British study of a day-in-the-life of families and their communication choices started to show some of the new frustrations, or irritations emerging as telecoms options have grown. For example, it was increasingly common for callers to try one channel, such as the fixed line, and then another one when the first failed or was occupied. However, sometimes this could happen too quickly. Or else, as the interviewee below indicates, it is precisely because this person was engaged in one call that she did not want to be contacted through another channel.

"One thing I don't like is when my husband tries the house phone and it's engaged. So he knows I'm on the phone! And (yet) he'll ring the mobile. By the time I get to it it's stopped. He often does that. It's really annoying." (Haddon and Vincent 2004)

Appropriate behaviour in these cases had not yet been worked out. Meanwhile the sheer increase in communications that sometimes followed from having more channels could be overwhelming.

"Sometimes it infringes on your privacy. I mean you want to be left alone and unless you switch the thing off [...] For example, my husband (calls and asks) "Where are you, what are you doing'. (And I think) 'Oh, leave me alone, don't drive me mad" (Haddon and Vincent 2004).

Turning specifically to the mobile phone, various studies have looked at how the mobile can be perceived as being disruptive in different public spaces.[4] This has given rise to observations about how users manage the relationship to co-present others when they are called—be that people they are with or just others in the vicinity—as well as with the interlocutor (e.g. Ling 1997; 2004; Fortunati 2003). For example, when do they go off to one side to receive the call, when do they indicate to others that the call will not be long? They now have to think about how to manage relations with the interlocutor in those situations, perhaps indicating the situation and the time that they can spend on the call. Meanwhile, how people control and manage their availability on the mobile is an issue people now have to think about, developing policies about who they give the mobile number out to, and strategies about when they switch the phone on and how they deal with particular calls—answering immediately or sending it to voice mail (Licoppe and Heurtin 2001; 2002).

There have been various issues related to texting on the mobile phone, with problems arising sometimes in relation to peers in social networks. One such issue is when it is or is not appropriate to manage communication by text at all as opposed to some other channel or face-to-face (e.g. when ending a relationship with a boy or girlfriend). Another problem to be managed was dealing with expectations about how quickly to return the gift of a text message (Taylor and Harper 2001)—although this could also apply to expectations regarding replying to phone messages or emails. And returning to intra-family relations, and another example from the British study, one teenager caused great anxiety at home and immediate phone calls back from his parents when he sent a text back from a holiday abroad just mentioning that there had been some problem. This illustrates the more general issue of when it is appropriate to send a text about what topic, and the consequences of doing so.

Similar questions have also been raised about the appropriateness of some emails, not so much spam but from and to known social networks. This had led some to comment on how this medium is still relatively immature, when it can lead to 'unnecessary' emails (almost like spam—when one can be overwhelming), emails that find their way to the wrong people, or emails that create misunderstandings. Once again, people have started to develop strategies for dealing with all of

4. In the 1996 survey, 47 percent of people had a negative reaction to seeing people using mobiles in public spaces (Haddon 1998b). One would have thought that this reaction would have diminished as mobiles became more commonplace, but use, sometimes perceived as misuse, could still attract surprisingly high negative responses. In research for Eurescom in 2000 (Mante-Meijer et al. 2001), nearly two-thirds agreed with the statement that mobile phones disturb other people (Ling 2004).

these potential or actual problems, although some still remain frustrated by some of these problems.[5]

Conclusion

The very start of this chapter noted that understanding communications problems could throw some light on telecommunications behaviour. Clearly the examples provided above illustrate factors shaping the calls people are willing to make, if there are sometimes interpersonal pressures to limit calls, as well as to receive them (if some are disruptive). The examples show why some calls are made at certain times, in certain places (if we consider the privacy discussion), and, as our options increase, through one channel or communications mode rather than another (e.g. fixed-line vs. mobile, voice vs. text, etc).

The opening statement also suggested that this was one factor, albeit only one, of relevance for understanding the adoption of new channels and options (and, we can now add, amount of their use). This is important for the developers of new ICTs and services. There is a tradition in the telecoms industry, albeit slightly changing now, of looking at user needs. Perhaps in part this might be conceptualised as problems users experience, considering not just usability challenges but some of the more social, interpersonal issues described in this chapter. Maybe reflecting upon actual and potential problems of the kind described here might help to create opportunities for new products and services, or at least avoid aggregating existing tensions or creating new dilemmas. More generally, while telecoms companies would desire us to consume ever more of their products, some of these examples have shown the tensions created by the costs of the current levels of telecoms usage.

When we turn to the social consequences of what, for many people, is an expanded communications repertoire, once again we can start to approach this by asking how much any of the problems have changed. Have some been solved, have they been transformed, or do new communications options lead to new, and possibly more substantial problems? Often when we ask about social consequences, the question is one of how much has stayed the same, how much has changed, and is that change relatively superficial or more significant? In these examples, we see this type of question can be asked of negotiations about the costs of telecoms—it remains an underlying issue, but clearly some of the discussions and decisions within households are different from the 1990s situation outlined earlier.

5. This section reflects work currently being undertaken for the Oxford Internet Institute by the author, involving interviews with people about their experience of email.

To finish, and standing back from all these particular examples, we can pose the more general question of why something is felt to be a problem or why something had to be managed. What expectations exist, where do these come from, is some behaviour infringing norms that existed before new telecoms options? Such questions have been posed in relation to some problems with the mobile (e.g. Ling 1997; Ling et al. 1997), but they need to be asked more generally of each new medium or innovation.

Secondly, we need to pose the question of how much of the way we manage our communications repertoire is settled and how much is still in flux. In other words, people develop strategies for dealing with problems, but to what extent do tensions or frustrations still exist, to what extent are people still in a process of trying out different ways of dealing with problems and in a process of on-going negotiation with others?

References

Carmagnat, M.-F. (1995), *Les Telécommunications en Situation de Mobilité, Usages et Prospective*, CNET PAA/TSA/UST/4141, January.

Fortunati, L. (2003), 'Mobile Phone and the Presentation of Self', Paper for the conference 'Front Stage/Back Stage: Mobile Communication and the Renegotiation of the Social Sphere', Grimstad, Norway, 22-24 June.

Haddon, L. (1994), 'The Phone in the Home: Ambiguity, Conflict and Change', Paper presented at the COST 248 Workshop 'The European Telecom User', Lund, Sweden, 13-14 April.

Haddon, L. (1998a), 'Il Controllo della Comunicazione. Imposizione di Limiti all'uso del Telefono', In: Fortunati, L. (Ed.), *Telecomunicando in Europa*, Milano: Franco Angeli, 195-247.

Haddon, L. (1998b), *The Control of Communication. Imposing Limits on Telephony*, A Report for Telecom Italia.

Haddon, L. (2003a), 'Domestication and Mobile Telephony', In: Katz, J. (Ed.), *Machines that Become Us: The Social Context of Personal Communication Technology*, New Brunswick, NJ: Transaction Publishers, 43-56.

Haddon, L. (2003b), 'Research Questions for the Evolving Communications Landscape', Paper for the conference 'Front Stage/Back Stage: Mobile Communication and the Renegotiation of the Social Sphere', Grimstad, Norway, 22-24 June.

Haddon, L. (2004), *Information and Communication Technologies in Everyday Life: A Concise Introduction and Research Guide*, Oxford: Berg.

Haddon, L. and Silverstone, R. (1993), *Teleworking in the 1990s: A View from the Home*, SPRU/CICT Report Series, No.10, University of Sussex, Falmer.

Haddon, L. and Silverstone, R. (1995), *Lone Parents and their Information and Communication Technologies*, SPRU/CICT Report Series, No.12, University of Sussex, Falmer.

Haddon, L. and Silverstone, R. (1996), *Information and Communication Technologies and the Young Elderly*, SPRU/CICT Report Series No.13, University of Sussex, Falmer.

Haddon, L. and Vincent, J. (2004), 'Making The Most Of The Communications Repertoire—Mobile And Fixed', Paper for the conference 'The Global and the Local in Mobile Communication: Places, Images, People, Connections', Budapest, 10-11 June.

Jouet, J. (2000), 'Retour Critique sur la Sociologie des Usage', *Réseaux*, 100.

Licoppe, C. and Heurtin J.-P. (2001), 'Managing One's Availability to Telephone Communication through Mobile Phones: A French Case Study of the Development Dynamics of Mobile Phone Use', *Personal and Ubiquitous Computing*, 5 (2), 99-108.

Licoppe, C. and Heurtin J.-P. (2002), 'France: Preserving the Image', In: Katz, J. and Aakhus, R. (Eds.), *Perpetual Contact: Mobile Communication, Private Talk, Public Performance*, Cambridge: Cambridge University Press, 94-109.

Ling, R. (1997), '"One can talk about Common Manners!" The Use of Mobile Telephones in Inappropriate Situations', In: Haddon, L. (Ed.), *Communications on the Move: The Experience of Mobile Telephony in the 1990s*, COST248 Report, Farsta: Telia, 73-96.

Ling, R. (2004), *The Mobile Connection. The Cell Phone's Impact on Society*, San Francisco: Morgan Kaufmann.

Ling, R. and Helmersen, P. (2000), '"It must be Necessary, it has to Cover a Need": The Adoption of Mobile Telephony among Pre-adolescents and Adolescents', Paper presented at the 'Sosiale Konsekvenser av Mobiltelefoni Seminar', organised by Telenor, Oslo.

Ling, R., Julsrud, T. and Kroug, E. (1997), 'The Goretex Principle: The Hytte and Mobile Telephones in Norway', In: Haddon, L. (Ed.), *Communications on the Move: The Experience of Mobile Telephony in the 1990s*, COST248 Report, Farsta, Telia, 97-120.

Mante-Meijer, E., Haddon, L., Concejero, P., Klamer, L., Heres, J., Ling, R., Thomas, F., Smoreda, Z. and Vrieling, I. (2001), *Checking it out with the People—ICT Markets and Users in Europe*, A report for EURESCOM, Heidelberg.

Taylor, A. and Harper, R. (2001b), *The Gift of the Gab? A Design Oriented Sociology of Young People's use of 'MobilZe!'* Working Paper, Digital World Research Centre, University of Surrey, UK.

Vincent, J. and Haddon, L. (2004), *Informing Suppliers about User Behaviours to better prepare them for their 3G/UMTS Customers*, Report 34 for UMTS Forum.

From teenage life to Victorian morals and back: Technological change and teenage life

Richard Harper

Preamble

We are often told that mobiles, and that mobile texting in particular, has changed the lives of teenagers (Ling 2004; Nyiri 2003). One can easily imagine how, in the past, teenagers would wonder what their friends were up to, and would have to exercise their minds to figure this out: now, in contrast, they can call or text them. Thus the walls of teenage experience have been altered; what was once impossible is now achieved at the cost of only a few pence (for a review, see Harper et al. forthcoming). But is this change so great? One should remind oneself also that what teenagers find when they make these calls or texts to their friends is not something that will surprise us or them: one imagines that they discover that their friends are, like themselves, lurking in their bedrooms, sulking about too much homework and yearning to be elsewhere. And this indolence, this teenager ennui, one would readily agree, is hardly something new nor, alas, something that will vanish in the 'mobile age' (see Katz & Aakhus 2002; Brown et al. 2002; Harper 2003).

The particularities of teenage experience aside, the point here is that the nature of social experience is in part captured by recalling that individuals create a mental picture of the world, one which captures where they are, where others are and where both they and those others have been and will go. All people do this in various ways; it is perhaps the phenomenological philosopher and occasional sociologist Alfred Schutz who explores this most thoroughly. The centre of this experience, the heart, if you will, of this gestalt is the individual, and the measure of this world is how encompassing it is, how many people populate it, how many memories it carries and what prospects it holds for the future.

According to this view, the trouble with teenagers is that their attempts to create this world are rather poor: their attempts to do so are amateur, indeed, by definition adolescent. Instead of, say, creating a mental space through conversation and interchange with people of different perspectives and social positions, for example, they solidify their parochialism by intensifying their experience of a world populated solely by those in identical positions, by people of the same age, the same sex, the same class at school, and the same geographic area (for a more general version of the same argument, see Gergen 2002: 227-241). And they do this through idleness, insouciance, and purposeless endeavours; they just 'hang out' with their mobile in just the same way that they used to hang out on street corners before (see Grinter & Eldridge 2001). There is therefore no surprise that there is a tension at the heart of this experience, a tension having to do with how the character of these individuals matures, grows, develops and moves beyond this self inflicted myopia, this adolescence.

Exploring teenagerdom

How is this achieved? Is this achieved through constant connectivity to one's fellow teenagers (see Ito 2003)? Does an adolescent get more mature by being able to text all day and all of the night (Kaseniemi 2001)? Does being able to talk from one's own bedroom with one's fellow teenagers in their bedrooms lead one to grow up?

And thus, in a roundabout way, I come to the rub of this chapter. I want to explore what the nature of teenage experience might be, and in particular their life vis-à-vis mobile devices. I noted at the outset that much is said about how this life is being changed by mobiles, and much is claimed about how the future can be discerned in the current actions of teenagers (see Nyiri 2003; Plant 2002).

But is it what it seems? Is the future all around us in the sweaty hands of our children? Or is it somewhere else, to be glimpsed not in the glory of their angst but in the dullness of the past, not in their faltering attempts at freedom but in their invocation of old fashions, ones that we ourselves have long forgotten.

Whatever the answer to these questions turn out to be, I will suggest that a way of identifying them is through exploring how teenagers, like all people, create and sustain a mental world populated by friends, families and strangers, a world that is at once embodied in the things they collect around them and in the things that they do day in, day out. This world, again like all social worlds, is a morally sanctioned construct, done well, done badly, managed chaotically and managed efficiently. What distinguishes it is two things: first, the commonplace fact that 'teenagerdom' (for want of label) is a world in which individuals transit, from being socially irresponsible and carefree to being responsible and burdened (as it happens this is a shift as much in physical form as it is in social status). Second, it is also a world that is, in terms of experience for the teenagers themselves, myopic, yet a world that from their point of view is rent with agony, doubt, and arrogance; for them, their lives are indeed a melodrama. But in so being this world, and their performance of it, is, I will contend, all too ordinary.

I will explore this world by suggesting that there are a number of metrics used in everyday ways by teenagers themselves and those who have to deal with them (most especially parents), to indicate how well they are faring in the shift in social status. Two metrics in particular will be focused on. They are, first of all, the metric of financial cost—though not only of texts themselves, but the costs implicated in all forms of every day conduct. I will show how the financial management of mobile telephony and texting by teenagers stands as a testament for the management of these other costs, and thus how their spendthrift approach to, say, clothes buying is a refection of and is to be uncovered by assessing their competence or otherwise at managing mobile phone costs. The second metric relates to what one might call conversational turn-taking systems, including text communications. I will show how systems of etiquette and propriety governing mobile communication are used to create fine but often consequential distinctions between teenagers of different ages, gender and social connection, and this in turn is a reflection of the delicate yet complex systems of turn-taking propriety that govern the behaviours of all competent social adults, whatever their age. I will note, however, that it is individuals of the late teen years who seem most rigid and elaborate in the way they impose these systems, excluding some from communicating with them and admitting others strictly in accordance with certain rules of access that older and younger age groups worry less about.

By selecting two metrics it should be clear that I am not proposing to explore every dimension of teenage life; that would too ambitious, even if possible, which I doubt. These two are selected because of their salience in our data. As it happens they also illustrate the importance of matters which are often left out by much of the research on teenagers—whatever the reason for might be.

The cost of mobile phones

With this in mind, I now turn to the data I want to consider. It was collected with various colleagues on a project investigating the evolution of fixed and mobile phones in family life. This research was part of an ongoing series of projects with a major mobile network operator in the UK, and entailed diary studies and interviews of households in the UK and Sweden. Some 59 persons were interviewed and monitored, populating some 21 households. All had both mobile and fixed lines available. The research focused on the grounds for the use of either.

The assumption that has governed mobile operator strategy on the fixed and the mobile has been that cost is and will remain the primary driver. Since mobile operators have been able to charge a premium for their technology outside of the home they see no reason to reduce that premium to make a success of mobiles in the home. Our research was meant to identify ways in which they could leverage new opportunities without having to reduce their premium charging.

Our research showed that cost, though often mentioned as the key driver, especially in interviews and focus groups, rarely drove actual behaviour. Other factors, like use of the 'virtual address book' on a mobile, the convenience and ease of use of the respective devices "their handiness as well as matters of habit were all more important". Without going in to the details of all the findings, there was one issue that was particularly interesting. This related to the fact that the cost of mobile phones was indeed something that people were conscious of, but that the issue of this cost was not viewed as something that could be thought of separately from other kinds of costs. The cost of mobiles stood testament to costs in general. Let me recount one interview with a father in a UK household which conveys the gist of what I mean.

"You know mobile phone bills are about the only thing I can talk to my daughters about when want I really want to talk to them about is not eating things out of the fridge and not telling anyone. I mean, they have got to learn that there are other people in the house and the only way I can think of making them do this is by having a talk about mobile phone bills and then I can talk to them about money and living together and sharing things without coming across as pompous, like some Victorian patriach."

What was he getting at here? Was he wanting to exercise, as some sociologists would have it, his monopoly of power in the home? (see Ito, op cit; as regards power over space, see Massey 1994; for a somewhat more general version of argument see Foucault 1977) Or was he simply a little eccentric and somewhat rigid, unable to cope with the idea that kids do not worry about expense? I would like to suggest that he was simply being a normal adult, an ordinary run-of-the-mill dad trying to figure out how to help his kids grow up.

A vignette of family life

Let me explain this more carefully again by reference to this particular family. When the mobile phone bills—or direct debit statements to be precise—arrived, this dad would pick them up and open them, and leave them around for his two girls—late teenagers—to bump into. He would put them on the kitchen table or on the fridge so that he could guarantee they would see them. They would thus not only be aware of their existence but would be also aware that 'Dad had put them there since he wants to lecture us'.

He was not, however, concerned with the size of the phone bills. As he put it, 'That's up to them'. His concern was to discuss how the respective phone bills identified certain behaviours which he viewed as irresponsible, and these costs may have had nothing to do with the mobile phones themselves.

As a case in point, he had noted that when the girls were both at home (one had just started at University and had been home for two periods of holiday), his own fixed line phone bill went up substantially. His phone statement showed that this was primarily because of calls to mobile phones rather than to other fixed lines. Now, his concern was that for many of these calls it would have been cheaper had they been made from a mobile on the same network. He also believed that in many cases the girls' own phones were on the right networks for this. He believed it was the girls who chose to make the calls on the fixed line not simply or even partly because they knew their dad was paying, but because they could not be bothered to find their own phone. Their costly behaviour was simply irresponsible behaviour.

The reason why he wanted to talk with the girls, then, was that he did not necessarily mind paying bills, including their own, but he did mind paying bills unnecessarily. Bills could be reduced if individuals thought about the overall economy of the family. For him the issue was that the girls treated expenditure as primarily individual rather than collaborative matter, and so they did not act in a way that reflected concern for others. In crude terms, if the girls recognised that some costs were shared then he believed that their behaviour would be different. Their use of the fixed line phone when a mobile would have been cheaper would have been an instance of this. By addressing this behaviour he hoped that the girls would adjust their behaviour for all shared matters in the house, whatever they might be. To be able to conduct oneself with respect to others was a matter of vastly more importance than the actual costs of something in particular. It was, if you like, a question of morality.

Now the term power might seem to offer a nice sociological view on exploring the issues here: after all there is clearly a difference in power between the dad and his daughters, especially over economics matters, or, more bluntly, over who had the most cash. But there is no news in saying that dads have more power than their teenage daughters, and if the goal of sociology is to merely repeat what one might call common sense knowledge then it would have withered long ago. No, the purpose is to prise open the nature of social experience and unpack it into elements so that we can see it more clearly, and sometimes in new light. All this has to be done without compromising a concrete sense of the experience in question.

To illustrate this let me provide another example of the intercourse between father and daughters in this house. If the first example was about money and thus obviously about power, this second example is about altogether different matters. As part of each study, several visits were undertaken; during the first the cost of fixed to mobile came up. In a later visit, a very different yet oddly related topic came up.

"Look this sounds daft but I had some sausages in the fridge to make dinner and when I went to the fridge I found that (one of his daughters) had eaten them, well at least it must have been her. Now, they are only sausages—though they were special ones I had bought—and I don't mind them eating them but now there isn't anything to cook and I don't want to go up to (the nearest supermarket)."

We saw in the first example that the father did not worry too much about mobile phone bills but their arrival was the only pretext he could think of that would enable him to get the girls to sit down over dinner and have, as he put it, 'a rational conversation' about learning to share. In the instance he is reporting here, his real agenda was about the sausages, but he felt that the issue of sausages *per se* would be simply laughed at by his girls. He was probably right. Yet, only through addressing a matter that they thought was potentially serious, namely phone bills, could he indirectly address matters that they thought were inconsequential, though he thought them symbolic. In short, he wanted to use conversations regarding mobile phone bills to raise the possibility that they might start behaving in different ways regarding other matters.

One might put this in a larger context: when these teenagers had been children, they might have simply taken without asking and used without commenting, as they were getting older and, presumably, as leaving home became increasingly imminent, he wanted them to start living in a manner where shared responsibility was the norm. His view was that part of moving on from being a teenager has to do with the ability of taking on responsibility. One of these responsibilities is for household bills; another has to do with consumption of shared goods, like groceries. The girls should cease behaving with little or no concern for others in the same space; they should start considering how their own behaviours would affect others. In a phrase, he simply wanted his girls to start being like adults: recognising that if the fridge was stripped of food then others in the house might be left hungry by the end of day, having planned to eat that same food.

Nothing sinister was meant here nor yet can one accurately capture it by describing it as the exercise of an oppressive power. I have deliberately chosen this example as a way of highlighting the fact that the experience of teenagers is an essentially prosaic affair. Here is no melodrama, just the tiresome battle between adults trying to get teenagers to be less selfish. Of course at times this battle can take on the appearance of a melodrama, especially from the perspective of the teenagers: but this serves only to further underline my point; not a real drama but a false drama, not real battles over social structure but squabbles over sausages.

The social propriety of texting

The rub of the matter, then, for these teenagers and the household that they were part of is the difficult, socially organised process of movement from one social role to another. Here a father is trying to facilitate that in the best way he can; though doubtless his daughters thought his efforts at best harmless, at worse tiresome, almost certainly his actions caused them to giggle. But this change in social status is not solely achieved through the coercion and benign encouragement of others; teenagers also contribute to it themselves, albeit the way they do so—and the manifest consequence of this achievement—may not be so visible to themselves.

I will examine this by addressing the issue of turn-taking on mobile communications, texting being one genre of these communications. I will make a similar argument about the question of the social shift in the competence of teenagers, but will show in this case that the adoption of various socially accepted patterns of mobile phone use are closely related to age differences in teenagers: eighteen year olds being systematically more sophisticated (in their own terms) than thirteen year olds. I will explain that the prosody of calling and answering, of content and topic management with mobiles, becomes increasingly artful as teenagers age, so much so that after a certain age an inability to manage these issues gracefully is viewed as a measure of immaturity. In other words, as they grow, teenagers themselves start behaving in ways that distinguish those who are becoming adult and those who are not. These skills and competences have to do with the social rituals of when to address someone, how to address someone, and what to say. These are at once ornate yet everyday, prosaic yet artful. They are about the socially achieved skills of ensuring the appropriate intersections of time, place, content and persons.

Managing calls

Crudely speaking, new users do not know how to manage mobile calls, and this results in them using the phones excessively, and it is only gradually as they age from the impressive heights of the first year of teenagerdoom towards the middle and later teens that these skills become more astute and refined.

These skills have many forms and their evolution is itself a measure of the general social skills of the individual in question. In Kaseniemi's 'Mobile Message' (2001) for example, teenagers report how tiresome they find friends who have just got their first mobile: apparently they phone and text all the time. Once they have got over this excitement they start to use the devices more 'appropriately', we are told. What this means is itself variable and complex. The same set of subjects report differences in the behaviour of the two genders: girls treat what they share and exchange over the mobile as more private than boys. So girls modulate what they say according to the gender of the person they are calling.

In our own research corpus, and as we have remarked upon extensively (see Taylor & Harper 2003: 267-96), there are ritual communications that need to be undertaken when girls and boys are going out together: the goodnight text sent from a boy to a girl last thing at night is now a social requirement, for example. Failure to deliver the message results in a summons the following morning in the playground. Sending a steady stream of little notes throughout the school day is also a measure of devotion and adoration; the absence of the same is an indication that an 'item' (an idiomatic label for a couple) are not what they once were.

All these little differences, in content, in the frequency of calls, in who is calling who and so on, are in a sense not only visible to those involved and merely matters of private moment, they are also matters of public interest since all are subject to the same patterns, exchanges, and rituals. Boys complain to other boys about the oppressive need to send goodnight texts; girls about the slovenly failure of the boys to send them, and so forth.

These patterns are of course somewhat varied with different codes being applicable in different societies and cultures: in Japan for example, we are told by Riviere & Licoppe (forthcoming) that texting is used between persons of different social status so as to avoid the *faux pas* of interruption; between intimates such as husband and wife, no such fear is present and thus voice calls are made any time day or night. In contrast, in France, texting is used not so much to avoid the problem of interruption as to avoid the possibility of emotional violence that goes with close relationships; thus girls would prefer to text their complaints to a boyfriend since this would not result in a physical outburst from that same boy; the boys prefer to text their own concerns since the girls do not respond with tears and weeping. Somehow text not only avoids these all too real physical reactions being seen, they also make them less likely to happen; girls apparently find themselves less weepy when they communicate with texts, boys less prone to violence. Now I do not want to comment on what this says about the respective cultures, these being matters properly addressed in the papers in question. The point I am trying to draw here is that teenagers begin to develop fairly elaborate patterns for mobile communication amongst themselves and these patterns slowly become concrete as they get older; what was accepted when thirteen is laughed at and a source of embarrassment by the time they are eighteen (Kaseniemi 2001).

Who is talking to who

The research above is drawing attention to the self-accomplished sophistication of teenagers, a sophistication regarding the who, the when and the what of mobile connectivity. I now want to focus in particular on one aspect of this patterning of communication. I will do this by once again referring to our research on home life.

We found that one of the reasons why teenagers like to use the mobile when calling from their home, and one of the reasons why they like to call a mobile rather than a fixed line, is that they can guarantee who they will end up talking to. For a mobile phone is, despite what we have said above about cost, one of those articles that remains essentially one person's sole responsibility. Thus a call to that person's mobile will not be answered by someone else, but only by that person. By contrast, a call to a fixed line could summon anyone within the space in which that fixed line phone rings.

What is interesting about this is partly how teenagers in particular are loath to speak with their friend's families. "Oh they are so awkward", as one of our respondents remarked. Apparently teenager-parent conversation, whether they be within a family or across families are always difficult.

Another perhaps more interesting issue has to do with the virtual address book. We have used this term before. I mean by this the address book on mobile phones which enables particular names to be associated with particular phone numbers. This is possible since the GSM standard for mobile network requires that a caller's number is made available to the recipient (this is called 'caller line identification' or CLI). The virtual address book, when combined with the assumption that only one person has rights to answer a mobile phone, creates what one might call a tight coupling of social systems of propriety and technology.

In much of our other work, on teenagers gifting for example (Berg et al. 2003; Taylor & Harper 2002; 2003), as well as in our research on home life, the power of the virtual address book as a tool and instrument to manage the ritual patterns of human communication is paramount. This is highlighted by the fact that when someone no longer wishes to communicate with another, as in the case of a girl breaking up with a boy, the name of the person out of favour is ceremoniously—one might almost say ritually—deleted from the address book. This does not inhibit that person calling that phone but it does mean that when the call is made no name comes up on the screen: it is the summons of an anonymous person.

Now, it might seem natural to answer any and every call whoever makes it, and indeed this has been habitually the case with users of fixed line telephony, but with mobiles and with the technological infrastructure that provides caller line identification, the phones themselves are now used to let the recipients of a call determine whether they wish to answer or not. They do so by grading their decisions according to social rights. People who have the right to call have this right embedded in their 'presence' in the address book: those who do not have this demonstrated by their exclusion from the address book. Membership and exclusion is not permanent, it is flexible and is dependent upon the state of relationship between two persons.

What is curious and at once delightfully anachronistic about this is that teenagers, especially as they grow toward late teens, use this link of the virtual and the real to manage the details of their phone communications in ways that appears extraordinarily rigid. They really do avoid answering calls that do not have a caller ID. They do so on the grounds that it might be some one that they have excluded from their address book. In short, instead of being available to be contacted by anyone at any time, which is surely what the technology was developed to provide, in practice teenagers constrain their social worlds to those who have a right to contact them and exclude those who do not.

This severely managed social intercourse is, it seems to me, redolent of high class Victorian propriety, where visitors would not be accepted in to a drawing room unless they provided a card first, and this card would then enable the host to decide whether that caller had rights of access or not. How strange then that today, in the 21st century, this is what teenagers rely on; they use a technology to bolster the very social practices that, one would imagine, they would laugh at and mock if they saw it in their parents.

Conclusion

This is what one finds not only in our research but others too: in Finland (Kopomaa 2000), Germany (Höflich & Gebhart 2003), the Philippines (Ellwood-Clayton 2003), and many other places too (see Harper et al. forthcoming). The technologies are indeed allowing teenagers to work at their relationships more energetically than they might have done before. They are also allowing them to embody what might have hitherto been unfilled thoughts, ideas and ambitions about who can and cannot contact them. The social systems that result are at once complex, subtle, highly graded and rigid; and this is the work not of those who have power over teenagers, it is they themselves who create these tongue-tied processes.

Even so, this social world (and the patterns that constitute it), is endemically threatened by teenagers themselves; they make confused and often hazardous judgements about who should be in their address book and who should not, on when they should send a text and when they should not, and so on. Their judgements on these matters often conflict with the occasionally more sophisticated judgements of others, including on occasion, their fellow teenagers, most especially when these teenagers are of a different age and level of familiarity with mobile communications. In short, it is a world made up of complex and definable rules, but the ability of teenagers to act upon them in socially sanctioned ways is highly variable and often very faltering. But though this moral order is one of their own making, one should not be surprised that this occurs—they are teenagers after all.

This brings me back to the issue of whether the world is changing in ways we commonly expect or in directions that are always leading to a new, more liberated future. I asked at the outset just how much teenager life is really changing with mobiles. What I have wanted to do is show what the texture of teenage experience might be through the use of some empirical materials. In the first empirical section of the chapter, where I addressed cost, I explained that the actual battles between parents and teenagers that constitute an important aspect of teenage existence are enormously prosaic yet oddly emotional to teenagers themselves. Where they view their parents attempts to talk to them about the cost of texting as an invasion of privacy, the parents simply view it as a reasonable attempt to get those teenagers to recognise that others exist in the world. Whereas for one set of persons, the goal of such conversations is to make another group of individuals appreciate that they are part of society, the other group want nothing to do with same society, it being boring and uninteresting and, most offensive of all, 'old'.

In the second section of the chapter what we have seen is that it can be, in certain regards, the teenagers themselves who act in ways that can be described as old or conservative, in particular as regards conversational turn taking systems and summons-answer rituals. We saw that teenagers apply very strict rules about who can call them, when they call and about length, topic and so forth. The phrases 'not now' and 'enough is enough' might be associated with parents but it is teenage morals they most accurately describe.

References

Brown, B., Green N. & Harper, R. (Eds.) (2001), *Wireless World: Social and interactional aspects of the mobile age*, London: Springer.

Berg, S., Taylor, A. & Harper R. (2003), 'Mobile Phones for the Next Generation: Device Designs for Teenagers', Proceedings of CHI 2003, Florida, ACM Press.

Ellwood-Clayton, B. (2003), 'Virtual Strangers: Young Love and Texting in the Filipino Archipelego of Cyberspace', In: Nyiri, K. (Ed.), *Mobile Democracy: Essays on Society, Self and Politics*, Vienna: Passagen Verlag, 225-239.

Foucault, M. (1977), *Discipline and Punish: The Birth of the Prison*, trans. Sheridan, A., New York: Pantheon.

Gergen, K. (2002), 'The challenge of absent presence', In: Katz, J. & Aakhus, M. (Eds.), *Perpetual Contact. Mobile Communication, Private Talk, Public Performance*, Cambridge: Cambridge University Press, 227-241.

Grinter, R. E. & Eldridge, M. A. (2001), 'Y Do Tngrs Luv 2 Txt Msg?', Seventh European Conference on Computer Supported Cooperative Work, Bonn, Germany, 18-20 September.

Harper, R. (2003), 'Are mobiles good for society?,' in Nyiri, K. (Ed.), *Mobile Democracy: Essays on Society, Self and Politics*, Vienna: Passagen Verlag, 185-214.

Harper, R., Palen, L. and Taylor, A. (Eds.) (forthcoming), *Inside Text: social, cultural and design perspectives on SMS*, Amsterdam: Kluwer.

Höflich, J. & Gebhart, J. (2003), *Vermittlungskulturen im Wandel: Brief—E-mail—SMS*, Frankfurt am Main: Lang.

Ito, M. (2003), 'Mobile Phones, Japanese Youth, and the Replacement of Social Contact', Paper presented at the conference 'Front stage, back stage: Mobile Communication and the Renegotiation of the Public Sphere', Grimstad, Norway, 22-24 June.

Kopomaa, T. (2000), *The City in your Pocket. Birth of the mobile information society*, Helsinki: Gaudeamus.

Katz, J. (2003), 'A Nation of Ghosts', In: Nyiri, K. (Ed.), *Mobile Democracy: Essays on Society, Self and Politics*, Vienna: Passagen Verlag, 21-33.

Katz, J. & Aakhus, M. (Eds.) (2002), *Perpetual Contact. Mobile Communication, Private Talk, Public Performance,* Cambridge: Cambridge University Press.

Kaseniemi, E. (2001), *Mobile Message,* Tampere: Tampere University Press.

Ling, R. (2004), *The Mobile Connection. The Cell Phone's Impact on Society,* San Francisco: Morgan Kaufmann.

Massey, D. (1994), *Space, Place and Gender,* Minneapolis: University of Minneapolis Press.

Nyiri, K. (Ed.) (2003), *Mobile Democracy: Essays on Society, Self and Politics,* Vienna: Passagen Verlag.

Plant, S. (2002), *On the Mobile: the effects of mobile telephones on social and individual life,* Report commissioned by Motorola.

Riviere, C. A. & Licoppe, C. (forthcoming), 'France/Japan: major trends with respect to mobile phones', In: Harper, R., Palen, L. and Taylor, A. (Eds.), *Inside Text: social, cultural and design perspectives on SMS,* Amsterdam: Kluwer.

Taylor, A. & Harper, R. (2002), 'Age-old practices in the 'New World': A study of gift-giving between teenage mobile phone users', *CHI 2002,* Minneapolis, ACM Press.

Taylor, A. & Harper, R. (2003), 'The gift of the gab: A design oriented sociology of young people's use of mobilZe', *CSCW: An international journal,* Amsterdam: Kluwer, 267-96.

Section Two—Mobile Personalities

Emotional attachment and mobile phones

JANE VINCENT

Introduction

This chapter examines and explores the topic of emotional attachment and mobile phones. It discusses the way the mobile phone is used as a means of achieving continuous connectivity and how it acts as the conduit for emotional attachment by keeping friends and family in touch and enabling the need to maintain social and business networks. Indeed, it will be asserted that the mobile phone engenders intimacy and a feeling of being permanently tethered to loved ones as well as to less welcome callers. The chapter discusses evidence that has emerged from a variety of studies conducted over the last two years by the author, most particularly two studies for the global industry body the UMTS Forum (UMTS: Universal Mobile Telecommunications System) that explored the social shaping of 3G (third generation mobile communications), the new technology for mobile communications that is being introduced (see Vincent et al. 2003; 2004a). This technology augments the capabilities of a mobile phone device enabling voice and text, as well as access to the WWW (World Wide Web), with camera and video, music, radio, games and more. In the course of the discussion the chapter poses questions, offers ideas and opens doors for further study.

Examining the social practices of mobile phone users

People in the UK and Germany were asked about their relationship with their mobile phone and what they felt about it (Vincent et al. 2003; 2004a).[1] It was found that many of them felt emotional about the information contained on and delivered via their mobile phone and had

1. Questionnaires, diaries, interviews and focus groups were used to explore the use of mobile phones by families, young people and businesses for personal and business use in London, UK and Erfurt, Germany during 2002 and 2003.

come to depend on the device—at times too much. Some respondents talked about how they kept in touch with spouses and friends during the day. "My wife likes to call me on the mobile—she'd be lost if I didn't have it and she uses hers all the time", and mothers found they were talking more to friends "I love it because we are not restricted". However for some the attachment to the device was so great it made the mobile phone too precious to let go; "We'd agreed she'd give her old phones to her younger brother; I found out later that she hadn't been doing this but had been keeping them under her pillow—the text messages and the calls to boyfriends on these phones were so precious to her that she couldn't bear to think of her brother using the phones", and for another sustaining a distant relationship interfered with sleep, "I text my boyfriend to tell him to stop texting me so I can go to sleep". These examples demonstrate the role that mobile phones perform in people's everyday lives and in particular their effect on relationships with loved ones.

Although few people think about their mobile phone in emotional terms they do appear to be using it to achieve emotional goals and most use emotional language categories to explain their mobile usage. As can be seen from the research extracts above people do respond differently to their own and others' use of mobile phones. The research identified a range of emotions and concerns expressed about the use of mobile phones and these are summarised in Table 1.

Table 1: Summary of concerns about emotion and mobile phones (Vincent & Harper 2003).

Emotions	Concerns Expressed
Panic	Absence from the device; being separated from it
Strangeness	Between those who do and those who don't have mobile phones
'Being Cool'	Chilled out, tuned in to the mobile phone culture
Irrational Behaviour	Can't control heart over mind e.g. driving and talking
Thrill	Novelty, multi-tasking, intimacy of the text received in public
Anxiety	Fear and desire: e.g. not knowing and wanting to know about others versus too much knowledge

As the range of new 3G services become available, particularly those that offer location based data, it seems probable that people's emotional responses will be intensified, and not always for the better. The reassurance that the mobile phone affords is becoming tempered by the increasing intrusion of less welcome interventions such as the recording of private behaviours in public places and of the intrusion into the intimate space that exists between mobile phone buddies (Vincent 2005).

This 'buddy space' is one of many terms being used to describe the intimate private world of the community that each mobile phone user inhabits. Each time the use of the mobile is initiated it invokes the absent presence of the other buddies who can be accessed via the device, whether or not they are actively engaged in mutual communications at that time.

The thrill of using communications devices, the feeling of 'being cool' and the desire not to be left out of one's social group continue to dominate people's response to mobile phones. They are increasingly used for seemingly meaningless chatter such as this observation by one respondent, "I'm coming; I'm on my way... Sometimes calls are a complete waste of time really... I'm coming, you know, that's not important". There are some, though, for whom a mobile phone is not part of their life and they continue to resist their presence. "I don't own a mobile, never have and never will. I don't have children; my wife doesn't own a mobile phone. I am a sales manager—I make appointments to see people, I call them—they don't need to call me."

These emotions that people used to express their relationship with all that the mobile phone engendered were not consistent for all types of communication. Indeed a key finding of the research was that person-to-person connectivity services in particular engendered emotion but that person to WWW data does not achieve the same emotional value. The mass adoption of SMS text messaging that has resulted in a new person-to-person argot set against the mass rejection of WAP (Wireless application protocol), a person to information service, exemplifies this point. The price of these services has some bearing on the adoption, although even with free WAP services they did not capture many people's interest (Vincent 2004b). It would seem that people would be prepared to pay almost anything to talk and text each other. This desire for constant connectivity and reassurance afforded by the mobile phone can however result in a situation where a value paradox arises. Some people find their mobile phone has become too valuable to lose and they will leave it at home in some situations, "I don't take it to the club 'cause it would be terrible if I lost it."

Explaining emotional attachment to mobile phones

Some possible explanations for emotional attachment to mobile phones can be found by examining two particular aspects of the spatial interface or relationship that exists between the user and the mobile phone. Firstly is the assertion that the mobile phone is an icon for the user—an articulation of who they are. Each mobile phone is uniquely reflecting the users life at that point in time; so the device 'holds' the memories, the sentiments that are associated with the text messages and numbers stored on the phone, the appointments, the ringtones chosen and the pictures held on the phone and not in the wallet and so on. The mobile phone as an icon is about 'me, my mobile and my identity'. However, arguably none of this would be happening were it not for the second point, that people's attachment to their mobile phone is not the result of a solitary pre-occupation with the device but rather it is relationships with others that provide the stimuli for people's attachment to their mobile phone. Considering people's attachment to their mobile phones in these terms of the phone as an icon and of the social groups with whom the user communicates goes some way to establishing the focus for the emotional attachment but further explanation is still required. The common strand for this explanation is the assertion that the relationship between people and their mobile phones is a sentient one. We are sentient beings, constantly being changed and affected by our surroundings. Our mobile phones reflect who we are in any particular moment in time. We interact with a mobile phone in a way that we do not with other computational devices—we fondle it, we clutch it in times of crisis ready to turn to it and dial for help or solace, and we know that our loved ones are doing the same, probably at the same time. As living and ever changing sentient beings our lives are thus constantly affected by our own and others' mobile phones.

Maturana and Varela's (1974) work on self organising systems and 'autopoiesis' offers up a way of describing how people might be affected by mobile phones. The perturbations of everyday life that are manifested via the mobile phone affect the user and the emotional attachment associated with these events is thus enfolded in every individual's autopoietic state. Social practices surrounding the use of the mobile phone would appear to result in more intensive relationships. Examples of these are of friends constantly calling each other when they have nothing particular to say and of relationships being enhanced by constant texting when two people cannot be together.

The aforementioned research showed that people talk to people they already know and, as explained earlier, that they talk about their mobile in emotional terms, 'We often have a panic situation when the battery runs down' or 'I'd feel really, really lost without my phone now'. People are also using them to make changes to arrangements or simply set up meetings, business or social, at the last minute. 'Ring me to say where you are and I'll meet you there'. The mobile phone is thus an important part of our emotional cache in that it is a repository for storing links to things that engender emotional response, as well as performing a functional role in the management of day-to-day life. This use of the mobile phone on a day-to-day basis highlights a unique aspect of the relationship people have with the device itself. The very act of using a mobile phone involves the simultaneous engagement with more senses than we use for other computational devices as we simultaneously touch, hear and see via the mobile phone in order to keep connected with our buddies. Table 2 offers an interpretation of the manifestation of some of the social practices that were identified in the research. By associating them with particular senses one can consider the sentient aspects of our being that may be affected by our relationship with the mobile phone.

Table 2: Sentient relationships between people and mobile phones. The manifestation of social practices in the senses of the users (Vincent 2005: 226).

Sense	**Manifestation of social practices in relation to mobile phone use**
Touch	Carrying in pocket or about the person, holding or fondling the device, having it with you all the time Knowing that the people with whom you are communicating are also touching or close to their mobile phone, often at the same time as you speak or send a message
Hearing	Listening to others through the device in real time conversation or voice mail, or listening to the radio or music Creating ring tones and personalising other 'noises' made by the device—sharing the creative process with others
Sight	Looking at the address book and other personal data stored on the device, or looking at the phone to see who is calling, that you have dialled correctly, selecting the people who will receive a group text Looking at messages sent and received Showing and sharing images and text messages with others Creating screen savers and personalising colours and images
Smell and Taste	By association only, perhaps conveyed in words or image, that give a sense of place or occasion to the communication

It could be further argued that the senses are being invaded as a result of the use of mobile phones in ways that are completely new. Thus rather than our bodies being physically pierced by mechanical technology that might be developed to heighten the senses the mobile phone is actually piercing the senses themselves in a more metaphysical way. Maldonado (2003: 20) discusses the body and how technology is developing ways to emulate it, but, as he says 'One very important point is usually overlooked. A person's natural sense of touch does not consist only of contact, touching is not just touching. Our sense of touch perceives multiple factors even without true direct contact with our skin'. Thus it is for all the senses, each reaches much further than the simple function they would at first appear to perform. The sentient relationship between the mobile phone and the user invokes so much more than the physical contact achieved through the making or receiving of a call.

Conclusion

This chapter has provided, through reference to recent research, insights into the ways that people are using their mobile phones in their everyday lives and in particular it has explored and examined the concept of emotional attachment to the mobile phone. In offering some explanations for this seemingly unique behaviour it has highlighted the role of the social groups or buddy groups as the focus for the emotional attachment. The constant changes that occur in people's everyday lives frequently involve the use of mobile phones—even if the people do not have one of their own. The rearranging of appointments, the casual setting up of new ones, the relationships between lovers conducted by text and the reassuring contact between families all have some effect on the individual's autopoiesis. The multiple roles of the mobile phone in everyday life adds to the complexity of the debate but underlying the functional purposes is this constant and increasing emotional attachment. The assertion that this is in part due to the senses being pierced by all that the device engenders offers some explanation for this emotional attachment and is certainly an area for further study within the mobile communications social sciences and engineering communities.

References

Maldonado, T. (2003), 'The Body: Artificialization and Transparency', In: L. Fortunati, J. E. Katz and R. Riccini (Eds.), *Mediating the Human Body: Technology Communication and Fashion*, Mahwah, NJ: Lawrence Erlbaum & Associates.

Varela, F. J., Maturana, H. and Uribe, R. (1974), 'Autopoiesis: The Organization of Living Systems, Its Characterisation and a Model', *Biosystems*, 5, 187-196.

Vincent, J. and Harper, R. (2003), 'The Social Shaping of UMTS: Educating the 3G Customer', UMTS Forum Report, no. 26.

Vincent, J. and Haddon, L. (2004a), 'Informing Suppliers about User Behaviours to better prepare them for their 3G/UMTS Customers', UMTS Forum Report, no. 34.

Vincent, J. (2004b), 'The Social Shaping of the Mobile Communications Repertoire', *The Journal of Communications Network*, 3 (1).

Vincent, J. (2005), 'Are people affected by their attachment to their mobile phone?', In: K. Nyiri (Ed.), *A Sense of Place: The Global and the Local in Mobile Communication,* Vienna: Passagen Verlag, 221-230.

The mobile phone and the dynamic between private and public communication: Results of an international exploratory study

JOACHIM R. HÖFLICH

The mobile phone as an "indiscreet medium"

The relationship between private and public is not static. There are numerous influences on the continuing redefinition of what constitutes private and public. Not least amongst these are the media, who contribute to a shifting of boundaries, or at least intensify such developments. In this respect the media not only leave their own mark but at the same time are themselves marked in a recursive sense. If there is a tendency towards a "tyranny of intimacy" as noted by Sennett (1990), then the media, first and foremost the mass media, play no small part (*Big Brother* being just one prominent example). The private, even the intimate, is exposed to the full gaze of the public eye. How great an impact the media exert on the direction of daily life remains to be discussed. However, the shifting of frontiers is now more readily accepted. Sensitivities as to whether and when something constitutes an indiscretion are also likely to change (see Weiß 2002: 68). In the wake of an increasing mediatization of daily life, various media previously based in the home have now been uprooted, for example TV being watched in public places, the Walkman or the mobile Internet.

In this sense the mobile phone is particularly topical, as well as controversial. According to Geoff Cooper (2002: 22), the mobile phone epitomizes an "indiscreet technology". This refers not only to the fact that this technology involves an indiscreet form of communication, but also that it notably causes the merging of hitherto discrete (i.e. separate) domains or categories—here the public and the private. That which remained hidden when using the phone at home, now becomes accessible to a broad audience; what once took place "backstage" is now played out "frontstage".[1] "With the mobile phone, phoning loses its intimacy, the private forces its way into the public sphere" (Burkart 2000: 218). It may even be possible under certain circumstances to use the telephone in public with fewer disruptions than at home. This is one attraction of the mobile phone, not least for young people, as it allows them to use the telephone beyond the parental sphere (thereby circumventing parental control). Occasionally this may also make it particularly attractive for someone to appear in public because it allows them to become the centre of attention—the mobile phone is used here as a means of manoeuvring oneself frontstage.

The mobile phone—Private and public

The mobile phone openly contributes to a privatization of the public arena, for instance where private or even intimate subjects are involved. It is an especially private medium because the network of linked media consists at its core of people who already know each other or who might even be connected by strong personal relationships. This is illustrated by the fact that only a limited circle of people have the user's mobile phone number: these numbers are not normally listed in the phone book, which in itself makes them private. "This means that the mobile enables people to find and to be found by those closest to them, in other words by a very limited social network. [...] Only this network is given permission to call, while actually reciprocal and official access is not allowed to subscribers as a whole" (Fortunati 2002a: 524). When the mobile phone enters the public sphere, it is simultaneously transformed into something private, with the consequence of an "uncontrolled appropriation of public space" (Fortunati 2002a: 522; see also Kopomaa 2000: 92-93). Phone users retreat from a given situation and form a kind of communicative island by looking for a hideaway where they can talk without being disturbed—a type of "improvised open-air wireless phone booth" (Lasen 2003: 19). This also means that they temporarily absent themselves from the actuality of their present situation. Other people may be ignored. Whether this can be reciprocated is another matter: third parties present are forced to listen to the phone conversation, even though they only hear one side of it. Not least through its obtrusiveness, the mobile phone disturbs the order of public communication; its ringing alone represents a nuisance. This becomes even more of a problem as familiar arrangements of closeness and distance are upset.

For life in big cities, in particular, we face having to create distance on a daily basis despite, or indeed because of, conditions of close

1. For the distinction between frontstage and backstage see Goffman (1969: 99 ff.).

proximity. Bahrdt (1969: 79) notes: "The distance between individuals, and between the individual and the totality inherent in the public sphere, is not only a negative condition necessitating the forms of integration of the public sphere, but also a constitutive factor. Public life owes much to its specific dynamism, vividness, variety and consciousness." In this respect, with a "carefully upheld distance", personality does not appear as a "whole", but only as one part of it. Avoiding awkward situations also means holding back personal matters not intended for others, and which would in this respect also disturb those in contact with them (see Bahrdt 1969: 66). Georg Simmel (1995: 123) talks about a reserve peculiar to the city dweller, resulting in "distances and steering clear", without which life as lived in the big city would not be possible. Part of this maintenance of distance, despite the close proximity that constitutes public life, is also what Richard Sennett calls "civility". By this Sennett means behaviour that protects people from each other and at the same time enables them to find pleasure in the company of others—civility aims at sparing others the burden of one's own self (Sennett 1990: 335). On the other hand, says Sennett (1990: 336), lack of civility means the opposite behaviour: namely burdening others with one's own self. But this is not just about keeping others at a distance or keeping our distance from others, but also about adequately dealing with situations of close proximity. For example, one mechanism that comes into force first and foremost in situations where we are within earshot of others is termed "civil inattention" by Erving Goffman. This does not mean ignoring others but acting as if they were of no interest, as if we (even if this is not actually the case) were not listening to them (see Goffman 1971a: 85; 1974: 294; 1994: 153).

The mobile phone upsets the established practices of proximity and distance. Parts of one's personality, which otherwise would have stayed hidden, are made accessible to others. In this sense such behaviour "lacks civility" because someone is troubling others, against their will, with the "burden of one's self". With the mobile phone actively forcing close proximity, the arrangements of proximity/distance and of private/public have to be redefined (see Ling 2005). But when the relation between private and public is taken not to be culturally invariant, and furthermore if a culturally different integration of mobile phone use can be expected, then culturally varied outcomes might indeed be expected. In Europe, for instance, there are clear differences in the assessment of locations where it is deemed acceptable for mobile phones to be left on or turned off. The French and Germans, Haddon (1998) reports, are much more likely to regard leaving the mobile phone on in a restaurant as a faux pas, compared to the Italians, Spanish or English.

In most cases, comparative studies are geared towards highlighting differences. However, what cultures share also needs to be taken into consideration. One might ask, as Katz et al. (2003: 85): Is there such a thing as an international mobile phone culture spanning continents? In addition, is there not also an international teenage culture where the mobile phone plays an important role? Are there cultural universals or near-universals in terms of the significance of communication in people's lives?

Results of the exploratory study

Tracing cultural differences and similarities in the use of mobile phones in various European countries was the aim of an interview-based study we conducted between November 2002 and January 2003. This study should be seen in the context of a comprehensive research project focussing on the growing saturation of daily life by telecommunication media, as well as the inherent change in routine communicative practices (see also Höflich/Gebhardt 2003; 2005). The study takes the form of a pilot survey, intended to be complemented in time by additional studies, including areas such as qualitative observational studies of communication behaviour in public places (Höflich 2004). Whilst the research project follows the strategy described by Glaser and Strauss (1967) as "grounded theory", it was decided, in contrast to commonly applied current methodology, to use a quantitative study as the starting point of our research. The intention was to obtain early insight into the relationship between private and public communication, and to use the resulting quantitative data to provide the impetus for further, more in-depth qualitative studies.

To approach mobile phone use and the dynamic relationship between public and private communication from a comparative cultural perspective, the question first arises as to which criteria to use in the selection of the respective countries used as the basis for study. In other words, it must be ascertained what "theoretical sampling" the study is based on (see Glaser and Strauss 1967). Whilst this issue is discussed very differently by various sources (see for instance Hantrais 1996; Przeworski/Teune 1970), we have used a selection strategy that follows Przeworski and Teune (1970: 31ff.). This is best defined as a strategy where the relevant countries are selected according to the principle of their greatest possible similarities ("most similar") as well as their greatest possible differences ("most different"). In this way only those countries have been considered that share a wide range of characteristics (for instance social, economic and political structures—though including here also the relative spread of mobile phones), but which on the other hand can be assumed to be significantly different in other characteristics. Eventually, Finland, Germany, Italy and Spain were selected for the study.

Rather than intending to be representative, this exploratory pilot study aims to generate hypotheses. In this way it becomes clear that even if the study refers to the collective communicative behaviour of, say, "the Finns", "the Germans", "the Italians" or "the Spanish", it cannot, and does not wish to, claim to make statements about the inhabitants of these countries in general. The important issue here is an effort to reveal potential areas of difficulty with mobile phone use and the dynamic between private and public communication, in order to obtain possible clues to establish future research studies. An expert workshop held in early 2003 at Erfurt University played a crucial role in the selection of research strategy. The quantitative data we had obtained was discussed with scientists who are experts in the field of mobile communication in the respective countries involved in the study. The aim here was to prevent the risk of too much of an "ethnocentrically" clouded perspective, and in this way to be able to better assess the validity of our data.[2]

One possible dynamic relationship inherent in mobile phone use in public spaces is outlined in the first instance by who usually uses the mobile phone to talk to whom and about what. This references the potential of the mobile phone to take intimacy out of the home, or, to quote Leopoldina Fortunati (2002b: 49): "This instrument enables us to capture the intimacy of personal relations while moving from one place to another, that is, in a public dimension, traditionally the place of extraneousness in social relations". Here, the significance of the mobile phone as an intimate means of communication is already shown in its

2. In this context I would like to thank in particular Prof. Leopoldina Fortunati (Italy), Virpi Oksman (Finland) und Prof. Santiago Lorente (Spain), who, through their comments and contributions provided valuable pointers for the interpretation of the data obtained by us. Their respective assessments are reproduced at different points in the form of written quotes from notes taken during the expert panel discussion at Erfurt University. Whilst the interview sample obtained from the respective countries cannot claim to be representative, the persons surveyed—100 interview respondents per country—were nevertheless selected according to a previously determined quota (e.g. sociodemographic characteristics and the size of their place of residence). Although a relatively broad cross section of the population was achieved, the proportion of students across all countries was high, especially in the German interview sample. Respondents from the public sector form the second largest group in the four countries examined. The majority of those interviewed were aged between 15 and 24, meaning that there is a higher proportion of younger people across all countries. Of the 400 respondents overall, 51 percent were female and 49 percent male, with a similar distribution of men and women across all countries. In terms of the size of their community or town, a range of respondents emerges, ranging from people coming from a community of fewer than 5,000 inhabitants up to a city size of over 500,000 inhabitants. The majority of those interviewed come from urban regions around Tampere (Finland), Erfurt (Germany), Udine (Italy) and Madrid (Spain).

development from a medium formerly used primarily in professional communication, towards a relationship medium. Meanwhile, in a way not dissimilar to the fixed-line phone, the main groups of people spoken to in mobile phone communication are partners and family members, as well as good friends and relatives: "In this sense mobile phones are essentially personal devices sustaining personal lives and commitment, holding those together that have already committed to relatively steady relationships" (Harper 2003: 194). The data obtained by us would seem to back this assessment (see Figure 1).

Figure 1: Regularity of communication with partners via mobile phone (n=400).

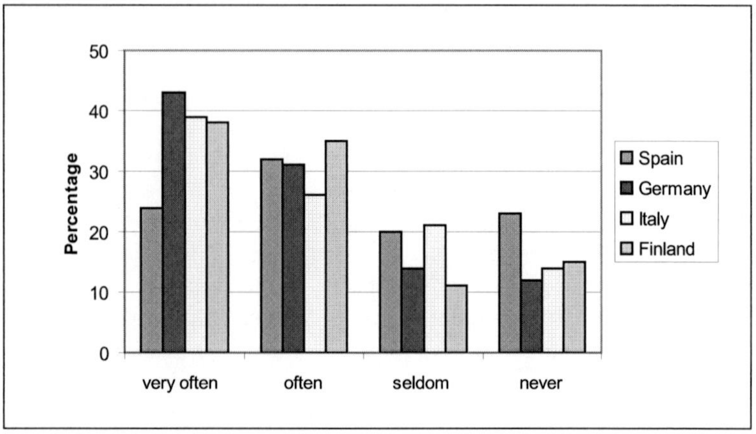

Alongside communication with partners, the mobile phone also operates as a typical family medium, although there are significant country-specific differences. In Italy, in particular, the mobile phone seems to be used most frequently to maintain communication with family members.

Using a mobile phone to communicate private matters in the public domain may not be advisable for a variety of reasons. Organizing proximity and distance between the communication partners on the one hand, and the third parties present on the other, represents a significant challenge in this respect. Managing proximity and distance in such a way firstly depends on the specific spatial and temporal characteristics of the communication situation (e.g. on the spatial distance to others, the size and spatial arrangement of the location, and also the noise level of both the conversation and its environment). Proximity and distance are also closely connected with the existence of specifically active social and communicative rules—for instance in relation to the question of whether using a medium or even a face-to-face chat with others is deemed acceptable. Of particular significance in this context is the degree to which using a mobile phone defaults on the commitment required in certain social situations (see Burkart 2000: 219). Such situational circumstances may be distinguished by the degree of commitment they require, in as much as these can be dominant or subordinate commitment requirements. Similarly, it can be assumed that there are locations where the use of a mobile phone is perceived to be more or less of a nuisance; this would then depend on how strongly its use is perceived by the third parties present to be an infraction of a mutually expected commitment. Table 1 shows situations where the use of a mobile phone is perceived to be a particular nuisance.

Table 1: Situations where the mobile phone is perceived to be a "particular nuisance" (n=400).

In the cinema, theatre or museum	92.0 %
At official events (e.g. a lecture)	91.5 %
In churches	89.6 %
In waiting rooms (e.g. at the doctor's)	70.8 %
In restaurants	57.5 %
At social events (e.g. a party)	47.5 %
At work	41.8 %
In public transport (e.g. bus or train)	37.5 %
In bars or cafés	34.4 %
At sports events	29.5 %
In other people's houses	27.1 %
In shops	25.0 %
In one's own home	18.3 %
In waiting areas (e.g. railway stations)	14.0 %
In the street	8.1 %
In public parks	7.0 %
In pedestrianized areas	6.0 %

Whilst the context of this chapter does not allow us to go into more detail about the situations listed, significant culturally-specific differences are apparent in terms of the assessment of mobile phone use in different locations. This in turn may suggest that the respective situations are embedded within the overall framework of a "situational balance"—the handling of which differs from culture to culture, and which may only be understood against that particular background.

With a view at least to the first four types of situation listed in Table 1, the data obtained by us was said to be "typical" for the countries studied by the participants on the expert panel. However, for the other locations and situations this was not the case. Santiago Lorente, Virpi Oksman and Leopoldina Fortunati all found the relevant data to be quite untypical for their countries surveyed and suggested that in Spain, Italy and Finland the use of the mobile phone in the context of the situations listed above causes much less of a nuisance than indicated by the results shown in Table 1. This particularly seems to be the case for the workplace, bars, pubs and restaurants, as well as for public parks and pedestrianized areas.

When considering the extent to which mobile phone use is perceived to create a nuisance in different situations, Leopoldina Fortunati pointed to the importance of the relative spread of mobile phones across a country. In this context Fortunati was able to show, on the basis of a questionnaire study conducted in 1996 across Italy, Germany, France, Great Britain and Spain (n=6609), that the mobile phone is primarily perceived to be a nuisance in those countries where mobile phones are very widespread—a connection which may be demonstrated by Italy in particular, but also by Britain (see Fortunati 1998). Whilst Fortunati's results point to Germany as a country where the public showing-off of private matters via mobile phones is viewed with the most scepticism, she did state, in view of the data obtained by us, "that the percentages relating to the second and third sets of situations are too high for Italy and probably also for Germany".

The framework of mobile communication may be characterized by the fact that the presence of third parties represents an integral part of the communicative situation rather than a marginal phenomenon. As for the reaction of the respondents from the countries we examined, the following facts emerge. Almost half of those questioned feel quite uncomfortable when strangers are present during a mobile phone conversation. Just under a third try to avoid such situations, almost one in five turn off their mobile completely, and as many as 40 percent actually find it embarrassing when the mobile rings in situations where others are present. In media communication processes, conversation partners often block out the presence of third parties, as well as the very fact that a medium is being used (see Gergen 2002). However, in the case of mobile phone use this seems to be different. Here, people are certainly conscious of using a medium in the presence of what represents a latent, if not actual, audience. In this respect, 60 percent of those interviewed categorically reject the statement "When I am talking on my mobile, I sometimes forget that strangers are present". Only just under six percent definitely endorse this statement. What is surprising here, however, is that despite the fact that mobile phone use in public spaces—in Italy in particular—has by now become a widespread phenomenon, it was notably Italian respondents who agreed with the statement "I feel uncomfortable making a call on my mobile phone if strangers are around me". This is illustrated in Figure 2.

Figure 2: Respondents to the statement 'I feel uncomfortable making a call on my mobile phone if strangers are around me' (n=400).

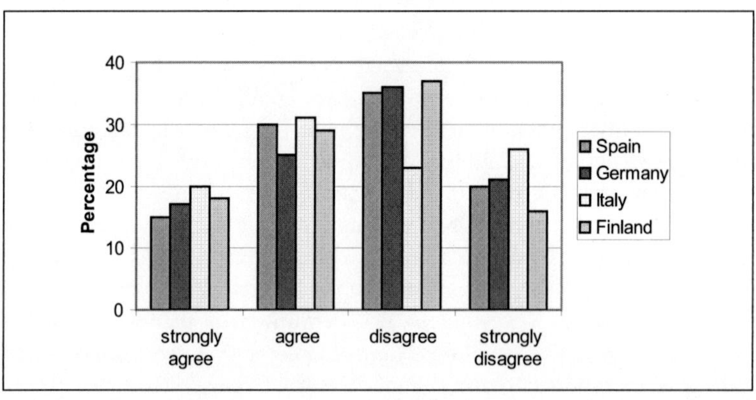

Similarly it is not possible to deduce from the responses received whether people actually lower their voices in the presence of others when using their mobile phone (see Figure 3). Along with Spanish respondents, Italian participants in particular disagreed with the statement "When I make calls with my mobile phone in the presence of strangers I speak quietly or turn away from others."

Figure 3: Respondents to the statement "when I make calls with my mobile phone in the presence of strangers I speak quietly or turn away from others" (n=400).

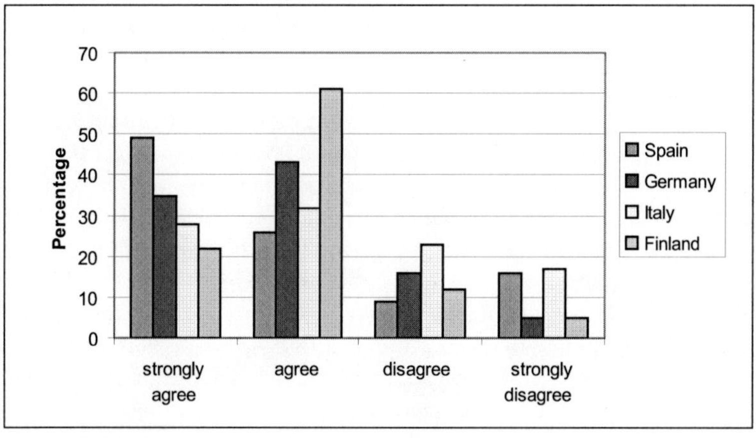

These results surprised Leopoldina Fortunati as well as Santiago Lorente, who commented on the above diagram: "My feeling is that these results are far too high for Spain [...], as talking on the mobile in the presence of others in Spain is becoming much like bearing an umbrella or simply talking in public with others [...]." As for the sound levels of mobile phone conversations in public, Santiago Lorente pointed to the fact that such behaviour patterns might, alongside elements that could be culturally determined, correlate most closely with the standard of education and received ideas of politeness: "More educated people usually happen to be the more polite and hence speak quietly or turn away from others." At the same time Lorente added that the opposite is also true: "In any case, it is true that Southern Europeans (e.g. Greek, Italian, Portuguese and Spanish) tend to speak more loudly in public than their Northern European counterparts." This assessment was confirmed by Virpi Oksman from the behaviour patterns observed by her in Finland. Nevertheless, it is certainly true that mobile phone use in various public situations is indeed perceived to be a nuisance. In addition, merely occupying too much "sound space" (Goffman 1971b: 71)—whether a phone conversation conducted in a particularly loud voice, or a ringtone with an overly loud setting—can become a nuisance. Many people even get annoyed just witnessing people fiddling with their mobile phone if this appears to take too much of that person's attention away from the particular situation.

A further aspect of private mobile phone conversations in public being perceived to be a nuisance stems from the fact that others may only hear one side of the telephone dialogue (see Ling 2002). However, in contrast to this assumption our study showed that this is not necessarily the case. Only just under eight percent of all respondents found it particularly annoying that they were only able to hear "one side" of the conversation. This percentage was slightly higher for Italian respondents (13 percent). The fact that people learn things about mobile phone users which they have no business knowing is deemed to be significantly more of a nuisance.

Even though ideas about appropriate behaviour in public vary from country to country, there are definite pointers to the fact that, regardless of their respective cultural background, people do have a desire for a private sphere in public space to be respected by others. The participants on our expert panel agreed with this, even though both Santiago Lorente and Leopoldina Fortunati expressed their reservations about the results detailed above. According to them, the oft-discussed phenomenon that you get to hear things about other people that you have no real business knowing would not cause any great irritation in either Spain or Italy. Therefore, in their opinion, the relatively large percentage of respondents who agreed with the above-mentioned statement is significantly too high. In contrast, Virpi Oksman was able to explain the high percentage in Finland (greater than 40 percent) by the fact that Finns feel a strong need for a private sphere respected by others—a phenomenon illustrated, amongst other things, by the fact that up to a few years ago public phone boxes in Finland used to be constructed in such a way "that no outsiders were able to hear anything about the private phone conversations at all...". Oksman qualifies this comment by adding that today Finns use the mobile phone to discuss all sorts of topics in public.

Summary

The mobile phone provides another reason to think about the degree to which the boundaries of public and private communication are shifting through the process of increasing mediatization of everyday communication. In particular it shows that the boundaries as such have never been static anyway, and that they consistently demonstrate historical as well as cultural differences. Whilst the comparison of cultures pursued here has been able to yield fruitful glimpses into the form of public and private communication spaces, it should be pointed out that such comparisons are always subject to the risk of cultural stereotyping.

Our study is less concerned with highlighting cultural differences—rather it seeks similarities in mobile phone use in the dynamic field between public and private communication. Nevertheless, utmost caution is advised with their interpretation, as evidenced by results from a whole generation of ethnologically oriented research. Comparative analyses of cultures always reveal that a whole range of the behavioural patterns observed in various cultures cannot be explained by the existence of cultural differences, but rather by socioeconomic factors unrelated to culture. However, culture cannot be discounted completely because that which may appear similar on the surface may be anchored in different, deep-rooted cultural structures.

References

Bahrdt, H. P. (1969), *Die moderne Großstadt. Soziologische Überlegungen zum Städtebau*, Hamburg: Wegner.

Burkart, G. (2000), 'Mobile Kommunikation. Zur Kulturbedeutung des "Handy"', *Soziale Welt*, 51, 209-232.

Cooper, G. (2002), 'The Mutable Mobile: Social Theory in the Wireless World'. In: Brown, B. /Green, N. /Harper, R. (Eds.), *Wireless World. Social and Interactional Aspects of the Mobile Age*, London: Springer, 19-31.

Fortunati, L. (Ed.) (1998), *Telecomunicando in Europa*, Milano: Franco Angeli.

Fortunati, L. (2002a), 'The Mobile Phone: Towards New Categories and Social Relations', *Information, Communication & Society*, 5 (4), 513-528.

Fortunati, L. (2002b), 'Italy: Stereotypes, True and False'. In: Katz, J. E./ Aakhus, M. (Eds.), *Perpetual Contact. Mobile Communication, Private Talk, Public Performance*, Cambridge: Cambridge University Press, 42-62.

Gergen, K. J. (2002), 'The Challenge of Absent Presence'. In: Katz, J. E./Aakhus, M. (Eds.), *Perpetual Contact. Mobile Communication, Private Talk, Public Performance*, Cambridge: Cambridge University Press, 227-241.

Glaser, B. G./Strauss, A. (1967), *The Discovery of Grounded Theory: Strategies for Qualitative Research*, Chicago: Aldine.

Goffman, E. (1969), *Wir alle spielen Theater. Die Selbstdarstellung im Alltag*, München: Piper & Co.

Goffman, E. (1971a), *Verhalten in sozialen Situationen. Strukturen und Regeln der Interaktion im öffentlichen Raum*, Gütersloh: Bertelsmann.

Goffman, E. (1971b), *Relations in Public. Microstudies of the Public Order*, Harmondsworth: Penguin

Goffman, E. (1974), *Das Individuum im öffentlichen Austausch. Mikrostudien zur öffentlichen Ordnung*, Frankfurt am Main: Suhrkamp.

Goffman, E. (1994), *Interaktion und Geschlecht*, Frankfurt am Main, New York: Campus.

Haddon, L. (1998), 'Il Controllo della Communicazione. Imposizione di limiti all 'uso del telefono'. In: Fortunati, L. (Ed.), *Telecommunicando in Europa*, Milano: Franco Angeli, 195-247.

Hall, E. T. (1966), *The Hidden Dimension*, New York: Anchor Books.

Hantrais, L. (Ed.) (1996), *Cross-national research methods in the social sciences*, London: Pinter.

Harper, R. (2003), 'Are Mobiles Good or Bad for Society?' In: Nyiri, K. (Ed.), *Mobile Democracy: Essays on Society, Self and Politics*, Wien: Passagen Verlag, 185-215.

Höflich, J. R. (2001), 'Das Handy als "persönliches Medium". Zur Aneignung des Short Message Service (SMS) durch Jugendliche', *kommunikation@gesellschaft*, 2 (1), http://www.soz.uni-frankfurt.de /K.G/ B1_2001_Hoeflich.pdf (4 November 2004).

Höflich, J. R. (2004), 'A certain sense of place. Mobile communication and local orientation', Paper presented at the conference 'The Global and the Local in Mobile Communication: Places, Images, People, Connections', Budapest, Hungarian Academy of Sciences, 10-12 June, http://www.fil.hu/mobil/2004/Hoeflich_webversion.doc (4 November 2004).

Höflich, J. R./Gebhardt, J. (2002), 'Mehr als nur ein Telefon. Jugendliche, das Handy und SMS'. In: Bug, J./Karmasin, M. (Eds.), *Telekommunikation und Jugendkultur*, Wiesbaden: Westdeutscher Verlag, 125-144.

Höflich, J. R./Gebhardt, J. (2003), *Vermittlungskulturen im Wandel. Brief, E-mail, SMS*, Frankfurt am Main: Peter Lang.

Höflich, J. R./Gebhardt, J. (forthcoming 2005), 'Changing Cultures of Written Communication. Letter, E-mail, SMS'. In: Harper, R. et al. (Eds.), *The Inside Text: Social, Cultural and Design Perspectives on SMS*, Dordrecht, Boston, London: Kluver.

Katz, J. E./Aakhus, M./Kim, H. D./Turner, M. (2003), 'Cross-Cultural Comparison of ICT's'. In: Fortunati, L./Katz, J. E./Riccini, R. (Eds.), *Mediating the Human Body. Technology, Communication and Fashion*, Mahwa, NJ: Lawrence Erlbaum, 75-86.

Kopomaa, T. (2000), *The city in your pocket. Birth of the mobile information society*, Helsinki: Gaudeamus.

Lasen, A. (2003), *A Comparative Study of Mobile Phone Use in Public Places in London, Madrid and Paris*, Digital World Research Centre, University of Surrey.

Ling, R. (2002), 'The Social Juxtaposition of Mobile Telephone Conversations and Public Spaces', Paper presented at the conference 'The Social and Cultural Impact/Meaning of Mobile Communication', 13-15 July, Chunchon, Korea.

Ling, R. (forthcoming 2005), 'Das Mobiltelefon und die Störung des öffentlichen Raums'. In: Höflich, J. R./Gebhardt, J. (Eds.), *Mobile Kommunikation. Perspektiven und Forschungsfelder*, Frankfurt am Main: Peter Lang.

Przeworski, A./Teune, H. (1970), *The logic of comparative social inquiry*, New York: Wiley Interscience.

Sennett, R. (1990), *Verfall und Ende des öffentlichen Lebens. Die Tyrannei der Intimität*, Frankfurt am Main: Fischer.

Simmel, G. (1995), 'Die Großstädte und ihr Geistesleben', In: Simmel, G., *Aufsätze und Abhandlungen 1901-1908*, Bd. I, Gesamtausgabe Band 7, Frankfurt am Main: Suhrkamp, 116-131.

Weiß, R. (2002), 'Vom gewandelten Sinn für das Private', In: Weiß, R./Groebel, J. (Eds.), *Privatheit im öffentlichen Raum. Medienwandel zwischen Individualisierung und Entgrenzung*, Opladen: Leske + Budrich, 28-87.

The role of interspace in sustaining identity

Michael Hulme and Anna Truch

What is interspace?

The term 'interspace' was defined as a result of the interpretation of a large-scale empirical qualitative and quantitative longitudinal study into mobile device usage and behaviours undertaken by the social research company Teleconomy in the UK and entitled 'Me, My Mobile and I'. The study has been conducted on an annual basis from 2000 to 2004 inclusive. The term was initially used to refer to the period which occurs between two separate but related events which are specifically located in space and time (Hulme 2004). This can refer to either the travel time between two events (e.g. home and work in the morning) or between the arrangement of a meeting (e.g. occurring on a Wednesday) and the meeting itself (e.g. occurring on the following Friday).

The importance and prevalence of interspace in everyday life is illustrated by Figure 1 in which an interviewee has drawn how and where they spend their time on a typical day (interviewees were not guided in their use of terms and were not instructed to define travel times, they were asked to define in drawing how they spent their time on a typical day). Notice the bounded ("20/10-15 mins") travel time emphasised between the main activities of the day. Over the whole sample there was also found to be a direct correlation to the 'balance' of work, home and social space/time (most individuals elected for these three spatial divisions) and travel and mobile phone use. The more balanced an individual's time was between the three broad space areas and the more the individual's travel time increased, the more their mobile phone use increased. This was subsequently interpreted as an indication of contention and struggle between 'fields', the need for 'active' maintenance, with moments of transit, or interspace, representing vital periods of active re-structuring (see later).

Figure 1: The 'typical day' of an interviewee.

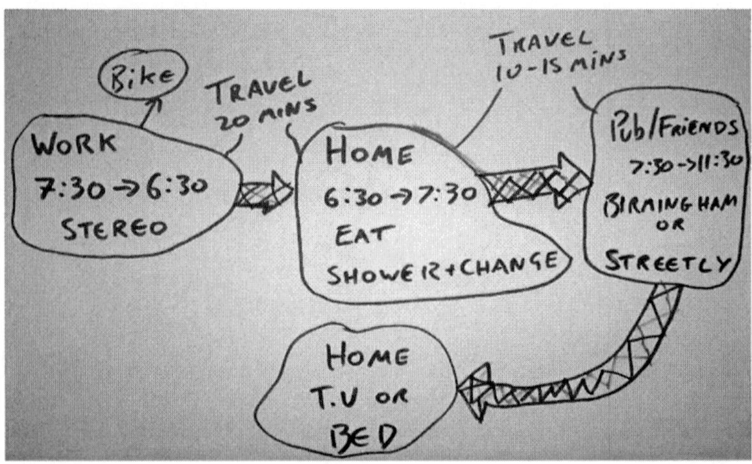

The initial conceptualisation of interspace, therefore, views interspace not as an 'event' in itself but as a 'transit' zone between two events. Figure 2 shows the conceptualisation of interspace as the transit zones between three main event environments which consistently appeared over the course of the research—work, home, and social environments.

Figure 2: Interspace as the space between work, home, and social places.

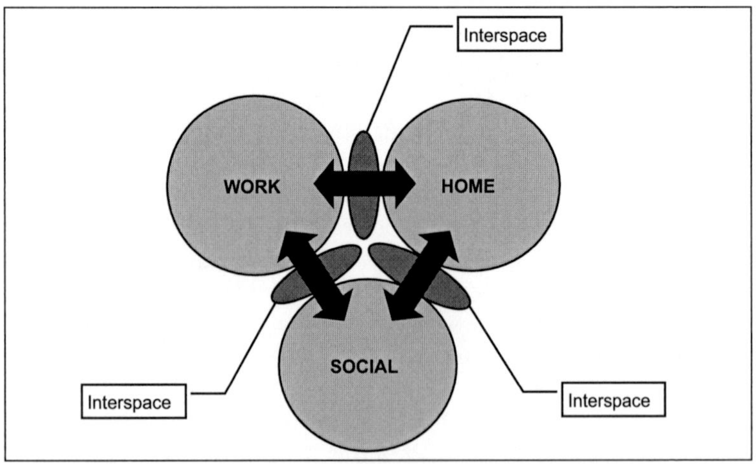

Following empirical research investigating mobile phone behaviour carried out by Teleconomy (Me, My Mobile, and I; version 2, 2003), the concept of interspace was revisited in 2004. It had become clear that the concept of interspace is greater than the initial conceptualisation; it holds more importance than the mere transition zone between two events.

Examination of the data indicated that some form of social field theory might provide useful insights for exploration. In particular Bourdieu's concepts of 'field' and 'habitus' were found to be useful in exploring and explaining the dynamics of interspace and the surrounding events seen in the empirical research.

'Field' and 'habitus'

Bourdieu used these concepts to consider social practice in the everyday lives of individuals. He maintains that 'fields represent a social space or arena within which struggles or manoeuvres take place over specific resources or stakes and access to them' (Jenkins 2002). The event environments shown in Figure 2 provide effective examples of 'fields'.

In perhaps one of his most succinct definitions of habitus, Bourdieu (1990) defines habitus as 'a system of durable, transposable dispositions, structured structures predisposed to function as structuring structures, that is as principles which generate and organise practices and representations that can be objectively adapted to their outcomes without presupposing a conscious aiming at ends or an express mastery of the operations necessary in order to attain them'. Habitus allows the regulation of behaviour without the strict adherence to a set of rules, thereby allowing individuals to maintain their own patterns of behaviour within social practices. Habitus also provides the links between different fields, which are, according to Bourdieu (1993), subject to 'invariant laws' or 'structural mechanisms'. He states that habitus is the 'unifying principle of practices in different domains' (1977).

A reconceptualisation of interspace using habitus

Beyond being a mere transition zone, interspace can be seen to have sociomateriality: 'sociomaterial space is the medium in which people act, intersect, move and locate themselves' (Freund & Martin 2001). At the same time, as a 'space between spaces' it can be seen to 'represent a boundary between fields in which struggle for dominance and maintenance of field integrity takes place' (Hulme 2004); in this way, it represents a space where subjective habitus emerges and supercedes any class habitus.

Interspace is therefore re-conceptualised as a 'space/time' environment in itself which consists of highly complex processes which are primarily concerned with the organisation of and negotiation between the boundaries of surrounding fields. The empirical research has even led to the conclusion that the interspace between two events could be more important than the actual events. This chapter explores these processes that occur in interspace and their importance.

Complexity introduced by the mobile phone

The longitudinal research study Me, My Mobile, and I (Teleconomy 2001-4), has shown that the space/time zone of interspace has become increasingly populated. The use of SMS and voice calls in interspace has been rising rapidly.

Before the introduction of the mobile phone, the use of time was defined by location of an individual (Geser 2003; Fortunati 2002). The regulation of communication between an individual and their social network was originally governed by physical disconnection. Fortunati (2002) holds that these are times of physical disconnection, 'these moments of pause, which were very precious, structured the network of relations inside a rhythm of presence/absence'.

With the introduction of the mobile phone, communication has been abstracted from the constraints of physical space—people can be reached anytime, anyplace:

> "In a very general way, cell phones introduce an element of entropy into all locational social orders, because they permeate them with communicative relationships which transcend system boundaries in highly heterogeneous and unpredictable ways." (Geser 2003)

People can stay in touch on the move, maintaining a 'nomadic intimacy' (Fortunati 2002). The social world has become a system of networked communities which are held together not by place, but by 'symbolic processes' such as trust building (Nyiri 2003). Communication and boundaries have become much more fluid. The result of this is that while people are physically in one place playing one role, they can be forced into another role in the same physical space, by a mobile call from someone from another context. Meyrowitz (1985) suggests that this presents a violation of the boundaries of place (physical space) and that this changes the social significance of where we are:

> "The old schedule of minutes, hours, days, and weeks becomes shattered into a constant stream of negotiations, reconfigurations, and rescheduling. One can be interrupted or interrupt friends and colleagues at any time. Individuals live in this phonespace and they can never let it go because it is their primary link to the temporally, spatially frag-

mented network of friends and colleagues they have constructed for themselves." (Townsend 2000)

In summary, a consequence of the mobile phone is that the layout, along the time axis, of activities and the roles with which they are associated, has become overlapping and unpredictable—simultaneity has replaced linearity.

Impact of the mobile phone on interspace

Translated into the terms of Bourdieu, the introduction of the mobile phone has added a dimension of complexity to the layout of fields and therefore the nature of interspace. As a result of people being contactable anytime, anyplace, the boundaries between fields have begun to merge and become less defined. The mobile phone has transformed the nature of interspace by allowing communication with other non-present people whilst in transit.

It is here that the initial conceptualisation of interspace becomes inadequate. Instead of being merely a 'transition zone', where fields in themselves do not exist, interspace becomes a space in which many fields can be seen to overlap; interspace can be seen as a space in which there is ongoing struggle amongst the surrounding fields for dominance and continued integrity. Within interspace there is a continual defining and redefining of boundary limits by means of constant 'conservation, succession, and subversion' (to use Bourdieu's terms). It can be seen that although interspace does not have the structure of a field itself, its 'topography', overseen by the subjective habitus, reflects the dominant fields within the space.

The configuration of interspace is influenced by the dominance of the surrounding fields. A number of factors are likely to influence the relative dominance of existing fields at any time. Belk (1975) provides a set of situational variables which are likely to have an influence:

Physical setting

- Geographical and/or institutional location and also the environment in which communication is received/sent.

Social setting

- Presence or absence of other plus social role and interaction.

Temporal perspective

- Time of day, time constraints, or other proximal issues such as date relative to another significant event.

Task definition

– Cognitive and emotional elements, situational influences upon the task, and nature of the task.

Antecedent states

– What the individual brings to the space, in terms of mood-related behaviours, knowledge, etc.

The introduction of mobile phones has perhaps also allowed more opportunity for the management of fields e.g. arranging social events by SMS while in a work environment. This presents a paradigm shift where the movement is from the need to be in a specific physical location to manage a particular field to the ability to manage any field from within any other field. This ability to manage fields from within other fields presents detachment of field boundaries from specific physical locations. This has at the same time however, introduced an element of 'entropy' (Geser 2003) and increased the complexity of the nature of interspace. With the occurrence of increasing fluidity of boundaries, a more conscious approach to field management is required in order to maintain the integrity of the boundaries separating them. This is where the role of interspace has become more pronounced.

Evidence of the use of the mobile phone in interspace is substantial. The use of interspace is demonstrated by data collected as part of the Me, My Mobile, and I research (version 3, 2003) which shows the major categories of SMS and voice call content (see Figures 3 and 4).

Figure 3: Content of SMS sent and received.

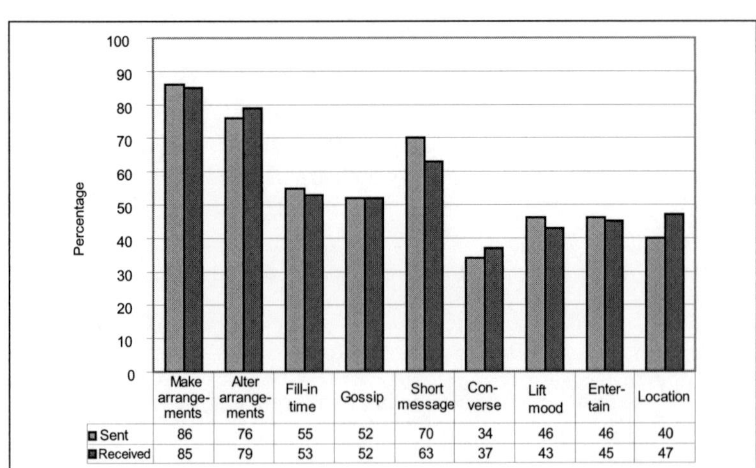

	Make arrange-ments	Alter arrange-ments	Fill-in time	Gossip	Short message	Con-verse	Lift mood	Enter-tain	Location
Sent	86	76	55	52	70	34	46	46	40
Received	85	79	53	52	63	37	43	45	47

The making and altering of arrangements demonstrates the management of field boundaries whilst situated in interspace.

As will be seen in the following discussion, the maintenance of field boundaries is crucial for sustaining the social identity of an individual.

Figure 4: Content of voice calls made and received.

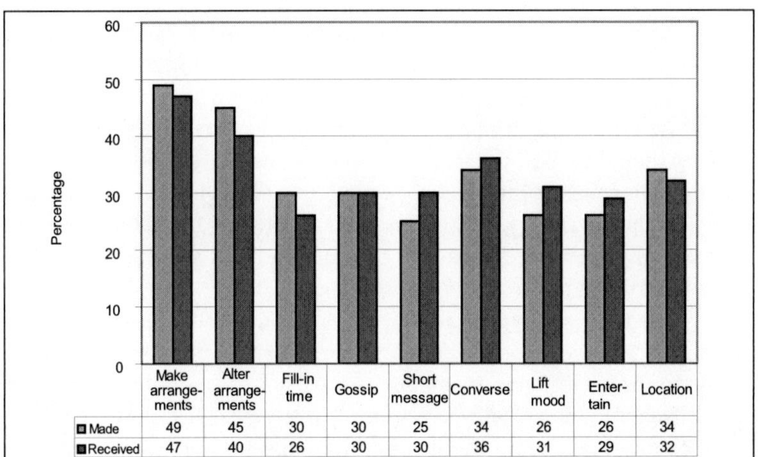

	Make arrange-ments	Alter arrange-ments	Fill-in time	Gossip	Short message	Converse	Lift mood	Enter-tain	Location
Made	49	45	30	30	25	34	26	26	34
Received	47	40	26	30	30	36	31	29	32

Social identity

Each individual has their own personal identity, that which they refer to as 'I'; each individual also has a set of social identities, conceptualisations of them that are held by other people. James (1892) made the following statement with regard to social identities: '*A man has as many social selves as there are individuals who recognise him and carry an image of him in their mind*' (which he later amended to 'there are as many social selves as *groups* of individuals who know him). [It is important to note that this 'multiplicity of self' is merely a metaphor as social identity is about an individual's attributes i.e. the unity of the 'actual self' is not questioned.] Social identities can, to a certain extent, be managed by individuals. They can choose aspects which are to be presented to the external world.

Before mobile phones, social identities were generally location-based. The social identity that is being portrayed at any particular point in time depends largely on the specific environment (field) in which the individual is placed and also upon whom they are with. For instance, if they are at home, they are likely to be maintaining the social identity of parent or spouse because they are with their families; equally, if they are at work, they are likely to be maintaining the social identity of manager because they are with their work colleagues. Each role or identity was closely linked with the surrounding physical environment and the co-located company. To a certain extent, the telephone began to change this, although it was initially immobile and located in a particular place. Therefore if someone answers the telephone, it will be generally clear to the caller and to the individual themselves, which social identity they are maintaining at that moment in time. Conversations will then continue accordingly.

With the introduction of the mobile phone however, it is not immediately obvious to the caller where the individual is located when they call. Equally, the individual does not know which of their social identities will be called upon at any time, given that anyone, from any area of their life, can theoretically contact them via mobile phone at any time. Because of the general relation of a social identity to a particular field, in the same way that boundaries between fields have become increasingly fluid, social identity boundaries have also become much more flexible.

The uncertainty that accompanies this flexibility in social identity boundaries can cause tremendous stress for the individual—with the 'anytime, anyplace' nature of the mobile, it is impossible to predict which 'social identity' will be required in the next moment—and also for those around them—the incongruity between behaviours 'on' and 'off' the phone can cause difficulties for co-located individuals who generally have a unitary image of that individual (Truch & Hulme 2004).

However, along with the increasing flexibility of boundaries between social identities, instigated by the introduction of the mobile phone, the mobile also provides a means of creating and maintaining these boundaries. This is where interspace comes into play—it provides the space for individuals to organise and maintain their identities and reflect upon how they want to present themselves to the world.

The maintenance of identities in interspace

The management of field boundaries within interspace can be conscious although the decisions made are more likely to be unconscious. Interspace can be used to sustain identity in a number of ways.

Firstly, interspace provides an opportunity to add depth to past and future events. In this way, the social identity of an individual within a particular field can be strengthened. If an individual is spending their time on the train to work in the morning by sending SMS to their social network, this ensures that they are strengthening their identity within that social field. This is an example of the struggle between fields within interspace—in this case, the particular social field maintains its dominance, whereas the work field, into which the individual could also be connecting but chooses not to, loses its influence on the topography of interspace at that time.

Secondly, the 'creation' and maintenance of social identity, sometimes called 'impression management', can now occur across a number of modes—face-to-face, SMS, voice call, email; this adds richness to the identity itself and perhaps strengthens it in a way not possible using only one channel of communication (Daft & Lengel 1984).

Thirdly, the ability to contact the social network while on the move can serve the vital function of reconfirming an individual's identity. As Thoits (1989) states 'psychological wellbeing comes from confirmation of identity'. As Weigert et al. (1986) maintain, it is through the examination of the individual's social relationships that the relevance of the individual's identity in that field is revealed. Heidegger (1962) also maintains that it is through using the world as a mirror that individuals receive feedback through which they are able to understand themselves and their relationships to the external world. Thus, through the feedback received from social contacts, an individual can reflect upon their identity and maintain it to a level which will promote psychological well-being. Interspace offers the opportunity for this feedback to be requested at most times.

Fourthly, the detachment of field and social identity from physical location can have a number of implications. The maintenance of identity remains possible with a reduced need to travel: 'Using my phone means I can cut down on travelling. Instead I'll text to bring people to me.' (Male, 29, Manchester)

The ability to communicate whilst in interspace, and unattached to any significant particular physical location, potentially allows the creation of identities totally unrelated to any physical location; for instance, the creation of totally virtual identity is possible through mobile communities, a phenomenon especially popular in Japan. The creation of new fields becomes possible in what used to be interspace.

Conclusion

Development of the concept of interspace through empirical research and the application of the theory of Bourdieu, has allowed the development of an understanding of the use of mobile phones and the sustenance of identity in 'the new real estate'. Interspace is viewed as an environment in which complex processes concerned with the maintenance, structuring and re-structuring of field boundaries take place. Alongside the maintenance of these field boundaries, the boundaries of social identities are challenged, managed and maintained. Mobile phones have led to an intensification of the flexibility of boundaries and the resultant 'entropy' in interspace. As such mobile devices can be seen as both maintainers of boundaries and new creators of boundary tensions, out of these tensions emerge opportunities for both maintenance and the exploration of new ways of developing and creating social identities.

References

Bauman, Z. (2001), *The Individualized Society,* London: Polity.

Belk, R. W. (1975), 'Situational Variables and Consumer Behaviour', *Journal of Consumer Research,* 2 (December), 157-164.

Bourdieu, P. (1977), *Outline of a Theory of Practice,* Cambridge: Cambridge University Press.

Bourdieu, P. (1980), *Questions de Sociologie,* Paris: Editions de Minuit.

Bourdieu, P. (1990), *The Logic of Practice,* Stanford: Stanford University Press.

Bourdieu, P. (1993), *Sociology in Question,* translated by R. Nice, California: Sage.

Daft, R. L. and Lengel, R. H. (1984), 'Information Richness: A New Approach to Managerial Behavior and Organizational Design', *Research in Organizational Behavior,* 6, 191-233.

Freund, P. E. S. and Martin, G. T. (2001), 'Moving Bodies: Injury, Dis-ease, and the Social Organisation of Space.' *Critical Public Health,* 11 (3).

Fortunati, L. (2002), 'The Mobile Phone: Towards New Categories and Social Relations', *Information, Communication, and Society,* 5 (4), 513-528.

Geser, H. (2003), *Towards a Sociological Theory of the Mobile Phone,* Sociology of the Mobile Phone, http://socio.ch/mobile/t_geser1.htm (14 July 2005).

Heidegger, M. (1962), *Being and Time,* translated by J. Macquarrie and E. Robinson, New York: Harper.

Hulme, M. (2004), 'Examining Interspace—A Working Paper Exploring Bourdieu's Concepts of 'Habitus' and 'Field' in Relation to Mobility Related Empirical Research', Paper presented at the Centre for Mobilities Research Conference, Lancaster University, 6 January.

James, W. (1892), *Psychology,* Cleveland, OH: World Publishing.

Jenkins, R. (2002), *Pierre Bourdieu,* London: Routledge.

Meyrowitz, J. (1985), *No Sense of Place: The Impact of Electronic Media on Social Behaviour,* New York: Oxford University Press.

Nyiri, K. (2003), 'Introduction', In: K. Nyiri (Ed.), *Mobile Communication: Essays on Cognition and Community,* Vienna: Passagen Verlag.

Townsend, A. M. (2000), 'Life in the Real-Time City: Mobile Telephones and Urban Metabolism', *Journal of Urban Technology,* 7 (2), 85-104.

Truch, A. and Hulme, M. (2004), 'Exploring the Implications for Social Identity of the New Sociology of the Mobile Phone', Paper presented at the 'Communications in the 21st Century' Conference, Hungarian Academy of Sciences, Budapest, 10-12 June.

The mobile phone as technological artefact

LEOPOLDINA FORTUNATI

Rationale

One characteristic of the mobile phone as an artefact is that it may be considered an emblem of the so-called "thumb culture". This term refers to the reduction of the hand to just the thumb. Since Aristotle, the hand has always been a traditional unit of measure, "the instrument of instruments". But why are we discussing this reduction today? Is talking of a thumb culture a form of minimalist approach or is there really a specific process of specialization of the thumb as opposed to the rest of the hand? As far as my competence will allow me, I will try to focus on a reconstruction of the sociological framework within which this shift from the hand to the thumb is occurring. There are two elements to which I would like to draw attention.

Firstly, there are two different types of organ in a machine (Maldonado 1974: 72):

"[...] indication devices (dials, meters, cathode ray tubes, visual and sound alarm instruments, etc.) and control devices (buttons, keys, switches, levers, pedals, knobs, and so on). To receive messages from the machine's indication devices, we use the sense organs (mainly sight, hearing and touch); to operate control devices, we use the organs of sense and the motor system (generally, the limbs). The first are also called 'receptor' organs, the second 'effector' organs."

Generally, in the current development of machines, indication devices tend towards hypertrophy and control devices towards atrophy. The mobile phone is in this sense an exception, given that its interface largely consists of control devices (keys), which require the use of fingers, thumbs included. This leads to the dimension of power of control over the machine, the same dimension of power that is present in the use of a remote control. The similarities here are no coincidence; some mobile phones can also work as remote controls. In reality, an important reason for the convergence between these two technologies might obviously be found in the "rapture" of power, which both of them transmit to their users. This rapture of power, with all the pleasure that it implies, goes some way towards explaining the huge popularity of the mobile phone.

The flip side of this pleasure is given by the transformation of the space occupied by the mobile phone. This space is very limited, as the mobile phone has taken great risks in its miniaturization. This miniaturization is paralleled by the gestures required for its use, which have become minimal (Montanari 1999: 187-88). For example, the bodily gestures needed to take the mobile phone from a pocket or bag are generally of a short trajectory. Those required for texting messages are not only minimal but also specialized. Message texting in fact needs great agility of the fingers and a certain amount of speed. Among adolescents it is girls who are keener than boys on text messaging, probably because of their greater propensity for writing.

The mobile phone is generally analyzed as a device that puts social behaviour in motion and is continuously re-interpreted and reshaped by it. But technological objects, says Riccò (1999), should be seen not only as shapes that release certain functions, but also as elements bringing about an aggregate of sensations. This is a path that should be further explored empirically. It would in fact be extremely useful to collect data regarding both the interiority of sensations and the exteriority of elements of the senses, such as sounds, colours and so on. As Simondon (1958) has taught us for all technologies, it is also worth looking at the mobile phone as a technological artefact, since this technical object is the site of important acculturation processes. The issue of the design of technological devices is crucial to the development of social studies on information and communication technologies (ICTs) and is an area of increasing interest to the scientific community, the terrain of theory development, and the field of empirical investigations (see, for example, Latour & Woolgar 1979; Maldonado 1987). Scholars who study communication and information technology share today a complex vision of its design: ICTs bring with them user design (Akrich 1992; Oudshoorn & Pinch 2003) but, at the same time, ICT users are increasingly able to invent functions and services and then to foresee future developments for these devices (Bijker, Hughes & Pinch 1987; Sørensen 2004). In other words, ICTs are seen as artefacts that change in a society in which they contribute to making change and which, in turn, changes them. Unfortunately, a limit to this debate is its abstraction and its lack of articulation in the production process of the specific technological devices (Stewart & Williams 2005). The mobile phone provides an excellent example for a concrete and specific analysis of this complex interaction between artefacts and users. Although, for reasons of space, we can only focus on two points: the mobile phone as "factish" and the design variants introduced by its users. We will try to develop them within this theoretical framework.

The mobile phone as "factish"

The aim of this section is to deal with the design and implementation of a specific technological device: the mobile phone. From this point of view, among communication and information technologies, this has not so far received adequate attention from scholars. To illustrate the current reading of the mobile phone as a technological device, let us begin by asking some questions. What are the patterns of behaviour that the mobile phone projects onto its users, to use an expression of Latour (1998)? What programme of actions is inscribed in the mobile phone? What are the affordances, but also ties, requisites, and side effects of the mobile phone, which impose conditions on the subjects that interact with it, completely modifying the nature of human communication? (Norman 1993) The mobile phone, as an "intellective" machine (Maldonado 1997), has an internal representation and design that presents increasingly complex problems, although the user has been subsumed in the production process from its very beginning. In order to understand them, we briefly recall and analyze various approaches from the general debate on technology.

The first approach is that of those who consider the technological device to be a neutral object which is only a transitory support for social relations. The users only are important, not what they have at their disposal. The technological artefact limits itself to satisfying some needs and to carrying out certain functions. This vision does not take into account the power that our capitalist system attributes to objects, commodities, as depositaries of exchange value. As such they have been raised in the social hierarchy almost to the same level as individuals.

The second approach is that of those, including Gibson (1986), who view each technological device as a vehicle for a script which conditions the behaviour of users, obliging them to act a certain role. In other words, the mobile phone provides not only itself, but also gives instructions, and indicates a communicative and entertainment function by its very presence. The abstractness of this perspective does not specify that this script is often generic, not very predictive, and cannot assure any automatic degree of constraint. Moreover, it would be much clearer to state that this script is the text in which the command and control embodied in each commodity, mobile phones included, is expressed.

The third approach is that of the protagonists of the German debate on technology and culture between Bismarck and Weimar (Maldonado 1991). They have seen another aspect, which is the creation of a new situation, not corresponding to the behaviour patterns that the user had in mind. Users may simply want to have a technological device in order to communicate, if need be, while on the move. But as they have a mobile phone, they do what can be done with it: talk when they feel like it, anywhere they feel like. There is an Italian adage that fits this situation perfectly: opportunity makes a thief out of a man. Individuals with a mobile phone in their hand become a different person; they are changed. In this case, the scheme of command and the script that is embodied in the mobile phone produce changes in social behaviour that go beyond what has been prefigured and configured in the artefact. At the same time, however, these social changes (see Sombart 1911) rebound on the mobile phone, which is also forced to change. As part of this third approach we cannot ignore the fact that the mobile phone, probably more than any other intellective machine, is characterized by *metis* (the feminine intelligence of astuteness) (Latour 1998: 18).

Being a great bearer of invisible tricks, this technological device, in the eyes of the common user, has something magical about it. To borrow an expression from Propp (1988), the mobile phone seems to present itself as a "magic helper" par excellence. Although, as Weber (1918: 227) points out, technology in principle presupposes the "disenchantment of the world", this process involves more the macro than the micro-social sphere, where individuals' perceptions can still be placed under a spell by what appears to be magic. This magical aspect of the mobile phone is also referred to in the title of this section. To express the ambivalent and hybrid identity of the mobile phone, we have used the term that was chosen by Latour (1998: 32) to describe the special status of technical or scientific objects: "factish" (fetish and fact). Here we concentrate on the first term: fetish. The mobile phone is a typical fetish, because we project on to it, mistakenly, fantasies, work, feelings, emotions, dependence and memories. So this device becomes an object to which we entrust the task of convincing us, through a process of inversion of the origin of the action, that it is it (the mobile phone) which creates the artificer, and not vice versa. Simmel (1900) had already observed this reversal of means into aims through technology. But in the particular case of the mobile phone, this shift is probably connected to the magical element strongly present within it.

Finally, there is a fourth approach, in which people twist the embodied script to create unexpected uses at a social level or even to introduce innovations in the mobile itself. These innovations on the part of users are so important that Fleck (1988) has suggested considering the innovation process a chain that continues in the sphere of consumption, calling it "innofusion" (innovation and diffusion). We will dedicate the next section to this fourth approach, in order to produce a taxonomy of the innovative behaviour of users, leaving further discussion of their meaning for another time.

On a physical level, the mobile phone has a highly mutant body, to the extent that in semiotics it is referred to as a highly variable geometrical machine (Montanari 1999). In relation to other communication and information technologies, the mobile phone is the most rapidly changing artefact because it is held very close to the body or stays on the body surface. This has led to its attraction to the sphere of fashion, that is, to that typical phenomenon of modernity defined by Simmel (1900: 41) as "the inconstancy in the domain of tastes and styles". The mobile phone is therefore the communication and information technology that is destined to change most in the future too. For example, it will be the technological device that is implemented with scents and perfumes and other senses, giving rise to new synaesthetic practices. In other words, it will have a greater possibility than other information and communication technologies to fight against the coldness and hardness that its technological frame and serial production lend it (Bloch 1973, original date: 1918-23).

As many authors have pointed out, there are several general tendencies for the bodies of machines, with a common denominator of avoiding the nightmare of the black box. In addition to becoming a "fashion object", another tendency is for it notionally to disappear and become a part of attractive surfaces that conceal their "new intelligence". Another tendency for the bodies of machines is to become softer, more coloured, less mineral and more biological and sensitive. This last tendency shows how women are today informally influencing the design of technology, shaping it in a more suitable way to their world. These general tendencies of course also include the mobile phone. Moreover, the mobile phone is the most suitable observation point from which to see the unfolding of these tendencies. In fact the mobile phone is being transformed into a more fashionable and seductive object, somewhere between accessory and jewel. In the same way as the computer, it is disappearing too, but inside watches, belts or even inside garments themselves. And finally, the mobile phone is becoming to all effects a soft machine. This last change obviously started from the materials used, which are today not only soft, rather than rigid, but also "intelligent".

The mobile phone is an artefact that is not only changing but is also multiform, multifunctional. It has become an agenda, pager, calculator, Internet terminal, video game, watch, alarm clock, radio, camera and more. In this sense, it shares with other technical objects the destiny, so well understood by Baudrillard (1968) many years ago, of becoming more complex than individuals' behaviour relating to these devices. The mobile phone's multifunctionality, as well as that of other ICTs, testifies to the desire for reunification that modern society expresses in the face of its opposing tendency to divide, fragment and pulverize. However, this need for reunification, which in this case is the assembly of many different functions, in the end clashes with the limits of lack of specialization. These machines, which apparently can do a large number of things, in reality do only one well and the others badly. Moreover, the dystonia between the complexity of the devices and the dream of simplicity which circles among users ends up resolving itself in a strong process of simplification.

Consumption and use mean severe selection of functions. In this sense, the mobile phone is an "open work" in which hermeneutics plays an important role. Finally, the mobile phone lends itself to being individualized by means of a particular logo, a special musical motif, a little teddy bear, or an original cover. Its domestication passes through the negation of its serialization and anonymity as a commodity. And this individualization works at a social level so efficiently that it is almost impossible to find a mobile phone completely equal to another. Attention to this process allows us to understand the behaviour by which we "humanize" its physical body, while research into its social representation helps us to understand how we "humanize" it mentally, by integrating it in our conceptual sphere. The destruction of the aura that surrounds the mobile phone as an artefact, as a product of an industrial process, is in a certain sense rebuilt in the consumption process. Here users liberate the creativity, inspiration and imagination compressed in the production process.

Design variants introduced by users

We have stated previously that the mobile phone is an excellent concrete example of how users change the behaviour patterns that are inscribed inside a technological device. So what are the design variants that people have introduced into the mobile phone? The answer is very important because when we speak in general of the active and innovative role of users we always remain on a vague level, giving at most one example: text messages. Whereas, from the research carried out so far, a very rich picture of user modifications emerges. A map of the design variants registered in the current literature should begin from the *individualization* of the mobile phone. Born as a mobile device to be used during commuting, walking, travelling and so on, that is, while the user is moving around, the mobile phone was very soon transformed into an individual technological device, used mainly by its owner. We can say that the mobile phone is the first communication technology that, through the precise initiative of people, has been put to a personal use and not a collective (familiar) one.

Another important variant is its *sedentary use*, which has been a secondary consequence of its transformation from a mobile technological device to a personal one. This transformation was brought about by a widespread desire for access to mobile communication, which ended up by individualizing the instrument. Despite the fact that the mobile phone was designed as a technology to be used while moving from one place to another, users have basically redesigned it as an instrument of individual communication. The inevitable consequence of this different reading of the technological object has been to use it anywhere where individuals might find themselves, so no longer specifically during their moving from place to place, but also at home, in the workplace, the restaurant and so on.

The third variant is the fact that the mobile phone, after being designed as a complementary and secondary means of communication to the landline telephone, has become the absolute protagonist of the scene, *overtaking the landline phone*. The mobile phone has not only been able to become the leading technological device among mobile technologies, but also, in the field of telephony, to cannibalize the landline market. This variant may be considered to be the result of the first two, but it also has a life of its own, since it has radically modified the core business of telecommunication companies and handset manufacturers, obliging them to reconfigure their planning and internal organization.

The mobile phone, and here we arrive at the fourth important variant, has also been the occasion for modern-day individuals to reconfigure public spaces by introducing a *new dynamic between the private and public dimensions*. In effect the mobile phone has allowed people to shake up the modern phenomenon of the cult of intimacy as a centripetal experience. The bourgeois idea of an aesthetic of intimacy, of separateness, of detachment, in short, self-reclusion and self-segregation, as a defence against the outside world, is no longer able to discipline the ritualization of sociability (Maldonado 1993: 8-10). The spread of the mobile phone, as if by enchantment, showed in the public space the two different sides of modern individuals: their "being bully heroes on the outside and humble anti-heroes on the inside." Although this contradictory attitude persists, the mobile phone has, in a certain sense, allowed people to open themselves out to the world.

A design variant which does not concern normal users but rather entrepreneurs, public administrations and so on, and which risks remaining hidden in the background, is the fact that these agencies, taking advantage of the mobile phone, have found a way of making people under them use it for work, *without paying for the costs*. From this point of view, the widespread use of the mobile phone has created a still more radical shift of the boundaries between the sphere of work and social reproduction or civil society and the silent re-appropriation by employers of part of the wages that should have been paid to employees.

In our list we now arrive at the most cited design variant created by mobile phone users (in particular, adolescents): the mass use of text messages, which had been conceived by the designers as a possibility for technicians to send each other short written messages during work. This function, in no way advertised by telecommunication companies, has been discovered and activated on a large scale by young people looking for a way of spending as little as possible to communicate. In this case it has been adolescents' lack of money that has led them to find alternative ways of "mobile" communication. One effect of this discovery has been the development in mobile communication of writing activity and a specific language.

Another design variant again comes from adolescents: the use of *special ring signals*, again sent for the purpose of communicating without paying. This is an international practice and is widespread in many countries. It has been a way for many young people to learn a new communicative register linked to strong ritualization and a non-verbal language. In this case the mobile phone, in the hands of individual children, has become the instrument for rebuilding a kind of virtual brotherhood and sisterhood. This practice has ended up by depriving adolescents of many hours of sleep, completely reshaping the moments of the days suitable for communicating with friends and girl/boyfriends outside of the home.

Still on the subject of variants introduced by adolescents, it is worth mentioning the practice of deliberately *calling random numbers* in order to widen one's social circle. If you think about it, only adolescents can allow themselves such freedom of behaviour. Their social identity, being still considered socially immature, might be a justification; moreover they can always, if things go wrong, put it down to a mistake or a joke. This communicative behaviour, however, reveals a difficulty in enlarging their social sphere, which too often tends to close in on itself and become sclerotic. At the same time, it also shows the intolerance of young people towards a schema of sociability that is too readily expected and inexorably local (school friends, district, sport etc.).

It is from a more composed world, however, that the use of the mobile to *interact with the media* comes (voting during programmes by means of text messages, phoning while in the car, etc.). The mobile phone fills a gap in the relationship between audiences and the media and has resolved some technical problems for both. The landline phone, for example, has never really been able to deal with the mass of people who want to take part in TV or radio programmes. The line has often been engaged and calls expensive; ultimately very few people have been able to express their opinions, respond to a quiz, and so on. The mobile phone has not represented a panacea for resolving every problem, but it is a useful aid. In this respect, text messages have turned out to be a great resource.

A variant that applies to everyone, unaffected by gender or generation, is the use of the mobile phone *to present oneself*. It is a fantastic resource for the construction of a public image, of self-assured and easy behaviour, to fill in gaps or empty moments with a precise rituality. In other words, it helps to overcome timidity and discomfort in one's performance and to maintain one's image in a public space, with its anonymous crowds or threatening emptiness. Women, when they are alone, in some situations use the strategy of demonstrating that they are using their mobile. As a form of self-defence, this display shows that they are connected to another person who can come to their rescue if need be.

One variant undoubtedly reinforced by women is the importance attributed to the *aesthetic aspect* of the mobile phone. Simmel (1900: 43) had already underlined that even machines can exercise aesthetic charm: "The absolute functionality and safety of movements, the reduction to a minimum of resistance and friction, the harmonious fitting of the most minute and the biggest components: all this gives the machine, even from a superficial view, a characteristic beauty." The mobile phone is probably the ICT that has most quickly transformed itself into a seductive and fashionable technological device. The reason for this may be that, much more than other information and communication technologies, the mobile phone stays close to or on the human body and has therefore been the technology most destined to fall under the influence of looks and more generally of fashion.

So far we have presented design variants regarding social changes that have been supported or made possible by the mobile phone. These social changes, brought about by people, are innovative and unexpected in relation to the behaviour pattern inscribed in mobile phones. But many of them concern society much more than technology or the world of telecommunications. There is, however, another type of design variant, which involves changes to the body itself of our technological device. Women, for example, have obliged telecommunication companies and handset manufacturers to remember that they often have fingernails that are much longer than men's. Therefore, these companies have had to modify the *keys* to allow women to press them more easily.

Moreover, a genuine design variant has been the attribution of *great importance to music* on the mobile phone. Starting from ring tones, but continuing with the possibility of listening to the radio on the mobile, young people in particular have imposed this additional form of convergence: between music and mobile phone. The widespread love of music by adolescents and young people in general has certainly led to the implementation of this component, which was totally extraneous to the original mobile phones.[1] It is sufficient to remember that music

1. On 2 September, 2004, the rock upstarts Rooster made history when they became the first band to broadcast a concert live by mobile phone. One thousand third-genera-

has been the main key by which people have been able to individualize their mobiles.

Our mapping of users' unexpected and innovative behaviour must end here for now. Our study, whilst necessary, is not yet sufficient because we need to also try and understand its meaning. Our impression is that, in order to achieve this, the theories at our disposal (co-construction, "innofusion", domestication, social learning theory on design) are in themselves insufficient. It might be more fruitful to refer to political economics and sociological studies on consumption (Codeluppi 2004). User innovations and modifications of the mobile phone must be seen first of all as the expression of consumer subjectivity. As buyers, consumers have to defend their purchasing power by trying to cut down costs and make best use of what they have bought, also in new ways. Secondly, these innovations should be seen as the results of users who have for some time begun to see themselves as an independent variable of the whole economic process. They try to use what they have bought according to their needs and desires, thereby avoiding the command scheme embodied in every commodity and applying all the modifications they consider suitable (the famous "dystonias of consumption"). In this context, seeing oneself as an independent variable of the capitalist process generally means at the same time keeping buying strategies secret (the acknowledged "unknowability" of buyers), whilst revealing those of consumption so that they will have a beneficial effect on the improvement of the technological devices to be bought in the future.

Conclusion

With this chapter we have merely begun to discuss the mobile phone as an artefact. A proper analysis would require much more space and time for reflection. We hope that this attempt will serve as a stimulus to draw the mobile phone more completely into the wider theoretical debate on technologies and technological devices.

---

tion (3G) video phone users of the UK mobile network '3' had to pay £5.00 to be able to follow the 45-minute show on their handsets. The broadcast of the band's concert at the Institute of Contemporary Arts in London was aimed at 18-25-year-olds (see Barton 2004).

References

Akrich, M. (1992), 'The description of technological objects', In: W. E. Bijker and J. Law (Eds.), *Shaping technology/building society: Studies in sociotechnical change*, Cambridge, MA: MIT Press, 205-24.

Barton, L. (2004), 'The first phone-in concert: Rooster herald new era of technology by broadcasting gig live by mobile', *The Guardian*, 3 November.

Baudrillard, J. (1968), *Le Système des Objets: la consommation des signes*, Paris: Gallimard.

Bijker, W., Hughes, T. P. and Pinch, T. (Eds.) (1987), *The Social Construction of Technological Systems*, Cambridge, MA: MIT Press.

Bloch, E. (1973), 'Die technische Kälte', In: *Geist der Utopie (1918-1923)*, Frankfurt/Main: Suhrkamp Verlag, 20-29 [tr. it.: 'La freddezza tecnica', In: T. Maldonado (1991), *Tecnica e cultura. Il dibattito tedesco tra Bismarck e Weimar*, Milan: Feltrinelli, 236-246].

Codeluppi, V. (2004), *Il potere del consumo*, Turin: Bollati Boringhieri.

Gibson, J. G. (1986), *The Ecological Approach to Visual Perception*, London: Lawrence Erlbaum Associates.

Latour, B. & Woolgar, S. (1979), *Laboratory life*, London: Sage.

Latour, B. (1998), 'Fatti, artefatti, fatticci', In: M. Nacci, *Oggetti d'uso quotidiano. Rivoluzioni tecnologiche nella vita di oggi*, Venice: Marsilio, 17-36.

Maldonado, T. (1974 [1959]), 'Comunicazione e semiotica', In: T. Maldonado (Ed.), *Avanguardia e razionalità*, Turin: Einaudi, 67-77.

Maldonado, T. (1987), *Il futuro della modernità*, Milan: Feltrinelli.

Maldonado T. (1991), *Tecnica e cultura. Il dibattito tedesco tra Bismarck e Weimar*, Milan: Feltrinelli.

Maldonado, T. (1993), 'Le ambiguità dell'interno', *Ottagono*, XXIII (3), 9-12.

Maldonado, T. (1997), *Critica della ragione informatica*, Milan: Feltrinelli.

Montanari, F. (1999), 'Dall'oggetto al fatticcio', In: G. Marrone, *C'era una volta il telefonino*, Rome: Meltemi, 169-192.

Norman, D. A. (1993), *Things That Make Us Smart. Defending Human Attributes in the Age of the Machine* [tr. it.: D. A. Norman (1995), *Le cose che ci fanno intelligenti. Il posto della tecnologia nel mondo dell'uomo*, Milan: Feltrinelli].

Oudshoorn, N. & Pinch, T. (Eds.) (2003), *How Users Matter: The Co-construction of Users and Technology*, Cambridge, MA: MIT Press.

Propp, V. (1988), *Morfologia della fiaba*, Turin: Einaudi.

Riccò, D. (1999), *Sinestesie per il design. Le interazioni sensoriali nell'epoca dei multimedia*, Milan: Etas.

Simmel, G. (1900), 'Die Herrschaft der Technik', In: *Philosophie des Gel-*

des, Leipzig: Duncker and Humblot [tr. it.: 'Il dominio della tecnica', In: T. Maldonado (1991), *Tecnica e cultura. Il dibattito tedesco tra Bismarck e Weimar*, Milan: Feltrinelli, 37-46].

Simondon, G. (1958), *Du mode de l'existence des objets techniques*, Paris: Aubier.

Sombart, W. (1911), 'Technik und Kultur', *Archiv für Sozialwissenschaft und Sozialpolitik*, 33, 305-347 [tr. it.: 'Tecnica e cultura', In: T. Maldonado (1991), *Tecnica e cultura. Il dibattito tedesco tra Bismarck e Weimar*, Milan: Feltrinelli, 136-170].

Sørensen, K. (2004), 'Cultural Politics of Technology: Combining Critical and Constructive Interventions', *Science, Technology & Human Values*, 29 (2), 184-190.

Stewart, J. and Williams, R. (2005), 'The Wrong Trousers? Beyond the Design Fallacy: Social Learning and the User', In: H. Rohracher (Ed.), *User involvement in innovation processes. Strategies and limitations from a socio-technical perspective*, Munich: Profil-Verlag.

Weber, Max (1918), *Wissenschaft als Beruf*, Berlin: Duncker und Humblot [tr. it.: 'La scienza come professione', In: T. Maldonado (1991), *Tecnica e cultura. Il dibattito tedesco tra Bismarck e Weimar*, Milan: Feltrinelli, 225-235].

The mobile telephone as a return to unalienated communication

Kristóf Nyíri

For at least one and a half million years, until about ten thousand years ago, human communication was invariably face-to-face, restricted to communication among people inhabiting a common physical space. According to evolutionary psychologist Robin Dunbar, language emerged as an instrument to maintain community cohesion in groups that were growing in size, enabling a constant, effective exchange of social information (Dunbar 1996). Dunbar's work had a marked influence on social science research on mobile communications. It was echoed by, among others, Kate Fox in her widely-cited essay "Evolution, Alienation and Gossip" (Fox 2001). As Fox has put it: "In the fast-paced modern world, we had become severely restricted in both the quantity and quality of communication with our social network. Mobile gossip restores our sense of connection and community, and provides an antidote to the pressures and alienation of modern life."

Mobile telephony amounts to a kind of return to primordial patterns of communication in a different way as well. According to another evolutionary psychologist, Merlin Donald, two main phases can be distinguished in the appearance of those patterns (Donald 1991). The first: the emergence of the ability to mime, i.e. to visually represent events. The second, beginning some fifty to one hundred thousand years ago, the emergence of the human speech system, the development of verbal language built upon the foundations of a language of gestures. Finally, some ten thousand years ago, there appeared entirely new patterns of communication, namely patterns of mediated communication, which came into being as a consequence of what Donald calls the emergence of external memory, the invention of pictorial, ideographical and phonological symbolic systems. We should note that some steps along this road brought not just better capabilities in communication, but also a growing disharmony between the primordial mindset and some of the new means of expression. My point in the present chapter is simply that recent developments in mobile telephony, while further, and vastly, improving these capabilities, also promise an opportunity to overcome the disharmony in question.

An initial slight estrangement between content and medium must have already occurred with the development of verbal language. This development allotted new tasks to the left cerebral hemisphere, but not everyone's brain was equally well suited to deal with these tasks. What today is called dyslexia in the broader sense—that is, difficulty with words—has an anatomical basis (West 1997: 271), and is quite widespread. Clearly, this difficulty did not become conspicuous before the rise of literacy. As West puts it, "certain special abilities and dyslexia tend to come together", but "in preliterate societies only the advantages would be apparent, not the disadvantages. And, because these conditions have prevailed through most of human history, it is not surprising that dyslexia should be relatively common and would not be evident as a problem until secondary and higher education (with their great degree of verbal orientation) is required for very large proportions of the society" (West 1997: 20). But to some extent dyslexia must have made itself felt in pre-historic times as well, when the masterly user of an elaborate gesture language and the inspired creator of cave paintings suddenly found themselves looking for words and stuttering. West cites Stephan Jay Gould quoting Goethe: "We should talk less and draw more. I personally would like to renounce speech altogether and, like organic nature, communicate everything I have to say in sketches" (West 1997: 257). The citation is from Gould's *Eight Little Piggies* (Gould 1993). As Gould puts it in that work: "Our attraction to images as a source of understanding is both primal and pervasive. Writing, with its linear sequencing of ideas, is a historical afterthought in the history of human cognition."

Generally speaking, the handing-over of inner mental contents to external memory devices liberates, rather than alienates, the mind. Marx criticised Hegel for equating *Vergegenständlichung* with *Entfremdung*, objectification with alienation; the propensity for objectification, beginning with tool-making, is an essential human trait. However, objectification does result in alienation when a system of imposed division of labour is the basis of the production of material goods. Marx believed that primitive societies were indeed characterized by a more or less natural or organic system of division of labour. In a well-known passage in his *Capital*, vol. 1, ch. 1, sect. 1 ("The Fetishism of Commodities and the Secret thereof", here quoted from the English edition of 1887) he refers to "the patriarchal industries of a peasant family, that produces corn, cattle, yarn, linen, and clothing for home use. These different articles are, as regards the family, so many products of its labour, but as between themselves, they are not commodities. The different kinds of labour, such as tillage, cattle tending, spinning, weaving and making clothes, which result in the various products, are in themselves, and such as they are, direct social functions, because functions of the family, which [...] possesses a spontaneously developed system of division of labour." As the young Marx had implied, there is a core of truth in romanticism: the early, "raw" conditions were, so to speak, "naive Netherlandish paintings of the true conditions" (Marx 1964: 78). Now we might say that there is a division of labour also between the visual, oral-aural, verbal, tactile, etc. communication channels. Unalienated communication presupposes a spontaneous harmony of these channels, but such harmony could hardly be maintained after the emergence of the first writing systems.

Pictorial and hieroglyphic writing systems were difficult to master, constituting priestly knowledge, and alien to the masses. Alphabetic literacy fostered democracy and rational thinking, but it also led, as the Platonic reaction shows and as Nietzsche emphasized, to excessive preoccupation with abstractions, to a neglect of the sensory world. As another distorting effect of alphabetic writing there arose, as McLuhan liked to point out, the dominance of linear thinking. And McLuhan's favourite, J.C. Carothers, was of course right in recalling in his seminal paper of 1959 that written words lose much of the emotional overtones and emphases that characterize vocal speech. As a consequence, written words "can much more easily be misunderstood; few people fail to communicate their messages and much of themselves in speech, whereas writings [...] carry little of the writer" (Carothers 1959: 311). Writing alienates us from ourselves and from each other.

Most importantly, during the centuries of writing and of the printing press, we had become alienated from images. The main reason for this was technological. Prior to 1400, when picture printing was invented, there existed no proper technology for duplicating illustrations; and until the age of photography, as Ivins stressed in his *Prints and Visual Communication* (Ivins 1953), no faithful representations of particular objects were possible. Also, it was much easier, both for the author and the printer, to deal with texts instead of pictures. In his 1924 work *Der sichtbare Mensch* ("The Visible Man"), a book dealing with the aesthetics of film and one that had considerable influence on McLuhan's Toronto circle, the Hungarian poet, playwright, and film critic Béla Balázs observed that it was as a consequence of printing that all forms of communication other than reading and writing have receded into the background. However, the new medium of film, Balázs wrote, would bring back the happy times "when pictures were still allowed to have a 'theme', an 'idea', because ideas did not always first appear in concepts and words, so that painters would only subsequently provide illustrations for them with their pictures" (Balázs 1982: 52). Balázs's hopes were premature. As late as 1967, cognitive psychologist Ulric Neisser could still note that eidetic imagery—mental imagery of a quasi-sensory vividness and richness of detail—is not uncommon in young children, but very rare among adults (specifically Western adults), consequently this capacity must somehow diminish with age. "Some visual factor connected with literacy", Neisser remarked, "may be responsible" (Neisser 1976: 149 f.).

Photography was a crucial leap forward that technologically enabled the faithful visual reproduction of the particular object, the particular person, and the particular moment; however, photographs, too, can deeply distort. The volume *Family Snaps*, published a mere thirteen years ago (Spence and Holland 1991), provides a depressing description of conventional domestic photography conveying a false sense of loving familial togetherness, excluding any suggestion of alienated relationships. Today, such a description has become obsolete due to the much-despised indiscreetness of mobile phone snapshots. Those shots are not designed to present idealized images to future viewers; they are meant to deliver, via MMS, authentic here-and-now visual information to intimates. You see something; you do not want to keep it to yourself, and you need not keep it to yourself.

Similarly with texts. You are haunted by a memory, you have a piece of news, you have an idea: you need not keep them to yourself, and indeed you cannot keep them to yourself. Carothers quotes a passage by an ethnologist reporting on illiterate Eskimos: "All the Eskimos we saw talked a great deal. A rule of Eskimo life is that a man must not keep any thought to himself—for if he does so he will go mad" (Carothers 1959: 314). Modernity's isolated thinker, Descartes' and Locke's epistemological ego, is an individual alienated from his community. With ubiquitous multimodal connectedness, and with devices dramatically reducing the effort necessary to think and to convey multimodal thoughts, a return to less-alienated conditions of communication seems to have begun. "Could it be", West asks, "that mankind might be entering a [new-old] stage, one in which [the dyslexic] set of traits might come once again to the fore [...]?" As he puts it: "it may be that we are now at a turning point where a new family of relatively inexpensive and powerfully visually oriented technologies is making it possible to complement the long-effective use of verbally oriented technologies" (West 1997: 23, 258). Certainly this transition raises philosophical questions of its own. After all, it was Descartes' and Locke's cognizing individual that created Western science and political institutions. Will a return to collective thinking not diminish the analytic and synthesizing powers of the Western mind? Or, will it, rather, amplify them?

For we must of course realize that while the internet, particularly the internet accessed through the mobile phone, represents a genuine revolution in communication, indeed no less than the reversal of humanity's centuries of communicational alienation, it is still true that real problems can arise with new information and communications technologies. I will mention four problems that must be confronted by both the technological and the philosophical worlds.

First: orientation on the internet. Anyone who uses the internet knows well that the level of information available means both a volume that is virtually impossible to manage and dearth of usable information at the same time. The demands of everyday life—establishing contacts, shopping, travel, entertainment and news consumption—are generally well covered on the internet; enter the more timeless and comprehensive ocean of knowledge, however, and you will soon discover that we are navigating without a compass. Today's search engines are fantastically efficient: entering your keywords results in countless apparently relevant documents; but finding a suitable starting point for more detailed information, or in some cases even knowing which documents to believe, often leaves us wishing for expert guidance. Such guidance can be found on internet portals, information collection points maintained by qualified organizations, which are common enough in the major languages of the world, though there is still a lack of portals in the lesser-known languages.

Another problem: chatting on mobile phones in public spaces—streets, trams, trains, airports, or waiting rooms. We are all familiar with the situation, and many of us suffer because of it. But what exactly are we suffering from? After all, private conversations have always been held in the presence of strangers in the widest variety of places. James Katz suggests that perhaps what disturbs the involuntary observer of a mobile call is the cognitive disharmony brought about by the unnatural situation where only one side of a conversation is ever heard—they are half-present in a communicational space that happens to randomly blend in with the given actual space (Katz 2004). Our third problem involves a related issue: the mixing of activity spaces in the wake of mobile communication, a phenomenon we have all experienced. Right now, you are listening to my talk, but at the same time you are receiving and sending SMS messages—you are simultaneously being active in a multiplicity of spaces. It can be disturbing during meetings when participants are communicating not only with each other, but at the same time they are in touch—virtually—with third parties who are somewhere else entirely. My fellow educators, from elementary school through to university, are positively livid when students pay attention not to them, but to their SMS partners. The phenomenon is real, but what does it tell us? Perhaps it tells us that organized gatherings of individuals are not always of the essence, that we happen to be exchanging words or pictures with our virtual communication partners regarding more important matters than the subject of the given meeting or class… At any rate, the arrival of an SMS message disturbs the given here-and-now communicational situation less than an incoming call: if the simultaneous accumulation of communicational situations could be separated and spatially arranged as side-by-side communications events, the problem of the mixing of activity spaces would immediately be more manageable.

And the fourth, again related problem: time management in the age of the internet and mobile communication. The given day's work schedule can be thrown into disarray at any moment by an e-mail, SMS message, or mobile call. We are frazzled and frustrated, frantic in several directions at once, and we can't focus on a given task. But how real is this problem? If I observe teenagers, I become uncertain. Incoming calls and SMS messages seem to enliven teenagers rather than disturb them. Their time management is different, and quite likely so is their concept of time: less linear than that of our generation and the previous centuries' generations whose sense of time were informed by the processing characteristic to the written/printed word.

We are the first generation to live in the world of these new information and communication technologies, and the last generation that was fully socialized in the Gutenberg galaxy. We are the first generation to be citizens of both worlds—the world of the written word and the world of interactive digital-multimedia communication alike. We have an enormous responsibility. Our activities must serve as an example showing that the internet can be a wondrous agent of cultural renewal and revolution. And the mobile phone is part of this new revolution in culture, not only as a new instrument of communality that is still reminiscent of the older communality, but increasingly as a tool of mass communication, as a medium: a new, interactive, individually-tailored medium. Yet the network revolution is not without its counter-revolutionaries—ignorant, but vociferous. Techno-pessimism is unfounded, harmful even; but of course it has always existed. Every era has its own techno-pessimism, each occurrence of which can seem somewhat silly in retrospect. Let me give a brief survey.

The founder of the Western philosophical tradition, Plato, lived in Athens in the 5th and 4th centuries BC, during a time when Greek society was moving from an oral culture towards a literate one. In his dialogues, he refused to trust the wisdom of philosophy to the written word, insisting that philosophical thought can only be properly conveyed through a live dialogue. In the 15th century, in the first decades following the invention of the printing press, the more refined reader was quite put off by mechanically reproduced copies. Early mechanical printing had to mimic the now-counterproductive solutions of handwriting at the time, such as combined letters (ligatures), in order to be acceptable in cultivated circles. The last third of the 18th century saw an abundance of books, and people learned to read quickly and silently. Characteristically, the guardians of culture at the time eschewed silent and continuous reading, with its hours of back-and-forth head movements. Silent readers must take frequent breaks, stand up, and walk around; all this reading is bad for the health. The telephone was the big worry of the last third of the 19th century: social boundaries will collapse if just any stranger can call and impose themselves into the family home. Actually, the democratizing effect of the telephone for the last century-and-a-quarter is indisputable, and nowadays we haven't the slightest such qualms.

Neil Postman saw television as the cause for concern in the 1980s. His bestselling book, *Amusing Ourselves to Death* (Postman 1985), sheds a harsh light on the changing nature of political discourse as it increasingly resembles entertainment and advertising, but it is blind to the limitations books and newspapers impose on the democracy and effectiveness of open political debate. A few years earlier he had written *The Disappearance of Childhood* (Postman 1994), in which he bemoaned the weakening and even waning of the difference between childhood and adulthood in the age of television. Postman's analysis failed to provide a satisfactory interpretation for the historical fact that the sociological distinction between childhood and adulthood (as opposed to the biological differences) was a product of the late Middle Ages or the Early-Modern Age; if the cultural/sociological divide between children and adults is currently diminishing, we should regard it as a natural and healthy development.

When techno-pessimists, and today's techno-pessimists in particular, worry about how technology affects culture, they misunderstand the essence of culture. They think of "Culture" with a capital "C", whereas the focus should be on culture with a lower-case "c"—think of the candle as a cultural artifact. This is culture in the sense first referred to by Nietzsche in the last third of the 19th century: a tool of human evolution, an instrument of collective and individual survival. We should regard even knowledge as having just lower-case letters; knowledge is primarily practical, as opposed to theoretical. Small "k" knowledge. To know is to know how: to discover, to follow through to the end, to create, and to solve. Theory is just one of the tools of practice, of action: akin to other instruments, equipment, and devices. The bulk of our knowledge is embedded in the tools we possess. Human culture has always existed in our objectified tools; there is no natural human environment: the human environment has been human precisely ever since it ceased to be natural. From the point of view of cognition, human nature itself has always been tied to tools. Recall Merlin Donald's position according to which human memory characteristically functions through external tools (Donald 1991). Granted, we store an enormous amount of information in our brains, but the ultimate cognitive evolution was the evolution of tools, from cave paintings to the internet; the internet today is no less an external memory tool than books, handwriting, and cave paintings were earlier. The thinking individual has always thought with and through his tools; nowadays more and more through network communications and the tools of the internet. But then the techno-pessimist also sees cultural deterioration in the fact that, through the internet and mobile telephony, individual thought is inescapably and constantly connected to collective thought—pushing back the boundaries of isolated thinking. However, there is nothing really new in this pattern—recall Robin Dunbar's suggestion (Dunbar 1996) that language came about primarily as a tool of social intelligence.

Human culture is by necessity a culture of artificial tools. We can certainly ask whether our tools and instruments are developing in a promising direction nowadays, and whether this direction can be influenced at all. The position held by technological determinism, according to which changes in our way of life are determined by the development of our tools and technologies, is true only to a minor degree. Generally, the approach found in the concept of the social construction of technology is much sounder: we develop and use those technologies and technical tools that we require socially. The concept of social constructivism is a thought-provoking aspect of Carolyn Marvin's *When Old Technologies Were New*:

> "New practices do not so much flow directly from technologies that inspire them as they are improvised out of old practices that no longer work in new settings. [...] Media [...] are constructed complexes of habits, beliefs, and procedures embedded in elaborate cultural codes of communication. The history of media is never more or less than the history of their uses, which always lead us away from them to the social practices and conflicts they illuminate. New media, broadly understood to include the use of new communications technology for old or new purposes, new ways of using old technologies, and, in principle, all other possibilities for the exchange of social meaning, are always introduced into a pattern of tension created by the coexistence of old and new, which is far richer than any single medium that becomes a focus of interest because it is novel." (Marvin 1988: 5, 8)

The proliferation of mobile phones dramatically underscores the thesis of the social construction of technology. The mobile phone is a characteristic tool of communication in postmodern society. Here "postmodern" applies primarily to the radical decentralization and fragmentation of social communication, resulting in the casting aside of hierarchical structures, centralized control, and linear logic. There is no question that this state characterizes the disintegration of the late twentieth-century metropolis into subcultures. The mobile telephone is an answer to the postmodern challenge—and at the same time it is, of course, a reinforcer of continued decentralization. This offers an explanation as to why mobile technology only really found its stride in recent years, even though all the elements were already present in the late

1940s, including the principle of cellularity. In the volume *Wireless World* (Brown et al. 2002), Anthony Townsend highlights the idea of the social construction of technology, which implies that societies develop those technologies that best fit the values, norms, and goals of the time. Townsend quotes from Herbert Casson's *The History of the Telephone* (Casson 1910): "No invention has been more timely than the telephone. It arrived at the exact period when it was needed for the organisation of great cities and the unification of nations." Townsend posits that the same convenient timeliness applies in the case of mobile phones as well: "Similarly, in the 1990s it seems that the mobile telephone arrived at just the time when it was needed to facilitate dramatic decentralisation of communications channels required by the new social systems in the postmodern age." But whilst fulfilling postmodern needs, the mobile phone, to sum up, is also a machine which corresponds to deep, primordial human communicational urges. Mobile communications point to a future which promises to re-establish, within the life of postmodern society, some of the features formerly enjoyed by genuine local communities.

References

Balázs, B. (1982), *Der sichtbare Mensch: Kritiken und Aufsätze 19221926,* Budapest: Akadémiai Kiadó.

Brown, B. et al. (Eds.) (2002), *Wireless World: Social and Interactional Aspects of the Mobile Age,* London: Springer.

Carothers, J. C. (1959), 'Culture, Psychiatry and the Written Word', *Psychiatry: Journal for the Study of Interpersonal Processes,* 22, 307-320.

Casson, H. H. (1910), *The History of the Telephone,* Chicago: McClurg.

Donald, M. (1991), *Origins of the Modern Mind: Three Stages in the Evolution of Culture and Cognition,* Cambridge, MA: Harvard University Press.

Dunbar, R. (1996), *Grooming, Gossip, and the Evolution of Language,* Cambridge, MA: Harvard University Press.

Fox, K. (2001), 'Evolution, Alienation and Gossip: The Role of Mobile Telecommunications in the 21st Century', Oxford: Social Issues Research Centre, http://www.sirc.org/publik/gossip.shtml (14 July 2005).

Gould, S. J. (1993), *Eight Little Piggies,* New York: W. W. Norton.

Ivins, W. Jr. (1953), *Prints and Visual Communication,* London: Routledge and Kegan Paul.

Katz, J. (2004), 'A Nation of Ghosts? Choreography of Mobile Communication in Public Spaces', in K. Nyíri (Ed.), *Mobile Democracy: Essays on Society, Self and Politics,* Vienna: Passagen Verlag.

Marvin, C. (1988), *When Old Technologies Were New: Thinking About Electric Communication in the Late Nineteenth Century*, New York: Oxford University Press.

Marx, K. (1964), 'Das philosophische Manifest der historischen Rechtschule', In: Marx-Engels *Werke*, vol. 1, Berlin: Dietz.

Marx, K. (1887), *Capital*, transl. Moore and Aveling, publ. by F. Engels, London.

Neisser, U. (1967), *Cognitive Psychology*, New York: Appleton-Century-Crofts.

Postman, N. (1985), *Amusing Ourselves to Death: Public Discourse in the Age of Show Business*, New York: Viking Penguin.

Postman, N. (1994), *The Disappearance of Childhood* (originally 1982), New York: Vintage Books.

Spence, J. and Holland, P. (Eds.) (1991), *Family Snaps: The Meanings of Domestic Photography*, London: Virago Press.

West, T.G. (1997), *In the Mind's Eye: Visual Thinkers, Gifted People with Dyslexia and Other Learning Difficulties, Computer Images, and the Ironies of Creativity*, Amherst, NY: Prometheus Books.

Mobile communication and the transformation of daily life: The next phase of research on mobiles

James E. Katz

In contrast to computer and internet technology, social science research on mobile communication technology has not caught on quickly among the scholarly community. Until recently, it was painfully accurate to decry the lack of scholarly interest in the mobile phone (Katz & Aakhus 2002). Happily, though, the situation is improving rapidly, not the least because of a growing international community of scholars dedicated to investigating social aspects of mobile communication technology.

Beginning in the mid-to-late 1990s, impressive progress has been made in tackling the scholarly study of the social aspects of this technology. Among the earliest efforts was a 1995 survey (apparently the first national poll to compare users to non-users of mobile phones) which focused on the social consequences of its early adoption (Katz 1999). Certainly a foundational thinker about the sociology of the mobile phone (and internet) has been Hans Geser, a Swiss researcher whose writings have been at once both prescient and influential (see his contribution to this volume).

Over the past several years, the leadership and contributions of Dr. Kristof Nyiri, both individually and through his far-reaching conferences arising from the Institute for Philosophical Research at the Hungarian Academy of Sciences, has been far-reaching. His work has not only advanced and broadened the field but has also helped create an extensive community among concerned scholars. Lara Srivastava is one of the astute and energetic commentators in this regard (Srivastava 2003; this volume). Her incisive, data-driven work has illuminated the status of many countries throughout the world. For his part, Joachim Höflich has demonstrated with precision the way use of urban space is affected by mobile phone users (see his contribution, this volume). Leopoldina Fortunati has written with great insight into the phenomenological and fashion aspects of the mobile phone (Fortunati 2002). In 2004, Richard S. Ling published a masterful and incisive summary of how the mobile phone appears to be affecting life in a variety of domains. For his part, Leslie Haddon has been a principal in the re-thinking technology's role in the domestic sphere, and is one of the originators of a framework known as "domestication," which explores the moral economy and device integration into the household (Haddon 2004). Scott Campbell has been using international comparisons of students perceptions of the mobile to explore further the Apparatgeist theory proposed by Katz and Aakhus (2002). Other important thinkers on the subject of mobile communication have also contributed impressively to the area. These include M. Hulme, R. Harper and N. Döring. Altogether, then, a highly insightful and comprehensive picture of mobile phone reception, use and impact is being drawn. These manifold efforts have led to an impressive corpus of knowledge.

Yet much is still to be learned. As the field moves forward, I would like to suggest three areas worthy of deeper investigation. These are (1) how space-time and attention to the physically present changes due to mobile communication technology, (2) the manner in which mobile communication technology affects self-presentational activities and the choreography of the body in public space, and (3) transcendental and spiritual uses of mobile technology. There are of course many other topics, a few of which are highlighted at the chapter's conclusion.

Meaning of time, self and life-space

An intriguing question that has caught the attention of researchers is how people understand the process of time and its change (Zerubavel 2003). Understandably, the question of how mobile communication technology is affecting people's understanding and use of time is paramount. It may be the case, for example, that the experience of one's day changes as a result of mobile communication; this would include subjective perceptions of time, its passage, and its meaning.

One phenomenological aspect might be what Ling and Yttri (2002) have dubbed "hyper-coordination," the sense that every moment is caught in a web of planning and interaction with others, and that plans can be changed quickly in light of circumstances and the actions of others. They also assert that mobile phones serve to soften one's sense of time. To put it differently, users of mobile phones appear to be more relaxed about re-doing schedules and altering plans if they are able to use the mobile phone to coordinating with others.

It is even claimed by some observers, perhaps with a degree of hyperbole, that the idea of being late may disappear altogether. Although such claims are extreme, it certainly seems subjectively that schedules are more readily able to be negotiated if there are changing circumstances, or even if internal subjective feelings change. Several studies reach this conclusion (Zernicke 2003), and it has even been suggested that "cell phones let us turn being late into being on time" (Reader's Digest 2004). By this it is meant that by calling to a waiting party that one will be late in meeting that can (with the proper excuse) redefine the appointment time to a later one. The essential claim is that it is now more acceptable to all parties involved to adjust social and business schedules. This certainly is the conclusion that Rheingold (2002) reached on the basis of having talked about this issue with mobile phone-using teenagers in Tokyo.

Related to this topic is whether it is indeed the case that mobile phones seem to fragment and isolate the self. Some researchers have focused on how mobiles reduce people's self-reliance, which in turn erodes their ability to react adaptively to unpredictable encounters. Geser (2003) for instance claims that mobile phones can blunt the development of certain social competencies. This is because of the constant availability of external communication partners (as sources of opinion and advice) as mobile phones enable people to retain primary social relationships over distance. This affects people's self-reliance, making them unable to operate alone and leaving them dependent on the mobile as a source of assistance and advice. Witness, for example, increasing numbers of people using their cell phones while shopping in grocery stores or video rental shops, asking their family or partners what they should get.

In terms of the mobile phone as the device for filling unoccupied stretches of time, some people in Tokyo (Moseley 2002) expressed concerns about how the mobile phone is used to avoid being alone with one's thoughts. In Japan, the traditional ways of killing time (i.e., reading books, comics, newspapers, etc.) are losing out to mobile phones. Fortunati (2002) shows how the use of mobile has encouraged more productive use of time. There can be little doubt that time spent commuting, waiting in queues at banks and airports—time ordinarily considered wasted—can now be used to communicate with others via the mobile phone.

Among the analysts who have considered how the mobile phone is altering one's life-space are Peters and Hulme (2002). In their view, the mobile phone is seen by users as an extension of their self. By the same token, the loss of a mobile phone is felt not just on the material level but also on the level of one's sense of physical self. Indeed, some even see such a loss as the psychological equivalent of physical disintegration. Thus Moseley (2002) asserts that should a person leave home without the mobile phone, that person may have a definite sense that something is missing: "A human with a mobile in the pocket is appreciably different from the human without one" (Moseley 2002: 37).

Based on this discussion, it seems that the mobile phone may be altering in a rather profound way the ordinary structure of everyday life. Whether the structure is becoming more obscure to its members, whether it is indeed becoming more plastic, and whether it is an important question for researchers.

To take but one illustration of the way daily reality is being rearranged by mobile communication, we can inspect the problem area of pedagogy. That is, we can raise the question of how education is proceeding when both students and teachers are equipped with mobile communication devices. Yet that paper raised several questions concerning the changing nature of ordinary life resulting from the widespread use of mobile phones in educational settings. So to explore the issue a bit further, in early September 2004 I asked some questions of a class of Rutgers undergraduate students (most of whom are about 20 years old, and two-thirds of whom are female), about their cell phone habits and experiences, especially as related to classes; the figures are presented in Table 1. To begin, it is noteworthy that nearly all had cell phones: of the 53 students in class, all but 1 reported having a mobile phone and the one student who did not said he had owned previously but currently was unable to afford one. Of those having them, the majority (73 percent) had their mobile phones on during the class, even while the survey was being taken. Of the 38 who had them on during class, 13 percent said that they had received a call or message since the class had begun. No sounds were heard by me, and the students all said their phones were on vibrate mode. (It is worth bearing in mind that US students are much heavier users of voice services than SMS services.)

Perhaps even more interesting is the fact that about half of the students indicated that they had witnessed a professor taking a mobile phone call during class. This proportion of students, who have observed such behavior, unsurprisingly, seems to continue upward as the technology becomes more widespread, more commonplace, and as the elapsed years of experience increase.

Several examples of this were discussed among the class members. One incident revealed how a professor had lectured his students about the importance of not having the cell phone sound during class. The next week, his mobile phone began sounding. He took the call for a moment, and then apologized to the class. Other professors were more extensive in their use of the mobile phone during class, including engaging in arguments with their spouses. In another illustration, this one from 2003, a professor of information science received a call during a doctoral seminar. He excused himself from the room, saying the call was from a doctor whom he had been trying to reach for an extended time period. That left the students baffled as to what they should do until the professor returned several minutes later.

Although not subject of the college-level survey, it is worth reporting an event that transpired which was an even more extreme example of teacher misbehavior. This took place in an elementary school in December 2003. It was reported that a music teacher of 4th grade students (that is, children who were about 10 years old) engaged in protracted discussions of up to five minutes long during class time. He would go over to the classroom's windows to get better reception; meanwhile the bored students would begin trifling. In less extreme examples, another 4th grade teacher would excuse herself and tell the students that the call was related to her wedding planning.

Table 1: Opinions of students concerning experiences with mobile phones in educational settings. Date: September 9, 2004. N=53, percentages rounded.

Topic	N	Percent
Students in the class	53	100
– currently have mobile phone		98
– who had mobile phones on during class		73
– received mobile phone call during the first 25 minutes of class		10
– recall making a mobile phone call during another class		19
– have seen their teachers use mobile phone during classes.		49

One implication of this small-scale investigation is that the classroom is no longer the isolated learning environment that it once was. Rather it is blending into the rest of the life, creating an environment of perpetual contact. As mobile games proliferate, the trend towards "outside interference" will continue.

Mobiles as public choreography

Another aspect of mobile communication that would benefit from further investigation is the "urban environmental" effects of its use in public. To some degree, questions concerning this have been investigated by Höflich (2004) and Katz (2003). However, the physical performance of public communication, and its impact on the way others in the ambient environment behave, is an area not well developed.

In this section, I would like to call attention to the value of further exploration of the way mobile phones are consumed in public. That is, greater attention could be profitably devoted to investigating mobile communication processes as part of the physical performances that individuals undertake as they share, navigate, and occupy public space. Perhaps it would be useful to apply the term "dance" to this process. In part this is a dance because the use of the mobile phone in public by one party often requires that the user's co-present partner adjust themselves in space and pace. That is, they must engage in a bit of choreography. This phenomenon of choreography finds a theoretical framework in Edward Hall's (1977) discussion of "being in sync." This refers to the idea that people in interactions need to "move together," and if one of the interactants are not "in sync," other parties find the interaction "disruptive" (Hall 1977: 71). He further states:

> "People in interactions move together in a kind of dance, but they are not aware of their synchronous movement and they do it without music or conscious orchestration. Being 'in sync' is itself a form of communication. The body's message (in or out of awareness), whether read technically or not, seldom lie, and come much closer to what the person's true but sometimes unconscious feelings are than does the spoken word." (Hall 1977: 71-72)

Ling (2001) examines the way people manage their social interaction involving the mobile phone. Observations of mobile phone use in public places suggest that the emerging use of the mobile phone has introduced a new context wherein people need to move "in sync." Whether people are aware of their body movement or not, they adjust their body positioning once the face-to-face interactants start engaging in a mobile phone conversation, thus creating a kind of dance with the mobile phone. People involved in the interaction could be the partners of face-to-face conversation at the moment or people who happen to be physically present in public places, rather like the "forced eavesdropping" situation that Ling (2004) has described. The participants themselves could be mobile phone users, nonusers or rejecters. Regardless of their mobile phone use, they all have to take on the choreography of mobile phone use somewhat, in order to have a smooth social interaction.

The choreography of arrangement is informal, but seems remarkably consistent within cultures. For instance, it has been argued that in Japan, users in public conveyances emphasize manners and privacy, seeking to exclude others. What follows are summaries of our observation. First, the non-using partner has to engage in symbolic behaviors that suggest valuable activity. At the same time, there is lots of tacit and audible but indirect coordination. For instance, as the mobile phone user gets ready to conclude the conversation, the non-participating partner mysteriously is able to resume focus on the mobile phone user, and begin engaging the user visually.

There also seems to be a consistent set of postures that people display when using the mobile phone. These include:

- The bent over "into the wind" posture when walking and the phone is held against the ear
- The public pacing—just where are the users going when they pace?
- The cricked neck
- The multi-task contortion
- Encompassing the technology to create a world separate from the environment
- Draping the body on environmental objects
- The diamond (both arms to the side of the head, one hand holding a mobile to an ear, the other used to cup the opposite ear)

In addition, behavior tends to reproduce itself. In his discussion of "postural echo," Desmond Morris (1977: 83) observes that friends who are informally speaking with one another often adopt similar body postures. They do this, he says, "unconsciously as part of a natural body display of companionship". I would go further, and suggest that it is often the case that people adopt the postures and body positions of those around them whether or not they are friends. While Morris holds that this form of imitation is not deliberate, I would go further and argue that it is actually quite hard to resist. It can often only be done if one is consciously making an effort not to do so. At the very least, there is a continual process of body posture interaction that complements the postures of those around the actor.

In the case of mobile phone use, the co-present partner, who had not been using his/her mobile phone, will often be prompted to begin using his/her own phone. Certainly our surveys of students in classrooms reinforces this idea. Students often say that when they see another student using a mobile, it prompts them to begin doing so even if they had not originally been intending to do so. Mobile phone use in public therefore seems to beget yet more public mobile phone use.

From the viewpoint of human behavior and proxemics, a pas de deux is created. However, the "postural echo" in this case does not seem to be a sign of "companionship." Two friends who are physically co-present are more likely to be sending a relational message of "companionship" to the persons who are on the physically present other side of the situation. The person, who had not been using a mobile phone, in order to display companionship, still unconsciously echoes the behavior of the partner who is physically present and using the mobile phone. This would be predictable extrapolating from Morris's assertion, made decades before the mobile phone itself was publicly available.

Yet we also note that there is a constant attempt at communication coordination when one member of a dyad is on the mobile, and the other not. There is continuous checking the partner's expression when the partner is looking away, which will be followed by the phone person looking away and the partner then checking out the phone user's face. Looks and body language alone are not the complete picture of the mobile phone dance. There is "song" too. The tone and loudness of the phone person's voice signals the partner as to what the partner should expect in terms of distance and anticipated additional time on that the phone users will be on talking; this too helps coordinate the choreography of the dyad.

A corollary aspect of public phone performance is that sometimes the dynamic of mobile phone use is largely (or even exclusively) for those who are present. That is, talking on (or playing with) the mobile phone may be as much for the benefit for those "present" with a mobile phone user as it is for those who are "absent" and would be the putative subjects of the mobile phone use. (This is certainly confirmed by our research which shows about one in four mobile phone users say they have pretended to talk on the mobile phone when there was actually no one on the other end of the line.)

So the choreography of mobile communication performance needs to be better understood as an interpersonal communication phenomenon, as a physical as well as a psycho-social and organizational phenomenon.

The transcendental mobile phone

While the identity and personal meaning of the mobile phone has been extensively examined, especially in terms of teens and children, the same cannot be said in terms of the spiritual and religious, and extrasensory aspects. In particular, insufficient attention has been given to the way mobile phones have been adopted as transcendental devices. For many, the mobile device seemingly enables a crossing over from this life to a possible after life or world beyond the "here and now." This is becoming widespread in terms of religious practices. For instance, occasional Jewish worshippers at the Western Wall ("Wailing Wall") in Jerusalem will hold their mobile phones aloft so that their distant co-religionists can have their prayers be made audible at that sacred location. Comparable scenes are repeated at Buddhist and Hindu shrines by adherents to those religions. In India, some Hindu temples encourage the sending of SMS messages to supernatural entities represented by their shrine's telephone number. Users can also receive messages via their mobile phone, such as a service offered in the United States wherein subscribers get daily messages from the Pope.

According to press reports, "Okwap" (a brand released by Inventec Appliances Corp.) has taken advantage of Taiwanese interests in Matsu, the Chinese goddess of the sea, and who is a popular religious icon there. Okwap has created in 2004 a limited-edition model that comes with a Matsu holograph on the back of the phone, ring-tones featuring religious chants and Matsu wallpaper for the display pad. Most relevant is that all the phones have been blessed in a ritual at a Matsu temple (Textually.org 2004), and can download special Matsu music from the web. Originally only 2,000 phones were made (each selling for about USD 300); however the demand was so overwhelming that an additional 1,000 were produced before the run was permanently ended.

In August 2004, Ilkone Mobile Telecommunications of the United Arab Emirates (UAE) launched the Ilkone i800, a device that it claims is "the first fully Islamic mobile phone." (Ilkone is derived from the Arabic word for universe.) The phone boasts many features that would be helpful to observant Muslims. The GSM-standard phone includes the full text of the Qur'an in Arabic with an English translation, an automatic prayer call (azan) with full audio reproduction as well as a silence mode, a prayer alarm before and after azan, automatic direction finding for Mecca directions, a Ramadan calendar and a Hijri calendar converter. According to Saqer Tellawi, CEO of Ilkone, "consumers nowadays view mobile phones as devices which can add value to their self being and inner feelings rather than just a simple communication tool. Ilkone i800 is specially designed to serve Muslims all across the world to address their needs, and add value to their spiritual self being" (Ilkonetel 2004).

Transcendental matters concerning the mobile phone have been taken still further. Uses of it have extended beyond the "spiritual self" and have been applied to spirits themselves. As an illustration, it has become the case that the mobile phones are now used as sacrificial gifts and utilities for those beyond the grave. Boxes of sacrificial offerings to the dead, which include items supposedly needed in the afterlife, have been and made commercially available in Asian rim countries. Now some of these gift boxes include mobile phones; in Hong Kong for instance ready-made sacrificial packages are sold that include cardboard mobile phones and pagers. In Japan, mobile phone antenna dongles and mobile phone toys have been left on religious statues of shrines. A statue of the Hindu god Lord Ganesh holding a mobile phone in one of the many arms has been created and merchandized. When a young Italian girl was accidentally killed by Mafiosi, mourners placed mobile phones as memorial offerings on the tombstones.

Thus the mobile phone is taken by many not only as a statement of self, but also as a representative of the self that can transcend states of reality and transmit a sense of will and being beyond the realm of the senses.

Other areas sketched

Many other research topics are worthy of further investigation. A small sampling is offered here to suggest the range of issues that mobile communication is posing for us. These can be put in highly abbreviated form here:

- What does it mean to be "with someone" and how does the splitting of attention between present and distant locations affect respective social relationships? Could we be hollowing out our social relationships, or building, as R. Ling (2004) suggests, walled gardens around our social selves?
- Are we moving from a phenomenology of writing to one of image, as Nyiri (2005) argues?
- Are there going to be more semi-spontaneous and coordinated group activities in the public sphere? Will the modes of initiating contact for social relationship creation be modified as a result of this technology?
- Will the practice of democracy change as a result of the availability of mobile communication technology and new modes of information dissemination and social organization?
- How will international crime control and anti-terrorism efforts be affected by mobile communication? Already both the conduct of terror and efforts to safeguard people's lives are being affected by mobile communication, but who is gaining an advantage and with what results needs to be further considered.
- Are there net benefits from the constant "perpetual contact" that people increasingly experience due to their organizational involvement?
- How will peer-to-peer mobile communication technology affect institutions?
- Will mobile communication technology serve to hollow local commercial life as automatic and "self-service" and "do it yourself" approaches erase the retail and middle management classes? What will the experience of shopping be like when the clerks and petite-bourgeoisie are replaced self-service systems? How will this affect urban and suburban landscapes and social life? Will a "mobile divide" be created, especially to the disadvantage of the non-mobile elderly and already socially marginalized?

These issues are posed in the form of rhetorical questions. To investigate them thoroughly, they must be broken down into further components for detailed analysis. It is also the case that it will be difficult to gather good data on them. Yet despite these considerations, the answers to them will be quite important.

Conclusion

In 2004, Prof. Christopher Henshilwood of the University of Bergen discovered in South Africa what appears to be the oldest known jewelry—75,000 year old pierced and ocher-tinted tick shells. His discovery suggested the importance of jewelry and other forms of interpersonal communication and representation. Henshilwood asserts that "once symbolically mediated behavior was adopted by our ancestors it meant communication strategies rapidly shifted, leading to the transmission of individual and widely shared cultural values" (Graham 2004). If we agree with Prof. Henshilwood's assessment of the import of the initial use of symbolic display technologies (in this case, tick shell decorative jewelry), the implications for evolving practices of mobile communication technology may be even more significant than we generally assume. Specifically, novel forms of widespread mediated communication could alter the cultural values we embrace and transmit. They could also transform social structure, interpersonal processes and land use in ways we might neither anticipate nor desire.

The lines of investigation sketched above are important since the illuminate understand current and emerging social practices and their implications. Mobile technology allows unprecedented permutations and concatenation of innovations in communication at the levels of place and space, individual, group and mass, and creative new services offered from a range of entities from amateur creators to gigantic corporations. Therefore, we have an opportunity to structure services and social practices in a self-aware way that should be conducive to outcomes that are better than would otherwise be the case.

I would, for the purposes of argument, go further and suggest that it might be the case that the mobile communication is also likely to be a transformative technology.

References

Brownfield, P. (2004), 'Lack of cell-phone etiquette draws ire', *Los Angeles Times*, April 24.

Fortunati L. (2002), 'Italy: stereotypes, true and false', In: J. E. Katz and M.A. Aakhus (Eds.), *Perpetual contact*, New York: Cambridge University Press.

Geser, H. (2003), *Towards a sociological theory of the mobile phone*, Release 2.1, September, http://socio.ch/mobile/t_geser1.htm (27 October 2003).

Graham S. (2004), 'Ancient shells may be earliest jewels', *Scientific American.com*, April 15.

Haddon, L. (2004), *Information and communication technologies in everyday life. A concise introduction and research guide,* London: Berg.

Ilkonetel (2004), 'Islamic mobile phone launched', http://www.ilkonetel.com/UAE-Press.html (17 September 2004).

Katz, J. E. (1999), *Connections: Social and cultural studies of the telephone in American Life,* New Brunswick, NJ: Transaction.

Katz, J. E. (2003), *A nation of ghosts?* Presentation at the Mobile communication and social and political effects conference, Budapest, Hungary.

Katz, J. E. & Aakhus, M. (2002), 'Apparatgeist', In: J. E. Katz & M. Aakhus (Eds.), *Perpetual contact,* New York: Cambridge University Press, 287-317.

Ling, R. S. (2004), *Mobile connection: The cell phone's impact on society,* San Francisco: Morgan Kaufmann.

Ling, R. S. & Yttri, B. (2002), 'Hyper-coordination via mobile phone in Norway', In: J. E. Katz & M. Aakhus (Eds.), *Perpetual contact,* New York: Cambridge University Press, 129-59.

Morris, D. (1977), *Manwatching: A field guide to human behavior,* New York: Harry N. Abrams.

Moseley, L. (2002), 'Digital culture: Rise of the thumb kids', *Newsweek,* May 6, 37-38.

Nyiri, K. (2005), See contribution, this volume.

Reader's Digest (2004), 'Only in America', *Reader's Digest* (April), 19.

Rheingold, H. (2002), *Smart mobs,* Cambridge: Perseus.

Textually.org (2004), 'Phones have been blessed in a ritual at a Matsu temple', July 1, http://www.textually.org/textually/archives/004381.htm (17 September 2004).

Zernicke, K. (2003), 'Calling in late', *The New York Times,* October 26, section 9, pages ST1, ST11.

Zerubavel, E. (2003), *Time maps: Collective memory and the shape of the past,* Chicago: University of Chicago Press.

Section Three—Industry Perspectives

Facing the future, changing customer needs

Raimund Schmolze

Within this chapter we discuss future changes in customer needs. We start this exploration of the future with a brief reflection of the past, and discuss how meeting existing customer needs has fuelled the past success of the mobile phone industry, and how meeting implicit customer needs will further guide the mobile industry in the future. As penetration rates continue to rise to saturation point, these needs will become increasingly heterogeneous. Only if operators manage to understand and meet the diverse and changing needs across all customer segments will they harvest the full future growth potential in the mobile industry.

Thirty years ago there was little reason to believe that mobile phones would become as successful as they are today. Life worked quite well with fixed line communication: fixed line telephony enabled people to communicate instantaneously over long distances, which was a huge improvement on previous times where communication involved either physical travel or lengthy delays while messages were transported. Thus, with the arrival of fixed line telephony people easily became accustomed to the fact that they had to arrange their lives around the technical means of communication. It was better to have a life built around the infrastructure for instant communication than to miss the benefits of this new form of communication. The mobile phone's success is based on the revolutionary concept of lifting this restriction. The mobile phone met the universal human need for unrestricted mobility.

This need cannot be underestimated. In some countries, like the former Democratic Republic of Germany, the people have come to overthrow their government, mainly for being restricted in their freedom to move. Thus, adding mobility to instant communication made a radical and very tangible change to consumers' lives. With the arrival of mobile phones, our customers' freedom to move extended tremendously. Where they previously could only move within the very limited space around the end of a fixed line, which was usually one or two rooms, or if one had cordless phone fitted, a house, they practically expanded their freedom to move, almost over night, to the reach of an entire mobile network. Admittedly, in the early days coverage was an issue. Networks "only" covered urban areas and there was no real ability to roam, but the ability to freely move within a town or a country (compared to the confinement of a house or an office) made a huge difference.

With hindsight the success of mobile phones is not surprising, it caters to a most basic human desire: the desire to be free. Step by step within the last 25 years this freedom to move has been geographically increased. Roaming is not an issue anymore, networks have been integrated and for consumers today's freedom to move covers the entire developed world.

There were some rather unsuccessful attempts to expand this freedom even to the under-populated parts of the world. Huge sums have been invested in the build-up of satellite based global networks. But the visionaries behind these networks failed to realise that they did not meet customer needs, since the vast majority of customers just does not want to spend long periods of time in Antarctica or on the tops of the Himalayas. And if they go there, they quite often enjoy that these far places are disconnected from their usual world, which makes them special places and worthwhile to go to.

This brings us to another basic consumer need, next to the true freedom to move, it is the true freedom of not having to communicate all the time. While the mobile phone originally increased the freedom to move it considerably seemed to infringe on our privacy. Consumers phrase this often as a loss in the freedom of not being reachable, the freedom of not having to talk, the freedom of going off and being on your own. It was this consumer need, the desire to reduce the immediacy of the mobile phone, which brought unrivalled success to the text message, the SMS. The text message allows consumers to send equivalents to a short telegram, messages that reach their addressee quickly and yet could be handled with whenever it was convenient for the receiver of the message. Combined with an initially highly competitive pricing, text messages became the most successful data application for mobile operators. Once one has understood that basic consumer needs were the foundation for the mobile phone's success, a much clearer picture of the future emerges.

While the traditional mobile phone catered to traditional consumer needs, a new phenomenon arrived that fundamentally changed our concept of space and time: the Internet. The Internet created a new dimension of mobility for consumers. It both enabled them to access geographically distanced places as well as created a new, virtual, world in itself. The geographical reach becomes apparent when students in Tokyo enter the catalogue of the Library of Congress in Washington. What today can be done from any computer with Internet access, required only thirty years ago some serious visa work, long travel and a lot of time. The internet has vastly changed our ability to move virtually. Rather than having to go somewhere in person we now can access places and information over the Internet.

Simultaneously, a virtual world has developed within the Internet. There are computer communities, online games and even online economies with their own currencies and exchange rates. This virtual world has become for many an integrated part of their lives. The relationship to their Internet friends has become closer and more intimate than many of the day to day relationships in their off line world. Ironically tough, the fixed line infrastructure of the Internet has again deprived consumers of their just gained freedom to move. The Internet brings the world to consumers' desktops, however, it requires them to stay just there, at their desks. It introduced a great new freedom of access and yet took the true freedom to move away. And it did so in a most radical manner since the Internet required consumers to actually face a computer screen! In the old days of fixed line telephony consumers could at least move within earshot of their phone, which could be an easy thirty yards. And with the introduction of cordless phones consumers could move up to 50 yards away from their fixed line. The Internet started again at the consumers' desks and asked them to stay exactly there. It was not until the arrival of Local Area Networks (LAN) and a considerable price drop in portable computers, that consumers experienced the cyberspace equivalent to a cordless phone.

Mobile operators have understood this contradiction between the newly gained virtual freedom of the Internet and the loss it brought to the true freedom to move. For mobile operators this contradiction provides a huge opportunity if they manage to meet both needs: the desire to access through the Internet distant and/or "virtual" places as well as the desire to move freely.

Although unlimited mobile access to the Internet is certainly the largest of all current opportunities, there are more customer needs that are currently answered by the mobile industry. It is through careful customer segmentation that operators identify and meet their customer needs. Good segmentations draw on a combination of attitudes and socio-demographic variables that are then overlaid with customer life cycle data. They allow operators to identify specific sub-groups and their very specific needs that exceed the generic needs for mobility in space and access described above. These segmentations are generally kept strictly confidential since operators see them as critical for their competitive positioning. Yet, the external observer can deduct their sophistication through operators' product offerings. For example, the success of the i-pod, a portable music player introduced by the computer manufacturer Apple in 2003, indicated a consumer need to have mobile access to vast varieties of music. Mobile operators catered to this need by providing unlimited mobility through the integration of music players with mobile Internet access to gigantic music stores. Their product offerings were distinct to the original Apple offering and they also differed among each other. Some catered to the youth segment, while others clearly addressed the more mature and sophisticated customer. This can be both an indicator for differences in their customer bases and their identified growth potentials.

Another example how operators anticipate and cater to changing consumer needs are digital cameras in mobile phones. Operators never set out to make a business by competing against digital cameras. The global digital camera market is far too small to be relevant for mobile operators and dedicated camera manufactures will always produce better cameras than the ones integrated in mobile phones. However, intelligent segmentation identified that there is indeed a customer need in younger and urban consumers to share moments rather than memories. This need is rather new and it developed playfully in accordance with the opportunities of technical development. Yet it became quickly a core need for highly relevant customer segments that made it worthwhile for operators to invest in the necessary infrastructure.

A further example of changing consumer needs is the consumer-need to play. Computer games have been around as long as the PC. Specifically designed mobile gaming devices have given a whole new dimension to these games. That these devices can also be used as a phone is of lesser relevance for the active gamer, for them they offer the ultimate integration of virtual and tangible reality. Admittedly, "computer gamers" are a very small consumer group, but operators certainly made this a better word to live in for the gamers when they offered them both the ability to take their games with them when they like to leave their houses as well as to integrated their real physical movement in to the virtual games they play in the Internet.

Mobile music, mobile sharing of moments and mobile gaming are just a few examples of how operators have identified higher order consumer needs that developed out of the basic needs for instant communication and global access to information. Music, games and pictures are only variations of these basic themes and there are others, like full access to our virtual office infrastructure. They all circle around the true freedom to move, and are all based upon changing the behaviour of consumers to embrace service offerings that help them to live their lives liberated of artificial constraints imposed by the infrastructure limitations of the past. Operators will have to continue to think creatively to further understand natural needs that develop with the removal of artificial infrastructure barriers. From an operator's point of view the opportunities are unlimited. This is a notion that gives great hope to consumers since more and more specific customer segments will find that new products and services offer them genuine further improvements to their lives.

Loading mobile phones in a multi-option society

PETER GROSS AND STEFAN BERTSCHI

In 1994, Peter Gross published a book called *The Multi-option Society* (Die Multioptionsgesellschaft), which became a best-seller in German-speaking countries (Gross 1994). It can certainly be argued that options, the choices facing people in their daily life, are further increasing in a mobile society. This chapter consists of an editorial introduction followed by an interview with Peter Gross, and reveals the connection between "multi-option" societies and the meanings a mobile phone may carry.

A "Multi-option society" refers to the "endless and competitive profusion of new possibilities" omnipresent in modern societies (Gross 1994: 11). This wealth of new possibilities is not only confined to supermarket shelves and the range of services available but also enters the spiritual realm. There is no sphere where the inhabitant of such a society is protected from the options on offer. The inhabitant, however, is by no means merely a passive victim. The underlying phenomenon resembles more the "will for more, to go forward, that is deeply embedded in modern societies and implanted in the heart of modern humankind" (Gross 1994: 11). This striving for "more" is the background noise that has accompanied humankind since the Enlightenment. Modernity is founded on such striving. "Which is why, if you wanted to summarize the comprehensive diagnosis of society made by Gross in a single sentence, you could say: Behind everything, something more, something better is waiting; everything that is more and better is waiting to be realized, and everybody has the right to demand more and better" (Abels 2000: 92). However, sometimes people feel overwhelmed, sometimes they realize too late that they have failed to choose the best option, or failed to even be aware of it (see Abels 2000: 101). Both the growing choice and the act of choosing (made more difficult by the increasing number of possibilities), lead to people feeling under pressure. They are increasingly subject to the pressure of piecing together their individual "jigsaw of life" (Gross 1994: 197).

This provides the background against which new consumer and user trends should be viewed. Due to the multitude of products and possibilities, people are increasingly struggling to find their way in today's "consumer world". In order to counter such "consumer confusion", products and services today are loaded in multiple ways, both in terms of their qualities and also in terms of communication (i.e. marketing). Amongst other things, it is possible to emotionally load products and services so that the consumer's heart—rather than brain—provides the decisive impulse to buy, binding them emotionally. Through this emotional loading, products and services are endowed with their own character, an image setting them apart from rival products. This is important for competition in today's saturated markets where products, viewed objectively, become increasingly similar. With mobile phones, consumer confusion is primarily due to the overload of innumerable functions, which—and this is the starting point for the concept of a multi-option society—thus far have always been desired (see Gross 2004b: 35). However, in most cases this plethora leads to the functions and services being tried a few times—if at all—then subsequently ignored. The fundamental dilemma between the fascination with the multitude of functions and the overload caused by such increased stimuli is sometimes called "consumer ambivalence" (Otnes et al. 1997). Avoiding ambivalence and confusion requires a clear strategy that is able to convey concise guidance to the consumer about the product and its functions and services.

As if this criterion alone was not difficult enough to meet, something else enters the equation: over time, certain products lose their primary use, which simply becomes taken for granted. The wristwatch offers a good example. The primary use—being able to tell the time—has disappeared (to the immediate benefit of the plastic watch manufacturer Swatch). Because the product's main use—with the mobile phone this would be communication—is no longer visible, it has to be loaded with additional uses. It needs to be assigned a new significance. Such an assignment however is not always advantageous, particularly if it involves emotions. Loading products with emotions may actually confuse the consumer further if these are emotions that the consumer does not wish to associate with the product. This is why today's mobile communication business makes intensive use of customer segmentation models. It is easy to see that, in the main, younger people have their own idea of the "qualities" a product should have, and in which way this product should communicate with them (or be communicated to them). To achieve this, "loading techniques" are brought into play. This means, "that products are not just products but have performance- and customer-related functions." (Gross 2004a)

In order to achieve the relevant loading, it is necessary to consider a product's functions as well as its primary and secondary uses. Whilst the product does not need to be reinvented, it must undergo rigorous communication training. Peter Gross names five registries for use in loading and training a product in this way: "The first and fundamental registry is 'synaesthesia'. People and things, offerings and products blend different sensory experiences" (Gross 2004b; see Vincent in this volume). A mobile phone may be handled, seen, heard and possibly even smelt. It may be given an optical, acoustic, haptic, olfactory and gustatory loading. Which sensory experience is brought to the fore depends on the individual product. This sensory-centred procedure represents one of the facets of "loading": one denotation of the verb "to load" is, according to Merriam-Webster, "to charge with multiple meanings (as emotional associations or hidden implications)".

The second registry available for use is "rhetoric". According to the communication model of Schulz von Thun (2000), an utterance has a four-fold content: factual information (what I am giving information on), self-disclosure (what I am revealing of myself), a relationship pointer (what I think of you and what relationship I have with you), and an appeal (what I want from you). Each product, each service and each offering carries these four aspects. As with synaesthesia, rhetoric asks the question as to what combination and weighting the contained registers should be used in.

The third registry for use in loading is "aesthetics". What is considered beautiful and harmonic is determined culturally and is reflected differently in a multitude of different lifestyles. The binary opposites of tradition versus the new, or simple versus the complex, could be used as registers within this form of loading.

The fourth registry contains "spatial-temporal" registers and denotes the space and the time window allocated to a product; comprising things like events and promotions. The fifth and last is currently the most commonly used registry for loading offerings: "branding" and "naming": "This also raises the question of when the register of symbols and their significance should be taken into account" (Gross 2004b). In order to be successful, the listed techniques need to generate added value for the consumer. Again, the wristwatch may serve to illustrate this point: its main use (i.e. telling the time) has virtually disappeared. Today, the watch is loaded externally with aesthetics, appeal, trends and brands. Soon, exactly the same situation looks set to apply to the mobile phone too. What then does it mean that products and services have to undergo vigorous communications training? "It means thinking about communication and its partially forgotten registers, no more and no less." (Gross 2004b)

However, subjecting the mobile phone to communications training also means understanding the desires and requirements of the user. One interesting approach, which may be able to marry communications training with these requirements, has been suggested by Christine Mussel (1992). Mussel's "discursive need concept" is based on the realization that a person's needs system is not consistent and contains major contradictions. The system constantly depends on exchange processes between the person and his or her environment. The system is not only affected by history and society but also by the individual person and his or her current situation. Such dependence makes the system highly instable: it therefore appears clear that needs can neither be ascertained (through market research) nor determined by expert deduction or systematic observation. Mussel's concept states that human needs can only be determined in a situational environment within a discursive process (see Gerstheimer and Lupp 2003). On a different theoretical level, George Kelly's "Psychology of Personal Constructs" (1955) seems to be of interest here. His theory emphasises that communality (social reality) and individuality (personal reality) need to be considered together in order to develop an understanding of the psychological processes. The key message of Kelly's theory is that the world is "perceived" by a person in terms of whatever "meaning" that person applies to it. The same can be stated for such an important tool as the mobile phone.

In actuality, the implementation of such approaches does not seem to function so smoothly. This may be due to the fact that market research and marketing tools are unable to anticipate individual realities. Therefore, what they are actually targeting is social reality. And ultimately it is here, at the threshold of individual and social reality, where misunderstandings arise. They arise because the mobile phone is fundamentally different from other products and services. In principle it is a product like any other. Primarily it is a technical device for the wireless transmission of speech and data. However, the mobile phone is both product and medium and occupies a higher order of media products. Neither the classic landline phone, radio, nor TV set has ever been endowed with such a massive lifestyle factor; they have never impinged on people's lives in such a fundamental way. This is why the consequences too are of a new order, and what we can learn here may be summarized in one sentence: "If design is defined as a complex of projectual acts intending to conceive products and services as a whole, the only way to design properly is to have the user in mind; and the role of marketing (a new marketing) is to have in mind the true project of the consumer, which, paradoxically, is not to consume but to be put in the condition to use properly." (Morello 1995: 70)

The aspects identified here as a starting point, and discussed in the course of the following interview, may be useful for a better understanding of certain trends and ways of reacting to them proactively. A good example is the trend described in the following extract: "People rush through the 'multi-option society' endlessly seeking to experience something more beautiful and better than what they have experienced to date." (Abels 2000: 104)

Interview with Peter Gross

Stefan Bertschi: If you want to explain increasingly mobile and global societies, I think your concept of the multi-option society has lost none of its relevance. Could I ask you to summarize what distinguishes your approach?

Peter Gross: My interpretation is different in that I try to bring together those drivers of modern society normally considered separately, and also to describe the consequences. What I refer to as "drivers" are: individualization (creation of autonomy, soloing), the creation of options, and the freedom from obligations (emancipation). These build the force field that we have to face in an open, free society—and the consequences of which (increasing insecurity, risk and the threat of exclusion) we also have to meet.

In connection with the multi-option society you saw a "panicked mobility" (Gross 1994: 28). Ten years on, how do you see this?

In the course of globalization, mobilization in general has become even stronger and more comprehensive. This means more and more desires arise, and ever more possibilities, which, however, we have less and less time to enjoy.

Do you believe that the effects of mobile phone communication influence your assessment today? Why, or why not?

As a cordless device, the mobile phone is a prototypical product of modern society. On the one hand it increases production through communication, on the other hand it compensates for the increasing distances and hurried mobility.

It can be assumed that mobile communication increases the users' range of choices in how they may shape their lives. At the same time this choice is made more difficult through the plethora of possibilities. How do you view this? Will it have more positive or more negative effects?

Every beginning is difficult, and that also holds true for the intelligent use of the mobile phone. Only once the device has disappeared, i.e. become taken for granted and integrated into daily life, will this problem be overcome.

Let us take this assumption further: Will human interaction become even more spontaneous and confusing through the influence of mobile phones?

Indeed, I see it becoming more chaotic and more varied at the margins where new users use new technologies. Meanwhile, at the same time "islands" will be created and communicative securities established, which will continue to stabilize the whole thing.

Can the trend towards the mobile phone not also be seen as an "ego hunt" (Gross 1999), as a search for oneself in the mirror of the communication partner? Is the mobile phone nothing more than a means of mutual reassurance? Or is there more to it?

Perhaps you could look at it like that. But I am thinking of "smartvote", an application with which you can be aligned with the identity of others.[1] Sooner or later there will be mobile services that make it easier to choose a product, for instance they might sound a signal when I pass the relevant shelf in the supermarket. Or they will tell me where to go dancing, which has direct implications for other people.

The mobile phone makes us contactable any time, any place. It can be foreseen that this will further blur the border between work and life at least. What role will a multi-optioned communications world play?

Naturally the new methods of communication mean that the border between the worlds of work and life becomes more porous. Here, everyone will have to establish their own boundaries so that these worlds do not get blurred together. I am thinking of, say, children upgrading the home PC and accidentally deleting business correspondence.

The contemporary family is a main strand of your research. In which way do you envisage the use of the mobile phone changing the family?

Using the mobile phone advances the most primal form of communication binding a family together: presence, evidence of being there, the mutual "I'm here".

---

1. Editor's note: "smartvote is a scientifically developed online election tool for Swiss elections at local, canton or national level. [...] Using factual and opinion-based questions, the political profiles of the candidates are collected and held in a database. Voters are subsequently invited to reply to the same questions, whereupon smartvote recommends those candidates for election showing the greatest political alignment." (see http://www.smartvote.ch/info.php?mode=idea). There are other "smart vote" initiatives around the world but none of them are equally well advanced (e.g. http://www.smartvote.info). In mobile communication between people, personal profiles will also gain in significance.

On a more general note, will the mobile phone help to dissolve social ties; will they become looser?

Not at all. In this, I am anything but a cultural pessimist or anti-technology. Mobile phone communication makes it possible to denaturalize social ties—which often brings advantages too, in so far as some people, for instance, are able to express themselves better through the new media and maybe even enjoy better social interaction. On the other hand, everyone who frequently uses a flight simulator strives for real flight. This also means the reverse can happen, i.e. that the dematerialized ties possibly ought to be re-naturalized.

What significance would you personally ascribe to the mobile phone today? Or, putting it another way: How would you describe the value mobile phone users allocate to it?

The mobile phone offers a kind of foothold on communicative solid ground in the modern world. Beyond that, it implies manifold secondary functions, such as belonging to a particular scene, lifestyle, etc.

How comprehensive can the multi-functionality of the mobile phone become? Will we ultimately only be able to manage our life with the help of this device?

It is possible that it would be hard for us to renounce this life-support device again. But no animal is as adaptable and disaster-proof as humankind. Humans would survive the end of mobile phone communication and, at the worst, return to smoke signals. But let us not dwell on such apocalyptic thoughts, although looking at the state of the world they do occasionally come to mind.

What happens when everything is within the grasp of technology? Let me couch the question in more sociological terms: Do you think that ubiquitous communication conveyed by technology increases people's fear of missing out on something, of not being able to take advantage of all possibilities?

In one sense that is indeed the case. However, the opposite is evident too: that modern means of communications confirm life in the subjunctive. This means that in principle they promise participation in all possibilities. The "could" is the decisive characteristic of modern life in open societies. The well-known Swiss film actor Liselotte Pulver phrased it like this: "What peeves me most is not receiving an invitation to a party I wouldn't have gone to anyway."

Recently you have been looking at "loading techniques" (Gross 2004a). What is the meaning of your statement that the mobile phone has to be "loaded" properly and to undergo rigorous communication training?

In a recently published paper (Gross 2004b), I systematically name the registers that can be used to load a product (see editorial introduction to this interview). All communication and presentation techniques that people learn also have to be learned by the product. This is why I say that in modern societies with "confused consumers", not (just) people but the products themselves have to be subjected to communication training. Think of the organist, who puts into place the registers of his instrument in order to be heard in church.

The mobile phone may be loaded in different ways. Which do you personally think are the most central?

Probably the primary *and* secondary functions, i.e. a loading with both the original communication function and, for instance, a user-specific lifestyle function. It depends on the product's life cycle, as well as on the user. Humans do not consist (solely) of their core function, i.e. procreation, but also exist in secondary functions. Humans do not eat just to satisfy their hunger, or drink only to slake their thirst—except for in emergency situations.

The mobile phone is loaded with meaning by both users and providers. Are these loadings similar or do they differ from one another? And why?

For too long, the mobile phone has only been loaded internally, i.e. with technological options. For too long, product management lay in the hands of the development departments and their engineers. In order for the mobile phone to properly become rooted in the markets, in the way that watches, glasses, and so on have, it has to be loaded beyond its core function (mobile communication) with secondary functions, i.e. with stories, myths, designs, scenes, idols.

What effect will such loading of the mobile phone eventually have on users and their everyday life? And what effect will it have on the communications industry and suppliers?

This will open up huge new markets for the communications industry. Users will want several mobile phones (we would better call them mobile devices) for different uses—as has happened with watches or glasses. And they will want to use them in a way specific to the task or situation. You can see the first signs of that already: for instance with the 'Mobi-Click'[2] three-button mobile phone, the colourful 'MYMO'[3] kids' phone, or Sony Ericsson's classic multimedia 'T 610' phone.[4]

To finish, let me ask you a very general question: Is mobile communication a social and cultural innovation accompanying the fundamental changes of our time?

That goes without saying. All transport systems, whether for products, for people or for news, have accompanied and counteracted those processes that we call industrialization and modernization, which have led to the split between work and life, between production and consumption, between job and relationship, between living space and friendships, etc. You could perhaps say that the increasing spatial, temporal and social differences of modern societies are being compensated by the multiple possibilities for transcending space and time and for social interaction.

References

Abels, Heinz (2000), 'Sich dem 'Mehrgott' verweigern: Zu Peter Gross' "Multioptionsgesellschaft"', In: Uwe Schimank and Ute Volkmann (Eds.), *Soziologische Gegenwartsdiagnosen I. Eine Bestandesaufnahme*, Opladen: Leske + Budrich, 91-107.

---

2. Editor's note: "The simplest mobile phone in the world", according to the Swiss manufacturing company, has only three large programmable buttons and is aimed at the needs of older people (see http://www.mobi-click.com). A similar development is seen elsewhere: "The most interesting device, from TU-KA, targets the elderly market, a rapidly growing segment in greying Japan. The 'TU-KA S' is only voice-enabled—no sexy features like e-mail, games, Web browsing, or camera—not even a small black-and-white screen. This no-nonsense Kyocera-made device features large buttons. [...] TU-KA promotes the 2G-phone with the slogan 'no manual needed'. There is a demand for these kinds of simple phones—the 'TU-KA S' is currently outselling all other phones from Japan's smallest carrier." (Blokland 2004)

3. Editor's note: "MYMO is the latest security device that parents can purchase for their children. It is a simple, easy-to-use mobile phone designed for children between the ages of 4 and 8. [...] MYMO is great for parents to keep in contact with their children in an emergency. As it can dial just 5 preset numbers, your children can contact you or another family member if they need you. You can track your MYMO and other family mobiles on the internet." (see http://www.mymoshop.com/html/mymo.html)

4. Editor's note: This mobile phone even has its own fashionable website which is designed as an "experimental global community of mobile phone photographers from around the world" (see http://www.t-six-ten.com).

Blokland, Arjen van (2004), 'Viewpoint: Simple Stylish Phones Tapping into New Market Segments', *Wireless Watch Newsletter. Commentary on Japan's Wireless World,* Issue No. 137, 12 December, http://www.japaninc.com/newsletters/index.html?list=ww&issue=137 (13 December 2004).

Gross, Peter (1994), *Die Multioptionsgesellschaft,* Frankfurt am Main: Suhrkamp.

Gross, Peter (1999), *Ich-Jagd. Im Unabhängigkeitsjahrhundert,* Frankfurt am Main: Suhrkamp.

Gross, Peter (2004a), 'Wenn die Nebensache zur Hauptsache wird—Aufladungstechniken', In: Belz, Christian/Bieger, Thomas (Eds.), *Customer Value. Kundenvorteile schaffen Unternehmensvorteile,* Frankfurt am Main: Redline Wirtschaft, 232-234.

Gross, Peter (2004b), 'Consumer Confusion und Multioptionsgesellschaft', *Thexis. Fachzeitschrift für Marketing,* 21 (4), 34-36.

Kelly, George A. (1955), *The Psychology of Personal Constructs,* 2 vol., New York: Norton.

Morello, Augusto (1995), '"Discovering Design" Means [Re]-Discovering Users and Projects', In: Buchanan, Richard and Margolin, Victor (Eds.), *Discovering Design: Explorations in Design Studies,* Chicago: University of Chicago, 69-76.

Mussel, Christine (1992), *Bedürfnisse in der Planung der Städte: Zur Theorie und Methode eines diskursiven Bedürfnisbegriffs;* Reihe Arbeitsberichte, Heft 106, Fachbereich Stadtplanung und Landschaftsplanung, Kassel.

Otnes, Cele et al. (1997), 'Toward an Understanding of Consumer Ambivalence', *Journal of Consumer Research,* 24, 80-93.

Schulz von Thun, Friedemann et al. (2000), *Miteinander reden: Kommunikationspsychologie für Führungskräfte,* Reinbek bei Hamburg: Rowohlt.

Mobile mania, mobile manners

LARA SRIVASTAVA

The importance of being mobile

Today's mobile phone has moved beyond being a mere technical device to becoming a key "social object" present in every aspect of our daily lives. Always-on connectivity and mobility will define not only the future technological landscape, but equally the socio-political one. This chapter focuses on two important impacts of the mobile phone on society: social etiquette and the growing problem of spam.

THE UBIQUITOUS MOBILE

The unprecedented and unexpected rise in the number of mobile phone users (see Figure 1) has a number of consequences and implications, but perhaps the most significant impact is on access, both to basic telecommunication services, and to other information and communication technologies as tools for economic and social development. It is also noteworthy that the phenomenon of mobile overtaking fixed has taken place across geographic criteria such as countries, regions, and continents, across socio-demographic criteria such as gender, income, or age, and across economic criteria such as the price premium for mobile (micro) or GDP per capita (macro). The cross-over point occurred in many developing countries (e.g. Cambodia) before it occurred in the developed world. The economy with the highest mobile penetration rate at the end of 2004 was Luxembourg, at about 120 per cent. Hong Kong and Italy hold second and third place respectively. Israel and the Czech Republic complete the 'top five' list. The largest economy, in terms of subscribers, is of course, China, which had over 330 million subscribers at the end of 2004. Overall, it is indeed the Asian region that boasts the highest proportion of the world's mobile users as well as the oldest 3rd generation mobile networks (under the IMT-2000 standards family),[1] which were launched in 2001 in Japan

1. International Mobile Telecommunications-2000 (IMT-2000) is the global standard

and Korea. After a relatively slow start, a number of additional third-generation networks were launched between 2003 and 2005, even in Europe where high auction fees had initially delayed 3G development. Already, research and development efforts are well under way for systems beyond IMT-2000.

Figure 1: Fixed and mobile lines (world), 2004 estimated, Source: ITU.

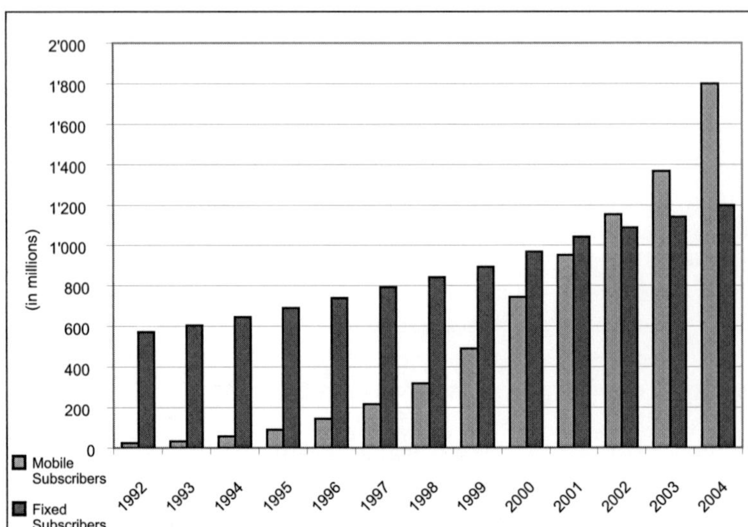

THE INTIMATE MOBILE

The mobile phone is probably the most talked about consumer product of the last 50 years and has been adopted at a staggering rate across cultures and nations. The English term "mobile" comes from the Latin "mobilis", which has the following meanings as set out in the 1975 edition of the Concise Oxford English Dictionary:

- Easy to move, movable, loose, not fixed, not firm;
- Pliable, nimble, flexible, agile, swift and rapid.
- Readily changing its expression. Able to change one's social status.
- In a negative sense, inconstant, fickle and changeable.

The "movable" and "portable" quality of the mobile is of course its key function. However, the mobile has come to mean much more, and the

for third generation (3G) wireless communications, defined by a set of interdependent Recommendations from the International Telecommunication Union (ITU).

etymological origin of the word may be rather more precise than imagined in describing this modern technology. Whatever its name or nickname, human beings have most certainly developed a fascinating and intimate relationship with their mobile phone.

The sheer physical proximity of this technical device to the human body cannot go unnoticed. Most users are no more than a metre away from their mobiles, at any time of the day. Many sleep with it near their pillow, and use it as an alarm clock. This distance will only be shortened with developments in wearable wireless computing. The Japanese, for instance, have recently released a mobile phone that enables users to listen to calls inside their heads, through a mechanism for the conduction of sound through bone (Srivastava 2004). The mobile phone has indeed become the most intimate aspect of a user's personal sphere of objects (e.g. keys, wallet, money etc). It seems to give users the impression that they are constantly connected to the world outside, and therefore somewhat less alone.

This physical connection with the phone is also accompanied by a strong emotional attachment. Losing a mobile phone can cause disruption and even panic in a user's life. The UMTS Forum concluded in its 2003 paper *Social Shaping of UMTS*, that users have a more "emotional" relationship with their mobile phones than with any other form of information and communication technology (UMTS 2003). The mobile is used to store personal telephone numbers as well as personal messages (e.g. SMS) and pictures that are cherished by the user. Often, these items are not stored on any other device. In some respects, the mobile phone acts as a "mirror" of the self, reflecting the identity of the user and acting as the basis for his/her social network. As a physical manifestation of a user's identity, mobiles have not surprisingly become important fashion accessories rather than mere utilitarian devices. Many young people show off their mobile phones to each other: the ring tones they use and the number and quality of messages stored on their mobile phones can serve to enhance or threaten their social status.

New technologies, new languages

It has been said that learning how to use a new technology is akin to learning a new language. A good illustration is the learning curve among children for new languages: it is widely known that children are much faster at absorbing new languages than adults. Similarly, the younger a user, the faster they take to a new technical development. Mobile phones are no exception, with young teenagers being the most avid users of both cutting-edge and established applications.

With the fast-paced evolution in communication technologies, humans have had to re-invent the language of social interaction. Plain old fixed-line telephones required us to learn to communicate in real-time without any visual clues. The advent of e-mail taught us how to be less formal in our written language and how to speed up our response time to incoming messages. The mobile phone has taken communication to a different level yet again. It is forcing us to discover how to communicate privately in public spaces, how and when to be contactable, how and when to end a mobile messaging "conversation", and so on. Young users and adults alike are even using new forms of SMS slang and spelling. The mobile phone has had a profound effect on language and communication, thereby challenging established and traditional norms of social behaviour.

Mobile and the evolution of etiquette

The private, the public and the polite

The ubiquity of the mobile phone in everyday life has meant that the distinction between the public and the private spheres of human existence has become less pronounced. Public places, such as restaurants and trains, are now commonly "colonized" by the private lives of mobile individuals (Geser 2002). As Sadie Plant (2001) has noted, mobiles have created a "simultaneity of place": a physical space and a virtual space of conversational interaction. In other words, there has been an extension of physical space, through the creation and juxtaposition of a mobile "social space". This has led to a constant "permeability" (Geser 2002) between the separate contexts of social life. For instance, individuals have often been observed talking on the phone at a restaurant table, while their dining partner either looks elsewhere or is similarly engaged talking or texting on their own mobile device. The intrusion (or potential intrusion) of remote others, in any given social context, has become commonplace, and even anticipated.

Although in some countries (like Japan), there have been efforts to regulate mobile phone usage in public, e.g. through restrictions on use in restaurants and public transport, in general, the tension between remote and co-present social interaction has not yet led to the establishment of any widespread social norms[2]. But some patterns of behaviour are already becoming evident. Two areas of complaint stand out:

2. See the 2004 ITU New Initiatives Workshop on "Shaping the future mobile information society" at http://www.itu.int/futuremobile (14 July 2005).

1. *The mobile voice:* many mobiles have loud ringing tones which disturb otherwise peaceful environments. The volume of mobile conversations can be disturbing in public places, forcing people to listen in on private conversations.
2. *Mobile multi-tasking*: the complexity of managing two sets of social environments and context, at the same time (Ling 2002).

THE MOBILE VOICE

It is widely accepted that, typically, a person speaking on a mobile phone (and indeed any phone) has the tendency to speak louder than if they were speaking to a person in their own physical space. Though no clear social norms have yet evolved, therefore, many who answer phone calls in meetings or quiet areas are subject to glances of admonition by others. Loud mobile conversations in public settings are unappreciated. Similarly, a ringing and unanswered mobile phone is often frowned upon.

Nonetheless, there still remain those who will interrupt a meeting with their phone call and carry on speaking in the room where the meeting is being held. There are also those who will continue to engage in staged mobile conversations, or speaking loudly on their mobiles in order to be heard and seen by others, seemingly to build their "social status". Interestingly enough, these mobile "actors" may even do so regardless of whether or not they are on an actual call.

FORCED EAVESDROPPING AS A FORM OF RELATIONS WITH STRANGERS

"Mobile loudness" in public places has meant that the mobile phone user and his/her conversational partner may not be the only ones "involved" in the conversation. Those around them, willing or not, may be privy to the one-way content of their telephonic exchange. This is why users are often seen avoiding eye contact or moving their head (even their entire body) away from those co-present when engaged in a mobile call. These are all means to manage the potential embarrassment underlying the public audibility of private conversations (Murtagh 2002). Most people will agree that they find it rather uncomfortable to be exposed to the private details of another's life. On the other hand, it can be argued this form of "forced eavesdropping" is actually defining a sense of "mobile urbanism", through the bonds it creates between strangers, for instance in a train or restaurant. Without having to speak to each other directly, strangers in urban public spaces can learn about each other through one-way mobile conversations, thereby establishing a form of 'invisible' understanding between those co-present.

Mobile multi-tasking

Mobile users have had to learn to juggle public physical surroundings with the private space of their mobile conversations. Face to face conversations can at any time be interrupted by a mobile text message or voice call. For instance, when a voice call is received, most users do not hesitate to step away from the social group in their physical space and engage in social interaction with a distant interlocutor on their mobile (Ling 2002). Many people do choose to text (use SMS or email) rather than talk, depending on the social situation they find themselves in. In meetings, participants might text instead of talk. Students sitting in classrooms, or in their room at bedtime, will prefer to text. Texting has the advantage, of course, of allowing users to continue to engage in conversation with those that are co-present, while communicating with a distant third party through furtive "thumb typing".

Clearly, we are a society that favours multi-tasking not only in the material sense, but also in the social sense. The mobile phone and the "synchronous social spaces" it creates are an enabler of multi-tasking, and in this respect responds to that age-old human need to control space and time. But does being at two places at once enhance or reduce the quality of each individual interactional space? Might "always on" mean that one is losing one's sense of the "here and now"?

A changing techno-social behaviour

Playing with punctuality

For most users, owning a mobile phone has allowed them to manage their day-to-day life more efficiently. For instance, they can call a friend at the last minute when they are passing by their neighbourhood, to check if they can meet. Appointments can more easily be made and shifted, and also cancelled if required. However, many people claim that mobile phones have led to a form of "impoliteness" among users. A survey conducted in September 2003 by Nokia found that a staggering 89 per cent of mobile users believe that people need to adopt better 'mobile etiquette', for example the use of ringing and messaging tones so as not to disturb others around them, and by not shouting and pacing while on the phone. However, according to the results of the survey, 71 per cent of users are now consistently late for social events because of the option to rearrange through a mobile voice call or text. In the United States, a similar survey by Harris Interactive in July 2003 found that 50 per cent of Americans believe that people are generally discourteous in their use mobile phones.

Keeping options open

Have mobile users become less definite about commitments? The "approxi-meeting" seems now to be standard practice: mobile phone users rarely set an exact time and place for a meeting, the excuse being that details can always be worked out later by SMS or mobile e-mail. The habit of "keeping options open" or the "multi-meeting" has also been enhanced by the use of mobile phones, i.e. users often make several approximate and tentative appointments, deciding only at the last minute the meeting they would attend (depending on the value they ascribe to it). On the other hand, it can be postulated that mobile phones have given users more responsibility and have facilitated accountability, e.g. between children and parents or employees and employers.

Spontaneity and the illusion of communication

Mobile phones encourage spontaneous communication, for instance through trends such as multi-player location-based gaming and "bluejacking" (the sending of short anonymous text messages to other mobile phones via Bluetooth). These may provide an outlet for passing the time, but do not necessarily strengthen existing relationships. While admitting to an overall increase in spontaneous and widespread social interaction, some argue that mobile phones may be reducing the quality of face-to-face social interaction. And the ambiguity regarding the social norms that mobile users are to follow in public or group settings seems to further dilute this quality.

Furtive text messaging, for instance, can often give an illusion of strong communication, whereas it is a medium which clearly lacks some of the principal elements of human interaction, e.g. tone of voice, body language, facial expression and touch. Some sociologists argue that texting teenagers run the risk of affecting their capacity to interact with each other on a voice or face-to-face basis: many choose to text rather than to talk, particularly in awkward or emotionally-charged situations.

Moreover, despite the overwhelming availability of communications media (e-mail, fixed-line voice, mobile messaging, mobile voice etc), people are becoming harder to reach. Users are aware of the fact that the mobile phone automatically records a missed call, and typically offers convenient voice-mail services. Therefore, users need not be so concerned about missing calls accidentally, whether this is occasioned by the low volume of the ringing tone or by difficulty of physical access (e.g. at the bottom of a purse). A deliberate form of missing calls, the "call screen", is becoming more and more commonplace, given that mobiles typically display the number of the calling party. As mentioned above, many now prefer to use the written language to communicate rather than the richer medium of voice. The mobile phone, universally recognized as a great facilitator of human communication, is now showing that it may also be assisting in the obstruction of it. For the mobile is intimately related to language, which is known to reveal and at the same time to hide, meaning and intent.

Commercial manners: The case of mobile spam

As users develop a more and more intimate relationship with their mobile phones, consumer protection in this area becomes increasingly necessary. Protecting the privacy of users is at the forefront of concerns. This section examines an important aspect of privacy protection, that is to say "freedom from interference". In this context, "spam" or unsolicited commercial communications is threatening to invade mobile phones.

No clear definition of spam has been agreed upon, as the scope of the problem is constantly evolving. Over the Internet, filters and blockers are reducing the volume of spam, but only slightly, and few can eliminate the problem entirely. Spam has now become a significant nuisance for individual Internet users, but is also leading to losses of productivity as employees spend much time clearing their inboxes. Spam includes advertising for dubious pharmaceuticals, from "get rich quick" schemes, gambling, pornography to offers of software and printer cartridges. Some spam messages are fraudulent and others may even contain computer viruses. One of the more serious concerns is the user of "phishing" (or spam and scam), a method using trick URLs. Phishing lets the customer believe that he/she is being linked to an official website (e.g. eBay or Citibank), and then asks the user to re-enter his or her account details.

Governments are attempting to thwart the facility with which marketing companies can currently send spam mail: the United States, for instance, has recently enacted the "Can-Spam Act" of 2003. Like industry self-regulators, governments are faced with the challenge of striking the right balance between fostering valuable commercial innovations and protecting the rights of users. With the use of location-based technologies, and technologies such as radio frequency identification tags, targeted advertising and promotions can reach users at the right time and at the right place. This might prove to be a very useful service for users; but it could also lead to an increase in the number of unsolicited messages appearing on mobiles. Clear opt-in and opt-out systems need to be put into place.

Although the amount of spam sent to mobile phones in most markets is currently much less than fixed-line spam, it will certainly increase dramatically if effective measures are not taken. Moreover, in some advanced mobile economies, like South Korea, mobile spam has even overtaken fixed-line spam as early as 2003. Spam over mobile networks may indeed pose an even more serious problem than Internet spam, given the personalized nature of the mobile phone, its growing use among young children, and in some cases the cost incurred for incoming messages. Spam also threatens future technological and commercial innovation in the area of mobile shopping, mobile marketing and location-based services. The GSM Association cites spam as one of the top four threats to the future of the mobile industry.

Forms of mobile spam

People trust the mobile phone more than any other form of information and communication technology. The receipt of unwanted commercial messages may threaten this increasingly intimate and trusting relationship. Where unsolicited messages have a visual component, e.g. MMS, illegal images may disrupt a customer's use of new services. Also, cigarette promotions or worse yet, pornographic material, may reach recipients such as minors. As mobile communications become more and more widespread (or "ubiquitous"), the potential for abuse is correspondingly greater.

On mobile phones, spam can come in the form of a text message that pops up on a mobile phone screen, advertising prizes or lewd chat rooms. At other times, it can be transmitted via Bluetooth inviting passers-by to a nearby coffee shop. A missed or 1-ring voice call, or an SMS, designed to solicit a premium rate response is another worrying example of spam, and can imply a direct financial cost to the user. Spam-type content, however, can vary, as does its precise definition. In Japan, for instance, most unsolicited messages, (approx. 80 per cent) advertise dating sites. Messages from operators advertising promotions and game prices are also common in some European countries. Recently, in Italy, citizens have received an SMS from the Presidency of the Ministry to remind them to vote for European elections. The question of how to define spam remains an open one[3].

Countering spam

The good news is that it is easier to detect mobile phone spammers than their Internet e-mail counterparts. Messages on mobile phones come from one of a handful of carriers, rather than thousands of traditional ISPs. Currently, it is also more expensive to send spam to mo-

3. See the 2004 ITU WSIS Thematic Meeting on Countering Spam at http://www.itu.int/spam (14 July 2005).

biles than to Internet e-mail addresses. The bad news is that this is set to change. First, the exploitation of free short-range technologies such as Bluetooth, will increase the number of location-based spam. Second, the shift towards interoperable mobile and wire-line messaging will mean that mobile phones will receive e-mail just like the fixed line Internet. Japan's mobile phone industry is a good example: a few years ago, the Japanese operator NTT DoCoMo, had already announced that spam was overloading its systems, even freezing some customers' screens. The operator took immediate action. From 25 December 2003, DoCoMo introduced a new anti-spam measure that enabled its mobile subscribers to block all e-mails from user-selected domains. The operator is taking aggressive countermeasures against spam mail sent from its i-mode network, such as limiting the amount of e-mails sent daily from a single i-mode account and suspending or rescinding the contracts of DoCoMo handsets registered to known spammers.

In the United Kingdom, in August 2003, Vodafone introduced programmes encouraging users to forward unsolicited messages to them free of charge. It plans to collate a consolidated report of all the unsolicited text messages forwarded. This consolidated report will be forward to mobile messaging regulators, such as ICSTIS (Independent Committee for the Supervision of Standards of Telephone Information Services).

Not only is industry making efforts to address the problem, but legislators are also looking for ways to counter spam. The U.S. Federal Communications Commission (FCC) announced in early August 2004 that it planned to set up a list of Internet domains used by mobile phone carriers to help keep spam off mobile phones. The FCC rule will allow marketing companies that don't want to contravene the national anti-spam law enacted last year to check the list to make sure they are not sending spam. The FCC hopes that the creation of a domain-name registry of wireless e-mail addresses makes sender compliance easy and inexpensive.

Of course, it is important for any legislative efforts in this regard to be "technology neutral", flexible enough to cover mobile phones, but also any future connected devices. It is also essential that direct marketing companies continue to develop and evolve their codes of conduct (Sipior, Ward and Bonner 2003). But perhaps one of the key mechanisms for countering spam is to address the main reason behind its popularity among marketing companies: its low cost. Sending spam via the Internet is the cheapest form of marketing. Although mobile spam is slightly more costly, it is still less than traditional print or television marketing. Thus, making mobile spam "uneconomic" may go a long way in tackling the problem. This can be achieved through national and international legislation maintaining or introducing calling-party-pays system (CPP) and through the withholding of interconnection payments in cases of spam. Operators should also be encouraged to put into place automated reporting facilities and effective response to customer complaints. Filtering mechanisms should be made available not only at the network end, but users themselves must be empowered to conduct self-defence activities on their handsets.

Conclusion

No one can deny the evolving nexus between technological innovation and the human condition. And it is in these early days of innovative energy that society, as a whole, has the rare opportunity to consider the implications of these new technologies. Serious thought needs to be given to the design and implementation of fair policy and regulation in the public interest, to ensure healthy market development, and to thwart disinformation and misuse. Mechanisms and safeguards to be developed by policy-makers should no longer be sector-specific as traditional telecommunication regulation has been in the past. Public policy for the protection of consumers should be wide in scope and include the prevention of abusive and harmful content (including spam and adult content) and the protection of privacy.

This chapter has examined two ways in which the mobile phone is impacting daily human existence: social etiquette and spam. With current advances in mobile technology, as with any new development, it is at, or immediately subsequent to, its introduction that suitable steps can be taken to ensure its proper establishment.

References

Geser, H. (2002), *Towards a Sociological Theory of the Mobile Phone,* University of Zurich.

Ling, R. (2002), *The social juxtaposition of mobile telephone conversations and public spaces,* Telenor R&D.

Murtagh, G. M. (2002), 'Seeing the "Rules": Preliminary Observations of Action, Interaction and Mobile Phone Use', In: B. Brown, N. Green, and R. Harper (Eds.), *Wireless World: Social and Interactional Aspects of the Mobile Age,* London: Springer.

Plant, S. (2001), *On the mobile. The effects of mobile telephones on social and individual life,* commissioned by Motorola, http://www.motorola.com/mot/doc/0/234_MotDoc.pdf (14 July 2005).

Sipior, J., Ward, B., and Bonner, P. (2004), 'Should Spam Be on the Menu', *Communications of the ACM,* 47 (6).

Srivastava, L. (2004), 'Japan's ubiquitous mobile information society', *INFO*, 14 (4), 234-251.

UMTS Forum (2003), *Social Shaping of UMTS: Preparing the 3G Customer*, Report 26.

Your life in snapshots:
Mobile weblogs (moblogs)

Nicola Döring and Axel Gundolf

"We used to take some 300 family pictures in a year. Now, with the camera phone, I can reach that number in six weeks. When one of my children comes back from school, when we go for a walk or shopping—I'll always take a picture and publish it on my moblog. If I carry on at this rate and post on average 6.5 family snaps per day, then I'll have 2,372 images in one year. If I had them printed out in a 10 x 15 cm format it would cost me hundreds of dollars. If you put them back to back, there would be a chain of photos 14 miles long. And all of this in just one year!"

Exhibitionism or journalism?

Julián Gallo is the name of the enthusiastic moblogger quoted above. He publicly documents his daily life in minute detail using a camera phone and moblog platform. Might the cultural critics be right who deem amateurs' publications on the Internet—personal homepages, weblogs or moblogs—in the main boring, useless and often even embarrassing? Who on earth could be interested in where Gallo went for his walk yesterday? More contentious than the banal snapshots of the allotment back home are exhibitionistic photos. This has already led to more than one hundred mobloggers using the moblog platform Yafro to protest against other Yafro members who on a regular basis place online nude pictures of themselves and their partners.

Those criticising this tidal wave of personal content stand on the opposing side of the debate to the prophets of a new democratised civil journalism. They argue that if camera phones, radio networks and moblog platforms enable more and more citizens to participate at any time in a free exchange of information and opinion, reporting live from important events all over the world, the information monopoly of mass media and professional publicists could be broken. The concept of a *moblog* carries associations not only with the mobility of keeping a mobile-based logbook but also with the mob as in a 'disorderly crowd of people'. According to Howard Rheingold this crowd may alter, through mobile communication and improved social networking, to become an 'informed mob' that exerts increased political influence (Rheingold 2003a). It was only natural for Internet pioneer Rheingold to encourage US citizens in the summer of 2003 to keep an eye on what was happening with the next presidential elections and to use their camera phones to report live from election events—"Moblog the Conventions!" (Rheingold 2003b). In the summer of 2004 this became reality. The University of South Carolina, among others, organised a major election event moblog—the Wireless Election Connection Moblog (http://wec.text america.com). Here, thanks to industry sponsorship, amateur reporters were given new camera phones, officially accredited as election reporters by both Democrats and Republicans, and interviewed by MTV as media stars in their own right.

From cult to commerce

The term "Moblog" or "MoBlog" (short for Mobile Weblog) was used for the first time by web experts Justin Hall (Hall 2002) and Adam Greenfield (http://www.v-2.org). In 2003, the latter organized the first *International Moblogging Conference* "1IMC" in Tokyo. Moblogs are regularly updated web publications comprising a series of chronologically ordered contributions. The crucial difference between moblogs and old-style weblogs that share the same structure is that moblogs may not only be uploaded from stationary computers but also, or exclusively, from mobile technology. This is usually a camera phone, sometimes a PDA or a notebook computer with a wireless connection. Moblog contributions usually consist of pictures taken with a camera phone together with some accompanying text. Only occasionally do they contain videos taken on the mobile or spoken word (videoblog, audioblog). Instead of "moblog", the term *wireless blogs*, *visual blogs* or *photoblogs* are sometimes used. For the latter, pictures from digital cameras are often fed in. So far, the reading or observing audience of moblogs is not mobile (via WAP or WLAN) but mainly seated at desktop computers.

In principle, moblogs serve personal publishing in the same way as homepages; allowing all media consumers to become media producers themselves. Also, Moblogs are part of the social media, as the content of a blog is not produced by a single person; normally several people participate directly and indirectly through links with other blogs and websites as well as public reader comments. *Collective blogs* are published by a team of authors, or are opened up to entries by third parties.

As with old-style weblogs, moblogs have access to specialized online platforms (Application Service Providers) enabling users to send in, save, edit and publish their contributions via e-mail or mobile messaging (SMS, MMS). *Moblog platforms* not only offer publication functions but also various community services. These enable moblog authors to establish personal profiles, exchange messages with other mobloggers (either direct or through forums), mutually list their names in public lists of friends, or form topical moblog circles. Not least, the platforms offer user statistics with information on which moblogs have the highest number of entries, the most up-to-date contributions, or the highest number of visits. The individual contributions eliciting the most comments, or users with the most comments, are registered in Top 10 or Top 100 lists.

Using a web template and mobile device, moblog platforms are relatively easy to use. They require very little knowledge of HTML and enable the user to immediately begin moblogging after entering the e-mail address and selecting a user name. All in all, however, basic moblog platforms offer more limited technical functionality than weblog platforms (see Sauer 2003). In moblog contributions, links to the web, so typical for weblogs, are fairly rare. No wonder: according to Justin Hall (Hall 2002). "A weblog is a record of travels on the Web, so a moblog should be a record of travels in the world".

However, on various platforms—such as German-language providers 20six.de, Blogg.de and Twoday.net—weblogs and moblogs are not accessed separately but in an integrated way. Whoever subscribes as a user for an *advertising-financed simple service* or a *payable premium service* can keep a logbook into which entries are fed by both stationary and mobile technology. Of course, moblogs are of economic interest not only for application service providers but also for the manufacturers of the mobile devices and the network providers who continue looking for killer applications for camera and video phones, broadband mobile phone networks, and related services. Meanwhile, with the 'Lifeblog' software for the Nokia 7610 phone, the Finnish information technology producer has also entered the moblogging market (http://www.nokia.com/lifeblog). Photos, videos, SMS, MMS and personal notes may be archived in chronological order.

Naturally enough, discerning mobloggers are not content with the standardized packages and design templates of the moblog platforms. They would rather use their own web servers to design their mobile logbooks with a higher degree of freedom. This has the additional advantage that they get to keep the exclusive rights to the content they produce, whereas commercial weblog or moblog hosts (e.g. Textamerica) often claim these rights for themselves. Standard blogging systems, typically through Perl, PHP and mySQL, either come with moblog modules (e.g. Pivot: http://www.pivotlog.net and WordPress:

http://www.wordpress.org) or complemented by moblog scripts including instructions offered by users with knowledge of programming (e.g. http://www.movabletype.org for MovableType). An open-source system with special moblog support is provided by EasyMoblog (http://www.easymoblog.org). Despite the trend towards commercialisation of the world of blogging, it is possible, with the relevant media expertise, to find and use free platforms, systems and tools. However, apart from the online costs, moblogging does involve substantial financial outlay for high-quality mobile technology as well as the costs of mobile communication.

Niche or boom?

Current surveys in the US reveal that weblogs are read, either frequently or infrequently, by 11 percent of Internet users, and written by 2-7 percent (Pew Internet & American Life Project 2004). Compared to a killer application such as e-mail, which is used regularly by over 90 percent of online users, weblogs are more of a niche medium. On the other hand, taken in absolute numbers, i.e. hundreds of thousands of bloggers and blogs, the blogosphere has attained remarkable proportions. The Blogcensus project (http://www.blogcensus.com) has registered over two million blogs worldwide, while the Technorati blog index (http://www.technorati.com) records as many as three million. German-speaking countries currently contribute just under 20,000 blogs (http://www.blogstats.de), many of which unsurprisingly progressed no further than the test stage or are barely maintained.

The world of moblogs overlaps to a certain extent with the world of the old-style weblogs, for instance where experienced bloggers now complement uploads previously made from a stationary computer by uploading contributions via mobile technology. Some mobloggers are committed camera phone users who never previously kept a weblog nor appeared in any other way as an Internet or web author.

In recent years, the number of moblogs has increased exponentially worldwide. Whereas in 2001 there were very few moblogs, in 2002 there were dozens, by 2003 hundreds, if not thousands, and now, in 2004, hundreds of thousands. The payable service provider Fotolog.net alone hosts just under half a million moblogs. The Photoblogs.org moblog index currently contains nearly 5,000 registered moblogs from 61 countries in 26 languages, clearly dominated by North America, Japan and Western Europe, and with English the most widely used language by a considerable margin. It is estimated that German-speaking countries are home to several thousand moblogs—with the trend increasing. It can be assumed that in the long term only a minority of Internet and mobile users will be moblogging. However, economically, a lucrative market does seem to be opening up. To illustrate this, the Blog platform www.blogger.com, which also allows mobile add-ins of text, images and sound, was taken over by Google for around US $20 million.

Between breakfast and the front line

The diversity of the contents of weblogs and moblogs matches its quantity. The Austrian moblog index of SMS.at, for instance, is divided thematically into at least 24 main sections such as "Cars and Motorbikes", "Arts & Culture", "Religion & the Spiritual World", "Business" and "Science", with dozens of subcategories. The predominantly young authors of the moblogs administered through SMS.at decide for themselves whether, and in which category, to register their moblog. The 3,000 or so moblogs registered in the index are distributed unevenly between the various sections. The most common are "About Myself" (1,061 moblogs), "Youth" (509), "Sports & Fitness" (245) and "Love & Companionship" (239). On this teenager platform, the sections "State and Politics" (7), "Science" (6) and "Health & Medicine" (3 moblogs) understandably occupy the lowest ranks. What has to be taken into account here is that a thematic division of whole moblogs is problematic because different contributions to the same moblog can deal with very different topics.

Teenagers' moblog contributions—with pictures illustrating their breakfast, their journey to school, their last party, or their pets and siblings—might seem trite, but so is life. They are not targeting a mass audience: most bloggers write, snap and design for themselves, as well as for real-life family and friends and for online acquaintances. Given the subject matter, advertising-style glossy aesthetics or mass appeal are neither possible nor necessary. While many bloggers insist they are publishing for themselves and for a small circle of readers, there are others who aim to generate more *attention*. For example, the administrators of the Fotopages.com moblog platform complained that some users were choosing the sexiest image possible for their most current photo on the platform's start page in order to attract people, even if the picture did not otherwise fit with the rest of the moblog (see Figure 1).

In August 2003, as part of the Blogcensus project, 776 blogs were selected at random (NITLE 2003) from around 500,000 weblogs archived at the time. It became apparent that nearly half of these blogs (47 percent) could be categorised under the *personal diary* section. Significantly more female (56 percent) than male (28 percent) bloggers were documenting their own daily life, with the remaining 16 percent of diary blogs comprising unspecified genders, or collaborative blogs run by several people. The American *Katie*, for instance, has kept a diary moblog since November 2003 and has since produced over 800 text image entries which document and comment on her professional and private daily life in graphic and humorous detail (http://steevie.text america.com/).

Figure 1: Start page of the Fotopages.com moblog platform.

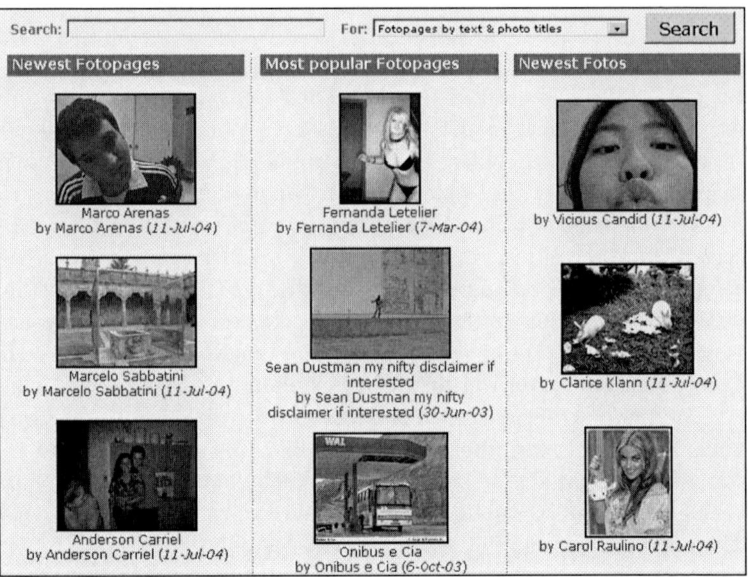

There are *personal weblogs* and there are *topical weblogs*. Subjects around online and mobile communication are favourites; the medium shows itself to be highly self-referential. The scientific research on blogs is also mainly documented and discussed through blogs themselves. No wonder: blog researchers and bloggers are often one and the same person and connect theory to practice. Elizabeth Lawley, Professor of Information Science at the Rochester Institute of Technology and an active blogger herself, criticizes the fact that scientists with no real experience of blogging often view blogs as a homogenous mass and only skim the surface of the medium. To treat all blogs the same, she says, makes as much sense as judging the entire output of books without considering the different genres (Lawley 2004).

In the Blogcensus study, only 6 percent of all blogs surveyed were categorised within the *political blog* section; here the gender balance was reversed from the diary blogs (84 percent male authors, 4 percent female authors, 10 percent group, 2 percent unspecified). Apart from topic-specific asymmetries, the gender balance of the blogosphere is almost equal, which is in complete contrast to nationality or age. Most bloggers live in the western world and are in the first half of their lives.

Amateurs versus professionals?

A mixture of personal diary and political logbook, frontline moblogs by US soldiers in Iraq are generating considerable interest on the Yafro platform (http://www.yafro.com/frontline.php). The soldiers offer photos of themselves and their comrades, of Iraqi civilians, war wounded and the dead. Moblog readers contribute patriotic slogans as well as anti-war protests, accompanied by jokes, compliments and flirtations ("You look great in your uniform!"). "CrashTheSoldier", who offers his moblog under the keywords "war, Iraq, beer, kill" (see Figure 2) defends his bloody pictures of the dead and injured by claiming a desire to document the truth of war at close hand and to counter the distorted reporting of the news channel CNN. In this sense he does show the conscience of a civil journalist, although one who naturally is also lobbying his own cause; promoting a more positive image of the US soldiers in Iraq. The "CrashTheSoldier" moblog is registered with Blueherenow. Blueherenow (http://www.blueherenow.com) is a platform for open-source news and moblog journalism reminiscent of Indymedia, but run by a commercial company (http://www.phrint.com). It presents a thematically sectioned mix of links to articles from established press bodies, complemented by links to moblog contributions.

Figure 2: Frontline moblog by CrashTheSoldier.

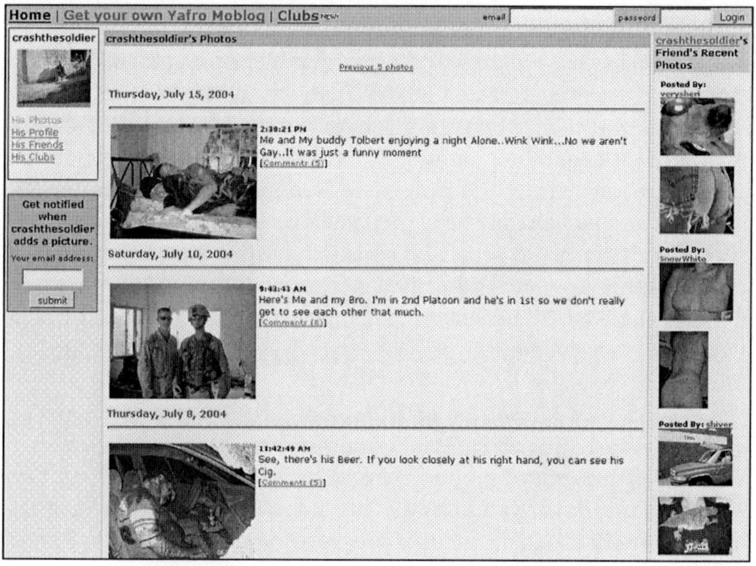

Useful as photos by amateur reporters may be, moblogs alone do not offer a sufficiently sound information base: they can only be put into perspective and interpreted in the context of other journalistic reports. In order for the three-step moblog process ("seen—snapped— posted") to become effective journalistically and politically, moblogs have to be promoted; they need readers in order to have any impact. Blogs only become known through recommendations on the Web and through reports in the mass media. It does not make sense therefore to celebrate moblogs as a replacement for professional journalism; both forms of publication complement and influence each other. It is no coincidence that moblog authors feature many professional publicists, authors, photographers and journalists. Through their personal popularity, as well as the quality of their blogs, they stand a good chance of being read, commented on and linked to frequently, thereby rising to the ranks of an A-list blogger.

Invariably, as in all freely growing networks with self-selecting links, there are a few dominant centres surrounded by large marginal zones. It is clear therefore that there can be no question of equal distribution of publicity influence amongst bloggers. This is not due to a failure on the part of the blogosphere, but more to a consequence of universal network laws (Barabási 2003). The Japanese Internet entrepreneur Joi Ito is without doubt one of the most famous A-list bloggers. Ito runs both a weblog and a moblog (http://joi.ito.com/moblog/) and according to press interviews spends some five hours each day reading and writing blogs.

The mutual surveillance and comments of active bloggers with each other is a form of quality control. For example, the team of the professional weblog *Phototalk* (http://talks.blogs.com/phototalk/) systematically examined Yafro's soldier moblogs in July 2004 in terms of their technical and photographic characteristics. The results showed that the vast majority of supposedly authentic front pictures from so-called amateur reporters in fact came from professional press photographers and had already been published online (Phototalk 2004). The spectacular first-hand reporting revealed itself as *picture piracy*. This means that fakes and falsifications are by no means restricted to the traditional media. To the extent that amateurs act as online and mobile publicists, they not only develop new expertise but also expose the failings that accompany it.

Alongside knowledge of and adherence to legal norms (in respect of issues such as copyright and privacy), arriving at an understanding of the ethical ground rules of blogging is equally important. An online survey conducted by the Massachusetts Institute of Technology in January 2004 amongst 492 bloggers (36 percent female, 84 percent under 40, 66 percent USA) showed that 36 percent of those surveyed had already encountered ethical problems (Viégas 2004). In addition, quite a few of the respondents knew other bloggers who had come into conflict with family and friends because of their blog contents (36 percent), or had even got into professional and legal difficulties (12 percent). Rebecca Blood, who via her blog (http://www.rebeccablood.net) managed the jump to professional author, dedicates a whole chapter of her weblog handbook to blog ethics (Blood 2002). The moblog covering the election event of the University of South Carolina quoted above is already working to journalistic standards.

Freestyle photography

With camera phones readily on hand in everyday situations and usable where cameras are often not an option, the opportunities for image production increase significantly. This extends to an invasion of the privacy of other people, whether family members at a dinner party, friends at a party, or strangers on the beach who might not appreciate their sun worship being lodged for posterity and commented on in sexually motivated moblogs. On the other hand, Howard Rheingold makes a valid point by referring to the politically emancipating significance of unwanted mobile snapshots. If, for instance, violence against demonstrators or minorities is captured and immediately published on the moblog, then this information cannot be erased even if the camera is confiscated or destroyed.

In contrast to analogue photography, the costs for individual pictures and copies in digital photography are dramatically reduced. Furthermore, the results can be viewed immediately. This accelerates the learning processes of amateur photographers, encouraging photographic experimentation. The camera phone makes these advantages of digital cameras accessible to even more people, and a popularisation of amateur photography can alter the way people perceive reality. Keeping and regularly maintaining a moblog means being on the constant lookout for new subjects and becoming more sensitised to interesting details in the environment that might otherwise have been overlooked. While some amateur photographers only have a patronising smile for the snapshots of eager camera phone owners, others appreciate this development, as one of the mobloggers in our online-survey commented: "Moblogging means that more people take pictures and start looking at the world rather than just perceiving it. I think that's great because photography is my biggest hobby. When I look at moblogs I like posting motivating comments." Generally, most of us are culturally illiterate at expressing ourselves through pictures. Multimedia messaging, camera phones and moblogs can make a small contribution towards developing more active visual competence and a sense of our own visual voice. This should not be seen as a rival for linguistic competence; in moblogs in particular, choosing the right caption and formulating suitable comments involves an astute handling of text-image combinations (Badger 2004). On the other hand, a purely photographic narrative promises an understanding across linguistic barriers not otherwise available on the text-dominated web.

The day-to-day photography popularised through camera phones and moblogs is mirrored in the current photo art. Under the title "Snooze Button", for instance, the Canadian photographer Dean Baldwin brings together a series of photos documenting his waking up every morning over the space of three years (see Figure 3). The snapshots, taken by a camera on top of his alarm clock, reveal the subtle differences in his daily routine. Baldwin deftly plays with the often-criticized banality of diary moblogs, opening up new perspectives on everyday life.

A detailed analysis of the content and formal structure of moblog contributions has not yet been conducted. Apart from their photographic content, one particularity of moblogs compared to conventional weblogs lies in their authors' mobility. The method of publishing straight after the event is particularly important for travel, major events, crises and disasters. It can, however, also be used for experimentation, to relieve boredom, to kill time, or to make further use of pictures already shot using the camera phone. Sometimes moblogging has a simple explanation—beyond headline-grabbing speculation about ethically dubious exhibitionism or recommended political activism: "It's a practical way of archiving the pictures taken when the mobile memory is exhausted," was the simple explanation one moblogger gave in our e-mail survey.

Figure 3: Snooze Button by Dean Baldwin (extract) (http://www.cbcradio3.com/issues/2004_04_30/index.cfm).

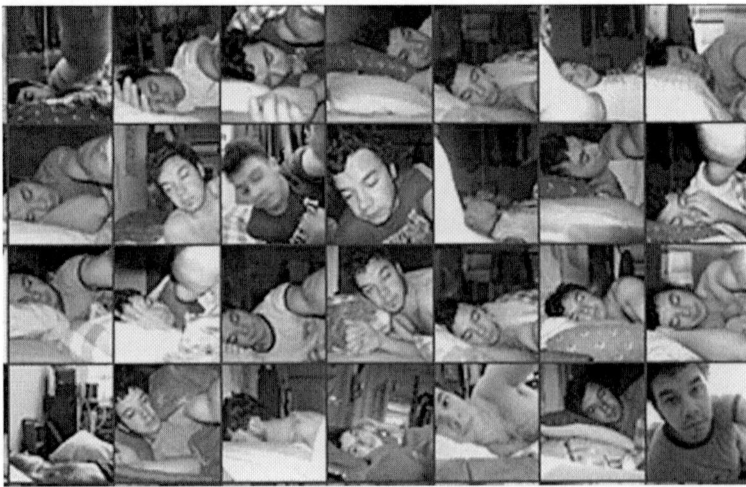

Mobloggers and their audience

Reading moblogs may be compared to leafing through photo albums of family and friends, or walking through a photography exhibition, or browsing in catalogues and coffee-table books. As there is no editorial selection or control, the differences in quality are as pronounced as on the web in general. Viewers have to decide for themselves what they deem to be *cat content* (bloggers' jargon for content of little interest) or relevant content. Naturally, for animal lovers, pictures of pets on a moblog are worth seeing as much as animals in real life. And apart from any moral criticism of adult content, in a cultural sense it is interesting to explore in more depth how and why men and women present their bodies and sexualities in moblogs. Not only in journalism, but also in the sex industry, online media contributes to increased participation by amateurs—offering specific opportunities and risks.

Moblogs that are regularly updated, gathering a loyal readership from both offline and online existence, develop regular, focused discussions about individual contributions and pictures. These include jokes and ribaldry, criticism and praise for photographers and subjects. "Well, it's just like looking at 'real' holiday snaps together—for instance, a place where you might ask 'where was that?' or comment on how slim the person looks or whatever," explains one female moblogger. For some, reading and commenting on moblogs is closely linked to personal ties; others use the medium out of curiosity or for entertainment ("because I enjoy thinking up 'intelligent' comments and making others smile or reflect", as one of the mobloggers we surveyed put it). The communicative function of moblogs is significant and can sometimes even take on the character of a lonely hearts service.

Other mobloggers are first and foremost interested in creative exchange, allowing themselves to be inspired by the photos other people have taken, and working harder on their own photography projects if they know that their moblog audience is waiting for new material. One of our moblog-survey respondents said: "For me the most important thing is the moment of the picture and the thought that goes with it. Also, I have all comments to my blog forwarded directly to my mobile; it's important for me to know who is following me 'live'." The desire to communicate cannot simply be dismissed as narcissism—it is one of the most fundamental needs humans have.

As with traditional online diaries (Döring 2001a) and personal homepages (Döring 2001b), moblogs are consciously used to acquire media competence and professionalism. It is no coincidence that the most committed mobloggers include many people involved in the media and photography profession. The compulsive picture-taking of the above-mentioned Julián Gallo is not just an obsession; in his role as photographer and lecturer in New Media at the Universidad de San

Andrés in Argentina, Gallo is reflecting the effects of photographic documentation in his moblog. In his own way, he is conducting a scientific experiment on his own person. A convincing moblog project may help a photographer establish himself or herself, as has been the case with some webloggers who are now published authors, have published their blogs as books, or report on blogging in magazines. After eight years of online publishing, Carola Heine (http://www.moving-target.de) describes her "private weblog value-added chain" as follows: "My own column in a PC newspaper, a non-fiction book on setting up a website, two non-fiction titles for young people, and again and again, with great pleasure, freelancing for the publications PCgo! and Internet Magazin."

From test account to moblog project

A public online logbook allows experiences to be shared with others, may open up new horizons, and can offer backup, encouragement and a sense of satisfaction. Just as in other aspects of life, the possibility of a lack of or undesired feedback cannot be excluded. Participants have the opportunity to operate using pseudonyms and/or to only allow selected persons access to their moblog in order to protect themselves from overexposure. This means that a certain amount of planning is required before launching into a blogging experiment with all its communicative and social dimensions. For pure documentation, traditional online photo albums are sufficient. These also offer the opportunity to order hard copies of the snaps (e.g. with Kodak, Foto Quelle, Media hype.de).

By no means all mobile users who start a moblog develop it into a long-term project. Of the 1,448 members of a popular moblog platform that had been active for more than a week, only 7 percent were still active six months later (Adar 2004). The average moblogger posts 14 images in the first week, one image in each of the second, third and fourth weeks, and none in the fifth week, suggesting that most lack the stamina needed for a continuous medium such as a blog.

However, this observation is no reason to dismiss moblogs generally as an aberration or mere hype. On the one hand, it is actually very sensible for users to say farewell to a medium after a short period if they see no added value in their day-to-day lives. On the other hand, it has to be conceded that meaningful and creative ideas only flourish when potential users are informed and inspired and find opportunities for social connection. Nobody knows how many good moblog projects would already exist if there were fewer financial and technical barriers, and if the blogging world, in some parts heavily characterized by academic discourse and insider jargon, seemed less elitist and more inviting to newcomers and 'normal' users. So far, not even the network and service providers have seriously attempted to really make mobile multimedia services and their application potential accessible and more relevant to everyday practice.

Is the future photo mobile?

It is unlikely that moblogging addiction will become a problem for society. Some bloggers do have phases of devoting a lot of time and energy to their project, but normally follow this with breaks. As Carola Heine blogs: "Weblogging is addictive but it always calms down again—personally, I have never fought against it but rather just go with the flow. The main thing is not to spend my day running after situations that would be useful for my blog—but to live." And Elizabeth Lawley (http://www.mamamusings.net) recently used her blog to report: "Haven't been blogging much lately. Am busy in the real world and enjoying time with my family."

In a way, in the context of the whole blogosphere, moblogs might be described as "a niche within a niche". They qualify neither for highest praise nor for complete rubbishing. It is all about the details and nuances of this new technical, social and creative form of expression. It makes little sense to pit bloggers against professional photographers, authors and journalists. There is partly an overlap of people involved in any case, and the publication forms are dependent upon each other through co-citation. To a certain extent, mass media and personal publications pursue, independent of each other, completely different goals. If a moblogger says, "My 81-year old mother, who lives 3,000 miles away, is always so pleased to see my pictures", then for her that is the best reason to be moblogging, with no attached thoughts of market share.

The generalised reproach of exhibitionism and voyeurism does not stand up either. The borders of private and public spheres are subject to constant cultural shifts and are shaped very differently depending on the individual. Of course there are dubious moblog contributions, but that holds true for all media—and issues of moblog ethics are under intense scrutiny. Also, blogs should be measured by individual standards instead of overloading them with utopian ideas. Monika Porrman, author and blogger (http://www.dailymo.de), describes the nature of a blog as follows: "A small pin bord in a long virtual corridor, in front of which you can stop a while in order to read what's on those little bits of paper hanging there. What goes on there—whether high literature, superficial blah-blah, demanding subjects, jokes, notes or brilliant ideas—is down to the author. The same goes for what is taken off. Nothing has to stay."

References

Adar, E. (2004), 'Usage Patterns for Cameraphone Driven Moblogs', http://www.hpl.hp.com/research/idl/people/eytan/moblog/index.html (14 July 2005).

Badger, M. (2004), 'Visual Blogs', http://blog.lib.umn.edu/blogosphere/visual_blogs.html (14 July 2005).

Barabási, A.-L. (2002), *Linked: The New Science of Networks*, Cambridge, MA: Perseus.

Blood, R. (2002), *The Weblog Handbook: Practical Advice on Creating and Maintaining Your Blog*, Cambridge, MA: Perseus.

Döring, N. (2001a), 'Öffentliches Geheimnis. Online-Tagebücher—ein paradoxer Trend im Internet', *c't* (2), 88-93.

Döring, N. (2001b), 'Persönliche Homepages im WWW. Ein kritischer Überblick über den Forschungsstand', *Medien & Kommunikationswissenschaft*, 49 (3), 325-349.

Gallo, J. (no year), 'Moblogs: The Map of Time', *ZoneZero Magazine*, http://www.zonezero.com/magazine/articles/jgallo/moblogs_time.html (14 July 2005).

Hall, J. (2002), 'From Weblog to Moblog', *TheFeature*, 21 November, http://www.thefeature.com/article?articleid=24815&ref=1858826 (14 July 2005).

Lawley, E. (2004), 'Blog Research Issues', http://www.corante.com/many/archives/2004/06/24/blog_research_issues.php (14 July 2005).

NITLE (National Institute for Technology & Liberal Education) (2003), 'Equal Numbers, Different Interests', 14 August, http://www.blog census.net/weblog/ (14 July 2005).

Pew Internet & American Life Project (2004), 'Online Activites & Pursuits', 29 February, http://www.pewInternet.org/report_display.asp ?r=113 (14 July 2005).

Phototalk (2004), 'Soldier Photography/War Photography', 9 July, http://talks.blogs.com/phototalk/2004/07/soldier_photogr.html (14 July 2005).

Rheingold, H. (2003a), *Smart Mobs. The next social revolution*, Cambridge, MA: Perseus.

Rheingold, H. (2003b), 'Moblogs seen as a Crystal Ball for a New Era in Online Journalism', *Online Journalism Review*, 9 July, http://www.ojr.org/ojr/technology/1057780670.php (14 July 2005).

Sauer, M. (2003), 'Jeder ein Publizist. Individuelle Online-Journale mit Blogs', *c't* (3), 166-169.

Designing the future:

Fables from the mobile telecoms industry

Laura Watts

Prologue

For a manufacturer of mobile devices (mobile phones, camera phones and the rest) the future is a matter of design: what can be made? What will be made? What will sell? The future is made into a product, an artefact. It is designed into being, condensing the multitude of necessary marketing and engineering compromises, negotiated over what may have been years of development. But which futures are being made possible by the industry?

What follows are two pieces of writing based upon a four month ethnography at the design studio of a major mobile telecoms handset manufacturer. They also draw upon my experiences working as a handset designer inside the industry during the 1990s. These writings express my desire to interfere[1] in the futures of the mobile telecoms industry—to make differences, rather than to just analyse and critique its practices. Many quotations and artefacts are taken directly from my ethnographic record, however, the events, locations, people and processes have been partly fictionalised[2], both to protect the anonymity of the company, but also to emphasise that the future is always fluid, transient—there are always other possibilities. Here, then, are two of them: two possible companies in two very different places, making two possible products and two possible futures.

---

1. As a project of 'interference' this writing draws upon Donna Haraway's notion of 'diffraction', a generative approach to interactions and differences, in contrast to the endless 'reflection' of critique (Haraway 1991). It is also, perhaps, a response to her question: "What if the study and crafting of fiction and fact happened *explicitly*, instead of covertly, in the same room, and in all the rooms?" (Haraway 1997: 110)

2. Bruno Latour suggests the genre of 'scientifiction' for such narratives that are partly fictional, partly ethnographic. See his story of the Aramis transport system (Latour 1996).

Ethnography of 'M-Phone' near London

I sat before a blank, red desk divider, feeling thin and exhausted. The incessant roar of the air-conditioning, photocopiers and monitors was steadily draining me away. The line of distant windows, a turquoise sheen against the sky, produced a kind of lifeless illumination that even the overhead spots failed to stir. This was a design studio and the ambient lighting was eminently well-suited for computer monitors, but I was not alone in longing for the white edge of a brilliant sun—one colour specialist had confided in me that she could only compare colour swatches (and do her job) by leaving the building.

A head appeared above the divider, smiling broadly (yet always with a slight sense of irony). It was Brian, the senior design manager and my indispensable company liaison; a man of geometric shirts and tireless enthusiasm.

"Ready?" He asked.

"Absolutely."

Brian had agreed to take me through their future design strategy at eleven (it was now half-past one). With my permitted ethnographic toolkit in hand, a pencil and decomposing notebook, I headed with Brian for the meeting room on the far side of the studio.

It was a move from spines of skeletal cable dripping from the ceiling, into a putrid mass of grey and yellow wires, seething over the chairs, over the floor, and down the walls. Those network and power cables seemed to fulfil a need for everyone to be always oozing into the creature at their centre—the company. A 'meeting' usually meant a queasy pulse of rhythmic interruptions and negotiations with other parts of the corporate body, rather than with those present. Brian was now generously offering his time to pass on what he could of the face-to-face aspects of a closed senior management meeting. As he walked in, however, his mobile phone chirruped. He left. He re-appeared, smiled, and his phone rang again. People constantly faded in and out of existence in the studio, as the pulse of the company made them ebb and flow around the world. Finally, he put down his phone, stepped up to the projector screen and began, rapidly, to pound through a hundred or so PowerPoint slides from a recent presentation.

"Okay, this one's from our consumer research group. Basically, the social trends for technology over the next five years or so are all about Storytelling, Sharing and Re-experiencing". The three words flashed up as a tag-line on a chart filled with a complex blur of graphics. "That's what it's all about for us. How do we help people tell, share and re-experience their lives?"

He hit the button to go to the next slide. "Physical contexts will continue to blur for consumers" he read, and shrugged. "Pretty self-explanatory, that one."

Thump. Next slide. "New communities formed." Again, he had nothing to add and began to pick up pace, blurring the next slides together, stopping periodically at a particular phrase or idea.

It was all fairly standard fare (and no doubt lost in the blur were more subtle nuances) but, from my own years in the industry, I recognised the moves: the mobile telecoms industry was (still) not in the business of Plain Old Telephony, but in the more refined and wholesome business of building relationships and communities. I sensed in this a technologically deterministic argument, as though the presence of a mobile telecoms network simply created new social relations, and thus more network traffic (more phone calls, more messages, and more business for the industry).

We cycled through several more slides, until Brian finally stopped in a flurry of graphics. We were done. My hand ached from taking notes on what I would never be allowed to keep, for the slides were too politically sensitive for me to have a copy. I had recorded what was regarded as the strategic direction for the company, so now the question was: how might that strategy become a device; how might the presentation and politics become embedded in a product?

It was time to move on for, as I write this account, I am fusing fragments of my ethnography, the many times and many places, into a narrative; a fable, accountable only to some material and historical fragments, but accountable none the less. The meeting with Brian, a senior design manager, was one fragment, a chance conversation with an industrial designer will be another.

As Brian faded into another phone call, I hurried out into the main studio and around the red, standard-issue desk pods to reach the industrial design area. As I approached his desk, Andy, who had been loitering on a sofa in the library, suddenly leaped to my side, friendly (as always) yet faintly suspicious (as always).

We exchanged pleasantries as I scanned his desk for inspirational flotsam: an embossed Japanese drinks can rested on a pile of papers by his monitor, and a small legion of Manga toy figures remained on permanent guard. I was particularly taken, however, with a delicate white-frosted glass bowl and some polished quartzite pebbles resting inside. I took one of the pebbles into my palm (see Figure 1), and quizzed Andy on its significance. He said he was interested in the texture of the bowl and stones for a recent camera phone design. I asked for more about the project, and he wove me this little tale, stroking his black goatee beard as he spoke:

"Senior management creates a set of priorities, the strategic requirements for the project: make it big and make it small. So it goes down to middle management, the heads of design and mechanical, who tell us to make it big and make it small. And we scratch our heads and try, and come back to middle management and say: well, we can make it big and make it big, or we can make it small and make it small. Middle management tells senior management, who go: no, we really need it big *and* small. So middle management say: okay, we'll tell them to try harder. So, we go off and the cycle repeats until senior management shout at us. And then they tell us: oh, but now we want it thin, that's the new priority."

Figure 1: This quartzite stone was collected from the desk of a designer at my ethnographic site.

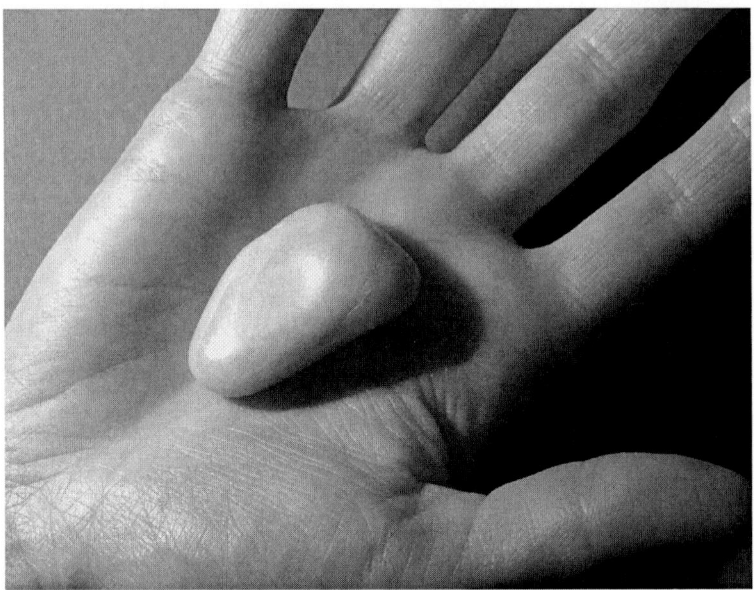

It was a great tale, told with fervour, and I thanked him, although it did leave me wondering what the translation between this tale of design practice, and Brian's tale of management strategy might be. Was there even a translation at all? As I pondered this, Andy asked me if I wanted to see the latest model of the camera phone, which had just arrived. And, of course, I did. He pulled open a drawer and extracted a small hard, black case, placing it carefully on the desk top. Lifting the lid, he revealed two glistening white camera phone models, held tightly in grey foam.

"These were about five thousand each. I think they're the most expensive models we've ever had made."

He picked one up, brushed his fingers over the frosted white front. I knew it was made of wood, sprayed to look like metal and plastic; knew from my own design experiences how it would feel slightly warm. Yet it was seductive. I looked back at the white bowl and translucent stones, sensed something of their luminescence in the soft white form of the models. As the smooth quartz pebble in my hand led my fingers to rub, almost absently, at a nagging imperfection, the bevelled edges and detailing of the models also demanded to be touched. But I was cautioned not to handle, or even breath on, their surfaces. The question of touch was a serious managerial decision. Focus group testing of new designs with consumers often only involved a plain block model and some illustrations (providing results that were both upheld and quietly derided, depending on the moment). These expensive, fully detailed models were reserved for impressing senior management and important customers who, I was constantly reminded, were the network operators, not the consumer.

Still fascinated by the models, I quickly sketched the white frosted bowl on Andy's desk (see Figure 2), thanked him again, and moved away; slunk back into my own temporary desk space and its baleful hum, the soft quartzite pebble, still held absently in my palm.

Figure 2: A field sketch of an opaque glass bowl, found on the desk of a designer at my ethnographic site.

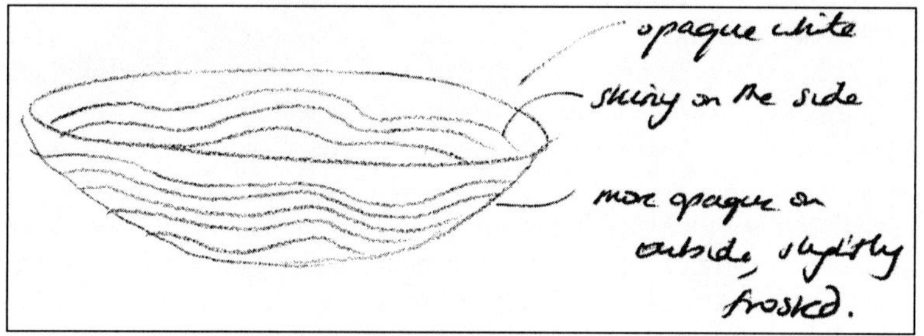

Ethnography of 'Sand14' on Isles of Orkney

"Oh, hullo there."

I looked up as Anne's bright self, in broad smile and red fleece, crept into the little room. Since arriving in a torrential downpour early this morning, I had taken to the odd central hearth to watch the black peat burn amber, and warm my feet over breakfast. I was in the Isles of Orkney, off the North East coast of Scotland, beyond John O'Groats. It was a treeless, wild place of broiling seas, wide low skies, and prehistory.

"We'd thought you might have been speared this morning by the rain. Absolute stair rods!"

I grinned. It was impossible not to grin when Anne spoke, her effervescence was infectious.

Sheepishly, I tugged at the ends of my trousers, still slightly sodden. "I think I was only out in it for thirty seconds, but it just blew under my umbrella."

"Och, umbrellas!" Anne waved her hand at the preposterous notion. "This is Orkney. It rains sideways here, you know. You'll need a riot shield not an umbrella!"

We laughed, as a rows of Orcadians armed with dripping riot shields marched through my imagination.

"Richard's suggested we all head off to the mill for coffee, did you want join us?"

Great, a meeting, an opportunity to see how the company functioned in practice. "Yeah, definitely." I scrabbled beneath the wooden chair for my rucksack, its pockets laden with recording devices, and a little reluctantly rose from the fire-warmed seat. It was a tradition at Sand14 that the fire was kept burning on the premises, so I threw another briquette on the hearth and left the strange little 'house'—holding the smell of peat in my lungs for as long as possible. The little stone building, just two rooms, one-up and one-down, formed the axis of a bright, ultra-modern domed interior[3]. Anne and I circulated south, past plants, spot lights, pin boards, and the other usual and less usual detritus of company life, leaving the dome of the main work area, to slip around and out into the foyer.

A small group had already gathered in the front of the building. Richard, the professorial managing director, was hopping with nervous energy from one foot to the other, and gabbling at high speed to Simon, who was calmly making notes and sketches. George(ina) was draped elegantly over the worn black sofa, ignoring all and staring out of the front doors, straight down the path to the towering monoliths in the field beyond. As Anne and I stepped into view, however, she leaped to her feet, and with business-like efficiency had us all out of the door, down the path, and inside the company 'bus' (a battered Land Rover with spare parts rolling on the floor) in moments.

As we drove the wet mile down the road to the café we passed into another world. Sand14 was inside one of the greatest prehistoric monument complexes in the world; a part of a five thousand year-old architectural project. In the field opposite the grass and slate dome of the company building were three, seven metre high monoliths, once part of a stone circle. As we drove East, we passed the dark entrance to the mound of a passage grave, a blur of a Neolithic village, another standing stone and, almost in a circle on the far hills all around us, beyond the rain soaked mist, were more standing stones, ever present on the edge of the horizon.

Once we had settled into the old mill café Richard held court as

3. For more information on the architectural principles involved in the construction of the Sand14 premises see Richards 1996.

usual, his strangely balding satchel overflowing onto the table. He leaned in, furtively, over his tea; black eyebrows bouncing up and down as he spoke.

"I have to say, I was a bit surprised at their sketches", he began, and I rapidly recollected that he had just been to visit a design consultancy in London. "I rather thought the illustration of the 4G phone I saw looked like a prop from a Nineteen Fifties B-movie."

"It's the whole retro thing." Commented George, sounding both bored and frustrated. "Silver and white, flashing lights, bulbous curves. It's just so totally uninspired. It doesn't engage at all with the world, it just fantasises about styles from the past. I hate it."

But Richard rolled on regardless, fingers weaving the air as though incanting a spell. "Well, I then wandered into the British Library. And I didn't realise, but some of Tim Ingold's recent work on multi-sensory communication talks about the importance of the 'lived experience' as opposed to the reification of the senses[4]. I think this is crucial for us. What we are doing is transforming, or rather translating[5], an experience of the world, not of the individual senses. It's the transformation, rather than the transmission, which is central. Our work is really about how to transform an experience, through silicon and radio, into something else."

"And into something no less magical..." murmured Anne.

"But we have been really focused on haptics and force feedback, recently." Simon, the interface designer, looked worried.

"Ah, don't worry, this is definitely not a redirection. I think we just need to keep it absolutely clear in our minds that we are not, we are *not*," he emphasised, "designing a multi-sensory communications device, as a kind of evolution of voice and camera phones. That would be quite wrong. What we are doing is generative. We are trying to translate a bit of the world into something else, which will hopefully be something a little extraordinary." He gave a sudden, quick, grin. "I guess it's more like painting."

"I don't think it's anything of the sort, Richard." Said George, piqued. "Okay, I accept it might be like photography, which is a quite bizarre translation of the world into a flat, timeless rectangle with a single point of perspective[6]. But it's not art. Storytelling maybe, but it's not painting."

---

4. See Ingold 2000: 243-287.

5. In a Sociology of Translation (also known as Actor-Network Theory) the notion of 'translation' includes the sense that things do not remain unaltered when they move; rather, the practice of changing the relations in which some 'thing' is embedded necessarily changes it (see Law and Hassard 1999).

6. David Hockney explores this transformation of the world by the photograph in his own artistic practice. See his discussions in Hockney and Joyce 2002.

The conversation bounced back and forth between the three of them for a while, with the two anthropologists, Anne and I sharing a quiet space between it all.

Finally George, who as both artist and businesswoman always insisted on the salient details, asked Richard how he might pitch the design concept to the mobile telecoms industry.

Richard winked conspiratorially to the rest of us around the table as he flipped over one of the pieces of paper, scattered in front of him. On it, in thick pencil scrawl, were the words: Storytelling, Sharing, Re-experiencing.

George read the words, and then laughed. "Brilliant. Yes, they'll love that."

When we returned to the 'house' (no one actually referred to the company premises as an office) I caught up with Simon, eager to understand how this latest move might impact his interface designs. We walked around the arc of flagstone corridor into the central domed atrium—always a blaze of sandstone, spotlights, and glass. He had set up a couple of tables and a floor of paperwork in front of the glass wall, with the mist and loch beyond. I scanned his desk: lots of paper and pens, an old CD player and chewed up headphones.

There was one of the white-frosted glass bowls on his chair (see Figure 2), still full of hot chocolate, the remnants of a French-style breakfast—they were always used for drinking chocolate here, but I wasn't sure why. There was also a large laptop, closed and leaning against the window, with a polished quartzite pebble resting on its clasp (see Figure 1). I picked up the pebble and asked Simon if it was important.

"Feel it", he replied.

I pressed the stone between my thumb and forefinger, and rubbed its surface, trying to sense something unexpected. I felt the coldness, the smoothness, but also a slight crease in the surface, a fracture, which drew my thumb.

"You feel the crease?"

I nodded.

"Well that's what I'm really interested in. The imperfection draws your fingers, doesn't it? But it's the colour, the translucency of the polished stone, that draws your attention."

"How does that lead to a mobile device?" I asked, alert.

He rummaged on his desk, pulled aside a few maps, and revealed a strange, glistening black object, shaped like a rounded and elegantly sculpted letter 'T'. It was not entirely black, in its depths were pale arteries of white. Nor was it completely smooth, it was etched with some grid pattern at the top. Simon held the maps back, and invited me to grasp the object. The shaft fitted easily down between my fingers and the handle snuggled comfortably into my palm. It was like holding some kind of designer bottle opener. The silken surface felt like sun-warmed marble, heavy, but gorgeous to touch. Instinctively I squeezed it, and felt the give of two pressure pads beneath my knuckles. A light appeared at one end, projecting down onto the floor. Then, extraordinary waves of what felt like cool water began to lap up and down my fingers. It was delicious. I realised there was a smudge of blue in the light on the carpet, put my other palm into the beam to bring it into focus. It was a picture of someone's hand dangling in lapping water, and I heard a slightly distorted voice from the object whisper: "Can you feel that?"

I could.

I didn't know what to say, almost dropped the device, and gave it back to Simon. "That's…" I gave up.

Simon grinned. "Isn't it just!"

Epilogue

Those were two ethnographic accounts of my research. Both accountable to a set of materials, artefacts and words I recorded during my four months at a mobile telecoms design studio. Both partly fictional, neither 'true'. Nor could there ever be a 'true' account, there are only fragments of an archive: dislocated notes and decaying artefacts, all stitched together through a kind of 'poetic archaeology'[7]. In the words of Marilyn Strathern, there are only ever parts, which are not part of any whole[8]. All that there is of my four months are my memories (always partial), my notes (always historical), and a collection of finds (always archaeological). In the space between my experiences of those moments and the archaeology of my records, there is the possibility for multiple accounts, and multiple stories, to be told[9]. As I followed and recorded a mobile telecoms company, I also made the possibility for other companies. So, the future gets made as a matter of size at M-Phone, and as a matter of experience at Sand14. The future is made in the mists and monoliths on the Isles of Orkney at Sand14, and in the pulsing networks and roar of air-conditioning near London at

7. 'Poetic archaeology' is a more sensuous approach to creating archaeological accounts from fragments of evidence, proposed and discussed by Michael Shanks (1992).

8. See Strathern 1992: 90-115.

9. In 'multiple' I am invoking Annemarie Mol's work on 'multiplicity' in medical anthropology. In her example she suggests that the multiple medical practices involved in diagnosing arthrosclerosis (x-rays and blood tests, for example) produce multiple versions of the disease; there are "more than one and less than many" arthroscleroses (Mol 2002).

M-Phone. Different places and different practices make different mobile telecoms products—and different mobile telecoms futures.

This is a small excavation of the futures of part of the mobile telecoms industry; a construction of the possibilities made by some fragments of evidence. This, then, is a practice of Future Archaeology.

Acknowledgements

Thanks to the many colleagues who have read and commented on drafts of this chapter, and in particular to John Law and Lucy Suchman. This research was made possible through the support of the Sir Richard Stapley Educational Trust, the Newby Trust and the Kathleen and Margery Elliott Scholarship Trust.

References

Haraway, D. (1991), *Simians, cyborgs and women: the reinvention of nature*, London: Free Association Books.

Haraway, D. (1997), *Modest_witness@second_millennium.FemaleMan©_meets _OncoMouse™*, London: Routledge.

Hockney, D. and Joyce, P. (2002), *Hockney on 'art': conversations with Paul Joyce*, London: Little, Brown.

Ingold, T. (2000), *The perception of the environment: essays in livelihood, dwelling and skill*, London: Routledge.

Latour, B. (1996), *Aramis, or the love of technology*, London: Harvard University Press.

Law, J. and Hassard, J. (1999), *Actor-network theory and after*, Oxford: Blackwell.

Mol, A. (2002), *The body multiple: ontology in medical practice*, London: Duke University Press.

Richards, C. (1996), 'Monuments as landscape: creating the centre of the world in late Neolithic Orkney', *World Archaeology*, 28 (2), 190-208.

Shanks, M. (1992), *Experiencing the past: on the character of archaeology*, London: Routledge.

Strathern, M. (1992), *Reproducing the future: essays on anthropology, kinship and the new reproductive technologies*, Manchester: Manchester University Press.

The future of mobile in the 3G era

Paul Golding

Introduction

Predicting the future is problematic. It is unseen, unheard and unknown. However, emergent themes and their connected possibilities are perhaps identifiable. We already find ourselves within certain technological landscapes wherein our journeys through them are apparently set in motion. One such landscape is the Internet. One such journey is the evolution of mobile technology, now in its Third Generation, or 3G. Given such starting points, plus knowledge of the rhythms of technology cycles, such as the lifespan of GSM, a consideration of the next ten years seems reasonable. I shall not describe specific services or technology roadmaps, such as processing power and battery power-weight curves. I shall suggest general *mobilisation themes* that will characterise the next decade of mobilisation. However, I shall examine a few technological developments, but within the context of the posited themes, as possible points of synthesis. It is not hyperbole to say that the process of mobilisation will affect our *lives*, not just our phone habits. Therefore, a discussion of the possibilities is a potentially important process in shaping our mobile futures.

Before outlining the likely themes for the forthcoming decade of mobilisation, I would like to make a couple of general points about the environment of mobile technology in what I am calling the *3G era* (a term I shall explain shortly).

Convergence as transformation

Firstly, I would like to comment on the often hackneyed and ineffable topic of *convergence*. As my book *Next Generation Wireless Applications* describes in some detail[1], the mushrooming mobile cosmos is going to be much bigger than the sum of its mobile-technology components.

1. Golding 2004; see my website for more details: http://www.paulgolding.me.uk.

Second generation (2G) mobile, such as GSM, was essentially a convergence of relatively few technological developments, mostly from the radio frequency (RF), telephony and real-time processing fields, which includes the colossal, crucial, and often overlooked contribution of silicon integration. A multitude of diverse technologies are already jostling for entry into the 3G mobile arena. These come from a wide gamut of technological possibilities, such as trust, security, payment, reputation, location and so many more. The possibilities are potentially overwhelming.

Technology is *transformative*, not merely additive[2]. Adding a drop of red dye to water does not result in a drop of dye and some water, it becomes something different. After the printing press, Europe did not simply become Europe with the printing press; it became a different Europe. Similarly, America, and later the world, became a different place after the telegraph. Our world is changing again, this time thanks to mobile. In the midst of technological evolution, the changes can seem gradual because they are ecological and we adapt to the evolving ecosystem. Marshal McLuhan said about immersion in media, "fish don't know water exists until beached" (McLuhan 1970: 191). Take a mobile away from many people today and they will begin to grope for its umbilical connection within hours, if not minutes. People notice and report the loss of their mobiles far quicker than the loss of their purses or wallets. It is perhaps not an exaggeration to think that some social mechanisms would falter, or even collapse, without mobile.

3G as era, not technology

Undoubtedly, 3G is a set of transformative technologies[3]. The essence of 3G is *not* its high-speed data promise. Rather, it is the myriad possibilities for *convergences* that it enables, totally unlike 2G, each with its own transformative potential. In essence, the real 3G—the *era* and not the mobile technology—is about an incredible convergence of various technology growth curves, many at their tipping points[4], spanning manufacturing, networking, processing and information technologies. It is a completely new set of possibilities.

In the early Nineties, most of us could not see the need for a mobile phone. Today, that notion is almost preposterous. In the 3G era, we shall see that carrying (wearing) a mobile device will become a pre-

2. For a complete discussion of this point, see Postman 1992.

3. Besides the general point I am making about convergence potential, 3G itself is actually a suite of technologies far more extensive than GSM and telephony. See the 3G Partnership Project for more details at http://www.3gpp.org.

4. By which I mean points of inflexion on the adoption (or growth) curve.

requisite for living in contemporary society, in which increasingly we shall live in information space, not just physical space. We can debate this point, but besides the evident IT revolution well underway, I refer to the likes of "management guru" Peter Drucker (and many like him) who consider that we are entering an age of "unprecedented change in the human condition", where "substantial and rapidly growing numbers of people [...] will have to manage themselves" (Drucker 2000). If true, this self-management ("survival") in what Covey calls the "Knowledge Age" (Covey 2004) implies a high degree of engagement ("24 x 7") with the information world. Information immediacy will demand mobility.

Essential themes—The four Cs of connectedness

At this juncture in the evolution of mobile, paradigm confusion is evident. The name "mobile *phone*" is increasingly problematic. Alternatives like "personal communicator" are more revealing, but still insufficient to describe its future eclectic role. In the prelude to *Next Generation Wireless Applications* (Golding 2004), I portray an imaginary character and her interaction with mobile devices[5] during a short lunch break. During the break, she does the following:

- *Organises* lunch with friends
- *Feels* messages notifications via her wrist "sleek device"
- *Finds* a popular meeting place
- *Sends* video clips
- *Locates* the meeting place
- *Hails* a taxi
- *Senses* a "friend of a friend" in the area
- *Compares* shopping prices (via barcodes)
- *Finds* somewhere to eat based on recommendations
- *Shares* the restaurant bill with friends
- *Pins* feedback about the eatery in mid-air
- *Announces* phone calls with an introductory tag line
- *Diverts* a voice call to a colleague's Instant Messaging client

Notice that the multifarious tasks (the verbs are in italics) are everything but talking (phoning)! This is illustrative of the convergence explosion and of the radically different nature of the *3G era* from the 2G one. Thinking about such mobile tasks, I believe that it is possible to

5. I assume, quite reasonably I feel, that we shall have more than one device in the future, which in this example includes a wrist-device, a pendant and a main "personal gateway" as per the Personal Mobile Gateway concept forwarded by companies such as IXI Mobile (http://www.ixi.com).

identify some fundamental themes for the next generation mobile experience, essentially from a user perspective[6]. The four themes are *communicating, consuming, communing* and *controlling.*

Communicating

The overwhelming function of a mobile device has been, and still is, to phone people in order to communicate via voice. The introduction of other modes, like video, is really an extension of this theme, nothing substantively new. Mobile devices are unavoidably and very essentially personal. Greater intimacy is hard to imagine, although the physical progression of devices is already unfolding to give us wrist-based, pendant and other wearable forms. Within the mode of personal accessory, or attire, devices are increasingly an expression of our aesthetic tastes. Fashion and personal expression have undeniably become parts of the mobile experience[7]. However, this is mostly a marginal theme in terms of any substantive revenue generation from mobile services[8].

The *person-to-person* (P2P) nature of mobile connectivity will remain a dominant overarching theme. Much of the development in mobile will be products and services that increasingly fold and embed P2P modes of interaction deeper into our daily lives. We can think of talking as being one mode of P2P interaction that we can assign to a super-category of personal *exchange*. The 3G era will be largely about services and devices that enable exchange to take place: exchange of ideas, contacts, thoughts, tastes, news, money, lists, preferences, opinions, interests, intelligence, intentions, and knowledge and so on, whatever digital form these take. The increasing digitisation of our personalities in the "Knowledge Age" will render the mobile an important instrument of exchange. I will mention some concrete examples later in the chapter.

Communication, or exchange, shall continue to develop through convergence and newer device possibilities. However, convergence is what makes the other themes possible. The Internet will play a central role in the convergence process and in all themes. Here I caution that the common notion of "Mobile Internet" as a kind of shrunk-to-fit ver-

6. It is worth stating however, that user perspectives for enterprise and consumer activities are different. Although various overlaps exist, our main concern in this chapter is the more horizontal consumer experience.

7. When the likes of Samsung and Vogue announce a co-marketing partnership, as they recently did, then we know that mobile-as-fashion has "arrived".

8. Although it is known that for some users there is a relationship between aesthetics and amount of usage.

sion of today's Internet is far from the mark. "Internet 1.0"—Berners-Lee's original vision for document sharing (now "content" sharing)—lacks the convergence power needed for the future of mobilisation. We need "Internet 2.0"—notably the *Semantic Web*[9].

Semantic description of digital information will allow convergence to deliver powerful services that exploit the P2P potential of mobiles that we have been exploring. Today we could stand in a shop and browse generic product information on our mobiles, albeit clumsily. Tomorrow, we shall ask our communicators questions like "which product in this store would Mr X buy?" where Mr X is some valued friend, guru, advisor or expert in the context of the question and to whom we can establish a P2P link, if only by asking this question. For the question to have meaning and for a meaningful answer to become available, the very substance of meaning—semantics—is required and needs to be digitally accessible. This is what the Semantic Web promises.

Computers are generally clumsy at figuring out what we want to do. Users can often overcome this by attempting various approximations to get what they want. However, mobile devices are even clumsier, so we need more precision or smarter interpretive technology. The Semantic Web can potentially offer both, which is why it seems a natural fit in the mobile ecosystem. Returning to Mr X for a moment, his purchasing records, wish lists, product reviews, web hits, web searches, and all manner of interactions within information space leave a digital trail. Gaining access to the trail and its semantics implies having permission to do. Thus, in addition to having the means to form P2P links, mechanisms are also needed to establish digital identity, trust and security. These are important sub-themes in the 3G episode.

This kind of P2P interaction will be possible and likely. Besides the infrastructural ingredients, like the Semantic Web, certain device interface developments will also serve to absorb this type of interaction into our daily routines, some of which I shall discuss later. The characteristic of these mobile P2P services is *information immediacy*. The sheer empowerment of immediate access to multifarious P2P networks and their content will be utterly compelling. Metcalfe's Law of networks is in play and the future of mobile is about increased and inescapable dependency on networks. A device being "always on" is not the point. We need it "always networked", with information being "always available" and "always relevant". Already, many broadband adopters have gravitated towards an *information-grazing* lifestyle. Broadband is not a fat pipe, but an information environment. The 3G era not only extends

9. See http://www.w3.org/2001/sw/ which contains a link to a paper by Berners-Lee first published in Scientific American, May 2001.

this experience, but also adds many new dimensions through its own convergence potentials. Once this process starts, we shall become like McLuhan's fish.

Consuming

Consuming is an obvious theme, especially with our increasing reliance upon digital information in our general patterns of consumption. New patterns of consumption might emerge because of mobile, but I focus here on supplementing existing mechanisms, in particular the monetary aspects of consumption processes.

Consumption involves financial transactions, a key component of which is personal authorisation of transfers. Today, all purchases are in effect authorisations. Handing over notes and coins is actually an authorisation. Credit cards and other forms of electronic transfer are clearly about authorisation. Substituting our wallets with some equivalent function on our mobiles is a seemingly natural progression. Various *m-payment* initiatives are surfacing, such as Simpay[10]. With the move by card vendors towards PIN authorisation at the counter, there is now no reason why a mobile cannot become a card substitute. Let us not worry here about various agendas for *m-payment* schemes. I am interested here in the end-user possibilities and the technological implications. The potential advantages of payment via "smart" mobiles versus "dumb"[11] cards are enticing for end users. Among them are the possibilities for financial management, budgeting, proxy-spending, group-spending, authorisation deferment, spending-controls, purchase logging, foreign exchange, loyalty schemes and so many more. In short, the user gains more control. This is central to Drucker's thesis of "self-management".

If the mobile is to take a major role in financial transactions, then reliable and secure connectivity is essential[12]. With the development of 3G, WiFi, Bluetooth and other emerging solutions, the 3G era will eventually herald an age of *perpetual connectedness*. This means we can deploy services with the cast-iron assumption that all active members of society are perpetually reachable via a network or networks.

---

10. Although in 2005 the Simpay initiative was ended by the participating network operators.

11. Modern chip-based cards are not entirely dumb, but compared to mobile phones they have extremely limited processing power and capability.

12. Note that it is not necessary for credit authorisations to go through the mobile's connection, but in some instances this is useful.

Controlling

Somewhat divergent from the overarching P2P theme is the idea of machine control, essentially remote control. As with "digital wallets", the control theme is mostly about substitution whereby personal devices assume the role of existing devices. *Personalisation* will be important, as well as *continuity* or *fluidity*. To give an example, consider the remote control of a home multimedia entertainment system, by which I mean a digitally networked television and audio system. Currently, such systems have dedicated remote control devices. It is an obvious substitution to use a personal device in place of the existing remote control, probably connected via Bluetooth. The remote control emulator on the device, perhaps displayed via the television, will invoke *personal* preferences and tastes, not generic ones, and on a per user basis. It will summon *personal* play lists, film reviews; content broadcast times and so on. The personalisation attribute is perhaps obvious, but what about the attribute of *continuity*?

Continuity is how a common networked device for all remote control applications will allow personalisation parameters to flow fluidly from one environment to another. For example, whilst listening to some audio content on the move, that same content will flow with us onto our home systems, available at the exact point of departure from our engagement in the car, train, or wherever. The control theme can include any machine. A machine might be a piece of medical apparatus in a hospital, a barrier at a subway station, or a baggage check-in machine at an airport. Desktop computers are machines too! Imagine never having to fill out forms again—whether ourselves or via some desk clerk at the hotel. The mere co-presence of a device will allow essential parameters to flow from it into whatever digital receptacle awaits them: online form, cash machine, car-park barrier, washing machine, vending machine and so on.

The notion that our personal device represents a kind of digital heartbeat is a powerful metaphor, with data-flow as our digital lifeblood. Just as the heart traditionally denoted the seat of the intellect in many ancient traditions, the digital heartbeat is its proxy in the virtual realm, a kind of digital *alter-persona*. It is our digital core. With a digital heartbeat, it will be easier to interface with machines. This is a new dimension to the mobile experience. We shall return to this theme later when we look at virtual kiosks and spatial messaging.

Communing

Community and social networking has already become a much-discussed and apparently important theme on the Internet. Indeed, the very definition of community is arguably undergoing transformation as it extends further into the virtual world. For this discussion, I take communing to be the bringing of people together with *common* agendas and interests and consider what the 3G era heralds for such activities. The strong P2P nature of mobilisation in the 3G era will inevitably put people in touch with each other on many levels. It will be much easier to "bump" into other people with common agendas and interests, both physically and virtually.

In training classes, I have often presented the concept of co-detection whereby one person detects another in physical proximity with a common interest. The initial reaction, perhaps not surprisingly, is usually one of apprehension. Aside from lack of experience to give insight, students envisage "frivolous" applications—not that we should condemn frivolity, otherwise perhaps much of the texting phenomenon would be outcast. Interestingly, when encouraged to think of a specific "non-frivolous" context, such as a conference or exhibition, co-detection seems more interesting and a sense of its potential emerges. Currently, a socialising tool such as this is unusual, but that does not mean it will be unlikely. The readiness of people to network online via tools like LinkedIn and Ecademy[13], suggests a willingness to try new means for an old game.

Possibly the greater potential for communing exists virtually, courtesy of the powerful P2P nature of the 3G era. The trend towards greater and richer modes of exchange—the communication super-category mentioned earlier—is such that people will inevitably come into contact more often in the virtual world. P2P exchange of information implies that increasingly we shall become content producers. We have also hinted that the semantic labelling of information will enrich this process. If I post a review on Amazon about a book on carpentry, it becomes accessible in the virtual world as a review. However, with semantics, it becomes the source of a potentially much wider conversation than a review page.

Imagine that I maintain a list of favourite carpentry tools. With semantic labelling, this list becomes implicitly connectable to my review. Returning to the shopper example earlier, imagine that I am now Mr X. The shopper, who hitherto has never met me, can connect to my tools list via my review. With mobile connectivity and semantics, a new P2P network can instantly form. The shopper could even attempt direct contact, which I can accept or deny via a multitude of communication means, such as voice, video, text etc. The process might cause my list to be amended or expanded, which enriches the potential for more P2P conversations of this ilk. This example is contrived and the details glossed over, but the 3G convergence process makes this type of *com-*

13. http://www.linkedin.com; http://www.ecademy.com.

muning immediacy possible, which is still consistent with the overarching P2P theme.

Some physical aspects of the 3G era

Let us turn our attention to some of the physical aspects of the unfolding mobile landscape. The mobile phone revolution thus far has been quintessentially a physical one, a conquering of physical technology limitations, mostly thanks to the unrelenting march of silicon integration. The 3G era is about conquering information space. However, interaction with information still has physical implications. There are too many device technologies and innovations to discuss in such a short chapter. I have chosen a few that seem significant in light of the aforementioned mobilisation themes, but which also have profound implications in their own right.

The mind's eye—Perpetual visualisation

The mobile revolution is largely thanks to incredible improvements in portable electronics, which also present challenges. Energy supply is one of them, but of immediate concern are device interfaces and ergonomics. Recall the bulky and impractical head mounted displays (HMD) of those early virtual reality (VR) immersions into computer-generated landscapes. Today, a tiny display can be added to ordinary spectacles with little additional weight and cosmetic alteration, as shown in Figure 1. Moreover, price erosion of HMD components suggests consumer viability within the 3G era[14]. Scepticism towards wearing such displays is understandable. However, perhaps the willingness to wear Bluetooth earpieces is an indication of our willingness to accommodate wearable devices. It seems inevitable that the immediacy of information access offered by HMDs might prove irresistible enough to overcome hesitations about wearing them.

The mobile phone has given us *vocal immediacy*. A mobile phone allows immediate fulfilment of the desire to talk to someone absent, a kind of empowerment of the *inner voice*. Even this potential has further to go. Imagine simply talking to a companion at will in order for them to hear your voice, and without any explicit connection process. With IP-based communication schemes, which 3G can accommodate, this is already possible. With HMD displays, we could readily see the *presence state* of fellow conversationalists using pictograms to indicate their

14. In fact the situation is that volume demand is all that is needed to bring the costs down considerably.

availability. With improvements in signal-processing technology, it will also become possible to talk very quietly, nearly whisper, unencumbered by background noise. Thus, we could potentially communicate within visually and acoustically masked "bubbles" that maintain privacy.

Figure 1: Wearable and affordable displays arrive in the 3G era. Reproduced courtesy of Carl Zeiss.

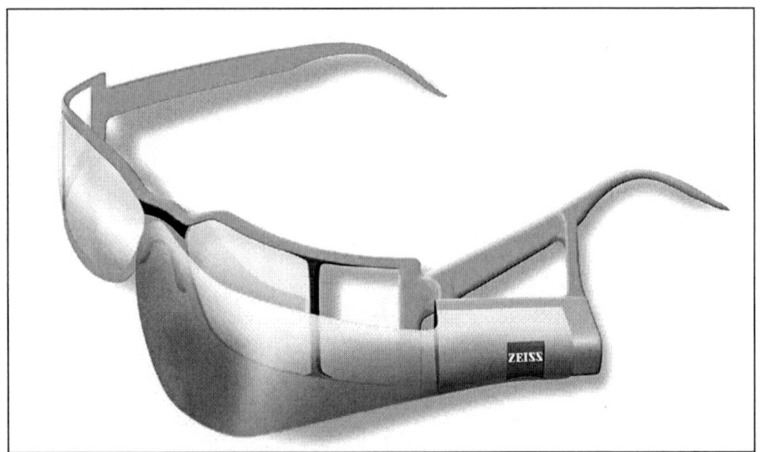

Visual immediacy will create new modes of interaction. Think of engaging in a conversation with someone whilst simultaneously viewing related information. Imagine that a co-conversationalist mentions a product, event or news item and within seconds, you are viewing its website. Imagine having multiple views, including perpetual web-cam feeds, such as from our homes or favourite tourist spots. The notion of being "here" and "there" at the same time becomes dramatically accentuated.

As well as improvements in voice control, gesticulation is a possibility for input control: using the movement of limbs and the body through definable gestures. The mobile device itself could become a pointing device that works in air, similar to devices already available, such as the Gyration™mouse. MIT Media Lab Europe are already demonstrating these types of interfaces in its palpable machines research program[15]. Of course, HMDs will also be useful for watching digital video, including broadcast modes (e.g. DVB-H), which may ultimately be a key driver for their adoption. As an alternative to wearable displays, portable projectors are emerging that are capable of self-stabilising the image to correct for movement relative to the illuminated surface.

15. See their project suite "Palpable Machines": http://www.medialabeurope.org.

Using similar combined-sensor techniques, already companies such as Canesta have successfully implemented projected keyboards, as shown in Figure 2. Other technologies, such as wearable or foldable display fabrics are possible. Display and input technologies will always have practical limitations, but the point is that the 3G era will herald solutions to many interface issues that currently seem to limit the imagination for mobile service innovations. In addition, new modalities will emerge altogether.

Figure 2: Light-projected keyboard. Reproduced courtesy of Canesta, Inc.

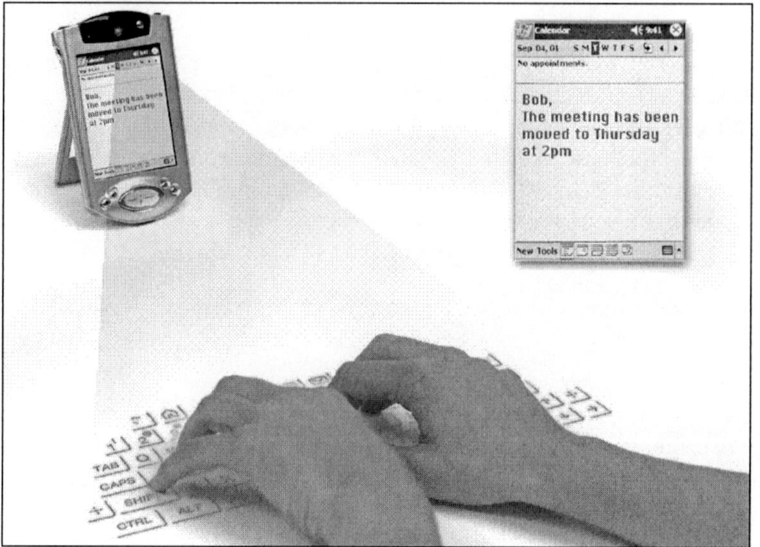

Total recall

In this section I shall look at the implications of high-speed wireless connections and the increasing price erosion of high-density memories. Broadband penetration is encouraging networked services such as networked storage to become more prevalent. Within a variety of contexts, we should expect networked storage to make perpetual archiving models possible, such as some email solutions today that already offer the "lifetime" potential of never having to delete old messages. Consequently, such trends are also encouraging improved indexing and retrieval methods. Any content generated or processed by the mobile could be perpetually stored, courtesy of a combination of networked storage, higher density device memories (e.g. hard disks) and high-speed wireless networks, permanent or nomadic. With camera phones, we shall never have to delete photos, nor explicitly back them up. This will be possible for all content, and not just the conventional mobile phone formats like contacts, call registers, text messages, pictures, sounds etc. All conceivable content could be stored, such as music files, location history, search requests, financial transactions, and barcode swipes (see later)—our entire digital trail.

More radical storage possibilities will also emerge. With effective voice coding techniques, it is possible to record all of our daily conversations, phone, or otherwise, and store them in the network. Offline transcribing and non-linear indexing methods will facilitate searching back through any conversation. Merged with pictures, location and any other event in the memory bank (e.g. a web search or shop purchase), glued with copious semantic data, an incredible *alter-persona* potential begins to emerge within the 3G era. "Where was I when I said X to Y?" "Who was I with when I took this picture of X?" The possibilities for perpetual memory are dramatic enough, but within the frame of powerful P2P networking and exchange, the transformative potential for this idea alone is difficult to comprehend fully. It is one thing to have a P2P network that connects person X with person Y, or a multitude. It is quite another to add the dimensions of time and memory—and location.

Spatial convergence

With the location-finding capabilities of new devices, we can tag *any* content or event (e.g. financial transaction) with location information. This is yet another dimension to the information landscape in the 3G era. It allows such concepts as *spatial messaging*[16]. A user can leave a message "pinned in mid-air" at any location, even a street corner, which is then accessible to other users, who could be anyone, or those in our chosen P2P or newly formed (even ad-hoc) networks.

Users and content producers can add spatial indexing to pictures, sounds, videos, songs, web links etc. Potential applications and implications are quite astounding, especially when we add semantic information that allows deeper content relationships to form, such as Figure 3 tries to show.

Privacy and authenticity is a concern. How can we leave private messages that are not accessible to unintended parties and how can we be sure that a particular message is authentic in terms of its authorship? This is a Digital Rights Management (DRM) issue. Already, DRM solutions exist that allow content protection against piracy. However, in the 3G era, everyone is a content provider! Therefore, we shall expect

16. For a more complete discussion of Spatial Messaging, see my online paper "Getting in The Zone with Splash Messaging", August 2003 at http://www.paulgolding.me.uk.

to see DRM technology deployed in a P2P context besides the more conventional "broadcast" modes of content distribution associated with DRM. Legal and ethical issues will arise concerning the blurring of private and public space. Interestingly, the same techniques that can protect and ensure identity in information space (as needed for secure messaging and financial authorisations) could also be used for audit purposes. With "digital fingerprinting", a photo taken by a device could be inescapably traceable to the device that took it. With low-cost biometric interfaces, which are already possible, the photo and the photographer can become indelibly linked. Clearly, these protective methods also have implications for social liberties. Such discussions will emerge during the 3G era and should not be overlooked.

Figure 3: Content, location and semantic links.

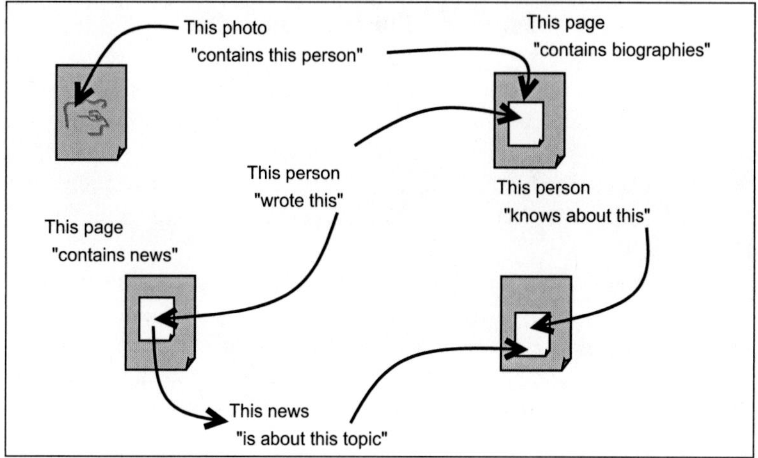

Other forms of spatial-virtual interplay will emerge with the increased usage of mobile-readable tags on products and other objects. It is possible to integrate low-cost barcode readers into mobile devices. Photographic scanning is also possible using the inbuilt camera, although it will not be as reliable as lasers. With suitable devices, we could scan product codes to access online information of all kinds, including web-based searches. Aggregator companies already exist to assemble bar code databases from various product manufacturers based on their bar code assignments.

Tagging need not be restricted to products. It is easy to tag any object and thereby enable proximity-based information access. Thanks to perpetual connectedness, tags essentially become low-cost information kiosks. A user can walk up to the tag, scan it and immediately access a web link. The linked information can take into account the location of the tag, if it is fixed. Users could also use tags to post messages back to a co-located virtual pin board. Tags need not be barcodes. They can be radio frequency (RF) based. The current retail interest in Radio Frequency Identification (RFID) suggests that it might figure in the mobile experience eventually, although barcodes still have a long shelf life. Proximity sensing is also achievable without tags. Techniques using Bluetooth or WiFi access-point co-detection are possible.

The overarching P2P theme remains pertinent to location. The ability to leave messages at a virtual "meeting point" will give rise to a vast number of parallel P2P conversations, not necessarily a chaotic splurge of graffiti. Some conversations will be private, some will be public, and some will be both. Merged with perpetual memory and semantics, the implications are dizzying.

Conclusion—The 3G Mobilopolis

I have attempted to predict some of the essential themes for the 3G era. It is an era and not a technology. This reflects the fact that this new age of mobile will be a convergence of variegated technologies, of which 3G—the technology—is only one. These convergences have the power to transform how we live our lives, which is the nature of technological change.

Mobile devices are essentially personal, including their person-to-person (P2P) nature. New modes of usage will greatly empower P2P networks. Today we communicate across established P2P networks. Tomorrow we will easily create new ones and traverse them in information space to *communicate* better than before, as well as *consume* things—real or virtual—*commune* with others and *control* machines: the four Cs of the 3G era.

In terms of experience, to vocal immediacy the 3G era will add information immediacy and communing immediacy, which collectively shall better equip us for the challenges of Drucker's "self-management" era.

Thus far, the mobile revolution has been a physical one, giving an old idea—telephony—a new form. The transformative nature of the 3G era will bring new possibilities altogether, many of which we do not yet have experiential paradigms for, like *spatial messaging*. However, whilst we might not recognise them now, or even think we need them, once in the *3G Mobilopolis* we shall become dependent, like McLuhan's fish. Of this, I am utterly convinced.

References

Covey, S. R. (2004), *The 8th Habit*, New York: Free Press.

Drucker, P. F. (2000), 'Managing Knowledge Means Managing Oneself', *Leader to Leader*, 16 (Spring), 8-10, As quoted in Covey, Stephen R. (2004), *The 8th Habit*, New York: Free Press.

Golding, P. (2004), *Next Generation Wireless Applications*, Chichester: Wiley.

McLuhan, M. (1970), *Culture Is Our Business*, Toronto: McGraw-Hill.

Postman, N. (1992), *Technopoly: The Surrender of Culture to Technology*, New York: Knopf.

Mythology and mobile data

Nick Foggin

Ten years have passed since the first GSM mobile networks were launched. Since then, well over 1.2 billion people around the world have purchased and made regular use of a 'Global System for Mobile Communications' (GSM) phone. No other technology has had such a rapid and universal impact—not even the Internet. Today there are more GSM mobile phones on this planet than there are computers, and mobile users outnumber active Internet users two to one.

But during the course of this incredible spell of growth, mobile operators have been forced into a rather uncomfortable position. The period of aggressive customer acquisition has all but ended in the West, and operators now find themselves in a position where, in order to grow their revenues, they must encourage their customers to use their mobile phone more. "More users", therefore, has been replaced by "more uses" and "more frequent use". The move from customer acquisition to retention and growth has given rise to a curious and unhelpful mythology—a mythology that is increasingly causing the mobile industry as a whole to veer off course and make potentially catastrophic mistakes.

Voice is dead—Long live voice

The first, and arguably most important myth is that for growth to continue in a sustainable fashion, an entirely new source of mobile revenues will be required. As a result, most mobile operators have singularly abandoned their core voice business, in strategic terms, and have begun the search for the next 'killer application'. So seriously is this myth taken, that the large majority of operators have built their businesses around it.

Look at the organisational structure of any mobile operator today and you will find senior executives responsible for data, for portals, for content and for Internet services; all of them with huge teams of busy people. At the same time, however, you will struggle to find a senior executive for voice. In other words, you will struggle to find someone responsible for the service that today represents upwards of 80 percent of operator revenues. You will struggle to find someone whose role it is to manage the development and growth of the only service that 100 percent of mobile phone owners use. You will struggle to find someone whose sole responsibility is the technical advancement of the core service offering of all mobile operators. So before we even consider data, we should perhaps remind ourselves that the real 'killer application' for mobile has been with us from day one. And that killer application still has huge latent value—value that is not being unlocked because it is afforded too little attention.

According to Ovum, a leading market research company, the global market for voice (fixed and mobile) will be worth upwards of $1,000,000,000 by the end of 2007. This should not come as a surprise. Total voice traffic has grown year on year at an astonishing rate, and for the mobile world, it will continue to do so on a global basis for the foreseeable future. This is largely because of continued subscriber growth in the developing world, which has surged in China, India and Latin America. As a result, mobile lines now outnumber fixed lines by several hundred million, and while fixed line growth has slowed very substantially, mobile is likely to continue its impressive trajectory for several years to come.

At the same time, mobile calls represent substantially less than one third of all calls made—the large bulk are still carried on fixed networks. And whilst volumes on both fixed and mobile networks are growing, the share of total voice traffic held by mobile is growing rapidly.

The extent to which this volume growth can be translated into revenues is dependent on the extent to which mobile operators seek to manage the strategic development of their voice offering. Mobile voice reliability remains substantially lower than the 'five nines' reliability of many fixed networks (99.999 percent call success rate)—a reliability benchmark that represents a downtime of approximately 6 seconds per week (Percy 2003). Similarly, mobile call quality remains lower than that of fixed; and both of these points serve to limit the perceived value of the mobile voice service as a whole.

But mobile networks are—theoretically at least—just as technically capable and substantially more flexible than copper wire networks, and of course, mobile handsets have received many hundreds of times more investment in research and development than their fixed equivalents, and it shows. Ten percent of calls made from European homes are made on mobile phones, simply because the device is easier to use, and in particular, contact numbers are much more readily stored and retrieved (Lehman Brothers 2003).

Since there is a well-established link between the number of contacts stored and the number of calls made, operators could rapidly accelerate voice volume growth by helping their customers to store more contacts in their phone or SIM card.

Simplifying tariffs would also help. One of the major barriers to greater mobile phone usage is cost, and even though the cost per unit of time is becoming increasingly competitive with fixed networks, customers remain wary of call charges, in no small part because they do not understand the structure of tariffs. Mobile operators do themselves absolutely no favours in this regard. One of Europe's leading international wireless operators presently has over 1,000 different tariffs in its top five European markets. Over 800 of those tariffs have been changed during the course of the last twelve months, leaving customers with an eternal struggle to understand the true cost of ownership.

The bottom line is that mobile operators have diverted their attention to data before they have optimised their core business. Second generation (2G) infrastructure—and the voice services provided by it—could readily be turned into a very healthy cash-generating machine. With most infrastructure written off in accounting terms, 2G has the potential to deliver very substantial profits. People call people, not places—and it is inevitable that mobile will ultimately become the primary voice communications medium for most of the developed (and indeed developing) world. Given such an opportunity, mobile operators should initially worry less about data and worry substantially more about how to extract long-term value from voice.

Mass demand for data

Mobile operators have managed to convince themselves that there is an unarguable, mass demand for data services amongst customers. But evidence from the fixed world would suggest otherwise.

The large majority of domestic Internet access is still based on a dial-up connection, as opposed to broadband or cable. Though this is partly because cable and DSL broadband operators have been painfully slow to roll out their infrastructure, it is also because demand for high-speed connectivity is limited. Even before broadband access has reached substantial penetration rates, operators are competing aggressively on price. There is a noticeable trend toward offering more bandwidth for less money, across the board. This suggests that for the most part, people are prepared to pay for 'fast enough access'—not 'as fast as possible'.

The other immediately obvious issue is that fixed broadband operators sell Internet access, and Internet access only. Their attempts at selling a broader portfolio of data services—as a means of increasing real and perceived value—have tended to yield very little customer interest. For example, early experiments with television over broadband have so far been an expensive failure—consumers do not see any inherent value in being able to download television programming that they generally receive either for free, or at a markedly higher quality, elsewhere. Only now are 'triple-play' services from companies like France Telecom and Homechoice (within the M25 region of London) beginning to combine internet, fixed-line telephony and TV over a broadband line in a way that is leading to decent numbers of subscribers.

Similarly, attempts to sell broadband appliances have tended to meet with indifference amongst consumers. Even the most popular networked device—the gaming console—is only just beginning to generate noticeable traffic volumes. And with its niche demographics, the gaming market is unlikely to confer a huge opportunity on fixed carriers, since their role is little more than that of a fat pipe.

Perhaps ironically, the services that have attracted greatest consumer interest—above and beyond Internet access—are simple communications services: e-mail, instant messaging, chat rooms and more recently, blogs (personal weblogs) and wikis (editable web pages). The popularity of these services hints at the colossal demand for services that allow consumers to indulge in conversations, self-expression and social activity. But their popularity does not infer the need for more bandwidth—they are all relatively low-bandwidth applications that can run quite happily on a dial-up connection.

Not surprisingly, in the mobile world, a similar pattern has arisen. The single most popular mobile service after voice is text messaging. Dominated almost exclusively by interpersonal messaging, the text market now contributes up to 20 percent of operator revenues. The next most popular service is voicemail—used by upwards of 50 percent of the customer base. These services—combined with voice—make up more than 98 percent of total operator revenues.

Other data services—which include ringtones, wallpaper and other downloads—make up less than 2 percent of revenues. And it is interesting to note that the large majority of these data services fall comfortably into the category of 'phone personalisation'—a category that is clearly linked to self-expression.

So what does all of this mean for the future of mobile data? On the positive side, it means that the very best place to start in the search for successful data applications is communications. Adding mobility, presence and immediacy to chat, instant messaging, blogging and other services has the potential to generate substantial value. The principle advantage of the mobile medium—its ubiquity—lends itself well to all forms of communications services. Already there is evidence that mobile e-mail, for example, is becoming extremely popular. E-mail specific devices such as the RIM Blackberry have demonstrated exceptional growth. And although each e-mail generates only modest revenues for operators on a per-unit basis, the sheer volume of e-mail sent suggests a very substantial total market. Consumers around the world still buy mobile phones for one reason—communications—and for the time being, this is the primary, if not only, market that operators should focus their resources on.

Content is King

At present, however, operators are focusing their attention not on communications, but on content—believing the myth that "Content is King". There can be no doubt that content generates colossal revenues. Newspapers, music CDs and DVDs, movies, pay-television, books and all manner of other published content generate billions of dollars in revenues. But there are two important issues here. The first is that the bulk of revenues from content go to the producers of content—not their intermediaries. The second is that whilst content revenues are huge, communications revenues have always been, and will continue to be, far greater. For example, even the largest and most successful global movie studios generate net revenues that are a fraction of those generated by a single-country GSM operator. So the notion that putting content over mobile phones will revolutionise the industry and generate billions in net additional revenues is entirely flawed.

According to Forrester Research, a telecommunications and technology research organisation, content over mobile phones is unlikely to generate substantial revenues. By contrast, however, conversations between users—conversations that are powered by content—have the potential to create a multi-billion dollar market (de Lussanet et al. 2002). Their research indicates that for mobile operators, downloads and content are substantially less important than the communications services that envelop them. The small-talk that has powered the massive growth of mobile voice can be further stimulated and grown, therefore, by using content as its raw material. Content becomes a means to an end, not an end in itself.

Bandwidth equals success

With a focus on content, mobile operators have begun to investigate—and indeed invest in—an increasingly long list of wireless technologies. Based on the assumption that ultimately huge amounts of content will be delivered to the mobile device, operators seem to be 'spread betting'—investing large sums of money in new technologies in the hope that they will deliver additional bandwidth which will translate into value for customers. To the already huge investment in third generation networks (UMTS/3G) is being added wireless LAN for local access; HSDPA (high-speed downlink packet access), which allows 3G infrastructure to deliver connection speeds of up to 10Mb/S; DVB-H (digital video broadcast—handheld) for digital television services, and several others. These technologies may well be extremely powerful, but they are also highly disruptive on several levels. First of all, consumers are already unconvinced by the need to upgrade to 3G. Add more technologies, and their uncertainty will rise—if operators cannot decide which technology is best, why should consumers? Secondly, the addition of each new technology increases the capital expenditure (CAPEX) burden on operators, making balance sheets even more difficult reading. And finally, each new network element essentially serves to compromise the window of opportunity for 3G.

There is no precedent to suggest that people have an all-consuming desire for bandwidth and speed. Moreover, there is little evidence that mobile customers see many meaningful uses for the bandwidth. Almost without exception, consumers buy a mobile phone for communications, and as intimated earlier, they may well be prepared to pay for 'fast enough'—but there is scant evidence to suggest that they will pay for 'as fast as possible'.

Everything belongs on mobile

The final myth that plagues the mobile industry is the notion that everything—from betting to banking, music to movies—belongs on the mobile device. This is simply wrong. The mobile device is extraordinarily powerful, and its capabilities are growing rapidly as a function of time. But that does not infer that consumers will ever see it as a panacea—capable of doing everything they need to do.

There is a clear social and practical context to mobile usage. Mobile is the perfect medium for voice, because it works virtually everywhere and is the one device that consumers carry with them wherever they go. It is the ideal medium for messaging and mail, because it is ubiquitous and immediate. It is the ideal platform for controlling other services—perhaps very many other services—but not necessarily for consuming them. And the separation of control and consumption is key. It is not inconceivable that customers will actively want to search for, order and pay for a movie on their mobile phone. But they will almost certainly prefer to watch it on a full sized screen, in the comfort of their own home. They may want to scan newspaper headlines, but they will want to read whole articles either on a large format screen or on paper.

The true position of the mobile phone—above and beyond its

role as a critical communications tool—is as the remote control. The remote control that allows customers to seek and find. The remote control that keeps customers informed. The remote control that allows customers to choose and pay. But resolutely not the platform for the consumption of everything.

Conclusion

So does all this spell disaster for mobile operators? No—but they must step back and look carefully at the foundations of their business. Starting with voice, operators must begin to realign their focus on the service that generates the large majority of their revenues and profits.

Instead of encouraging the erosion of voice margins through increasingly generous bundled tariffs, operators might instead focus on taking voice into its third generation. Most operators have assumed that the 'killer application' for 3G will be a data application, but there is no reason why that application could not be next generation voice service. Arguably the best way to displace fixed voice (and indeed voice over IP) altogether is to develop a sustainable quality differential. 3G networks have sufficient bandwidth and capacity to offer high-fidelity voice. Even stereo voice.

It seems ironic that operators have so far overlooked the opportunity to bring voice up to date. For too long customers on all networks—fixed and mobile—have put up with audio reproduction that is low bandwidth and low quality. High-fidelity, combined with universal mobility, would give mobile networks an invincible edge over all other voice media.

Operators must also recognise that content is not their business—communications is. As such revenues will be generating by developing communications services that take interpersonal interaction into new areas. That means leveraging all of the power of the mobile network and device. More particularly, it means making sure everything works. It is a sad truth that even today, customers can leave a store with a new, high specification phone that is not properly configured for basic services such as picture messaging and e-mail. If operators really want to see data revenues grow, they must ensure that a customer simply cannot leave a store without a phone that is ready to send and receive every meaningful type of mobile communication.

Operators would also do well to think about handset design. Adoption of even the simplest non-voice services, such as text messaging, are impacted by the wide variety of user interfaces and operating systems available in modern mobile phones. Get into a car—any car—and a user will be able to drive away. The headlights, the gear stick, the windscreen wipers and even the stereo are in a standard position—so the user immediately knows how to operate it. This is not the case on mobile phones, and operators must work to standardise interfaces—otherwise all but the most technology literate customers will simply not use the services.

And services—not bandwidth and technology—are what sells. Operators must focus on the development of a long-term suite of practical, meaningful and relevant services, and then decide which technologies allow them to deliver those services most efficiently—not the other way round.

Communications is King

The services themselves need not be complex or advanced. Indeed, arguably the simpler they are the more popular appeal they will have. And there are plenty of seemingly obvious mobile services that still do not exist. Users still cannot book a wake-up call with their mobile operator. They cannot send a post-it note to their colleagues. They cannot do a crossword puzzle on their phone.

In the end, the numbers are massively stacked in the favour of mobile operators—so failure will only ever be self-inflicted. Historically, demand for communication has grown consistently as a function of time, and as a function of new media and communication forms.

Within this context, the very notion of 'data' is irrelevant. If we accept that communications is king, then there is no need to arbitrarily divide the world into voice and data. Because ultimately customers don't—and won't.

References

de Lussanet, M. et al. (2002), 'Conversational Content Unlocks Revenue', Forrester Research Inc., *The TechStrategy Report*, July.

Lehman Brothers (2003), *Mobile Growth at Risk as Fixed Stands Firm*, Telecom Services, 30 May.

Percy, K. (2003), 'Five Nines, by the book', *Network World*, 14 April.

Conclusion—Delphi Report

People, mobiles and society. Concluding insights from an international expert survey

PETER GLOTZ AND STEFAN BERTSCHI

Introduction

It is difficult to estimate whether and how people will integrate mobile technologies into their daily lives, and how the usage of technologies will affect social life. In the survey presented in this chapter, we aimed to verify social 'situations' which derive from the use of mobile phones. Some of these situations are already in existence (at least in some regions or countries). Mostly, individual expert opinions have been used to detect tendencies and prospects of mobile phone usage in the past. To enhance this we use a method which has existed for approximately fifty years: the Delphi method (see Linstone and Turoff 1975). The Delphi technique is a questionnaire method for organising and sharing expert opinion through feedback.

Here it was used to get personal, but well-founded, opinions about actual status, incidents and developments in social effects of mobile phone usage. These opinions were validated throughout the process by discourse—during the process the participants were encouraged to build on their replies in the light of the anonymous replies of other members of the panel. The survey's aim was not simply to collect individual opinions but rather to find a consensus among experts of different backgrounds and origins.

Research on the social effects of mobile phone usage and their future should cover a broad variety of aspects. A preceding study of the literature and a public and media perception analysis helped to identify and narrow down important issues and cohesions (inspired by facet theory, see Borg 1977). An example, called the 'Honeycomb' and used in preparation of the Delphi survey, is shown in Figure 1.

We then went on to build preliminary questions which led to the final questionnaire. Furthermore, various impulses collected at an international expert workshop, held in the summer of 2004 in London and organised in association with T-Mobile International, were used for the development of the survey as a whole (which was conducted in the autumn of 2004). The results give an impression of the current state of research and about further needs and issues.

Figure 1: The 'Honeycomb' depicts issues related to the mobile phone.

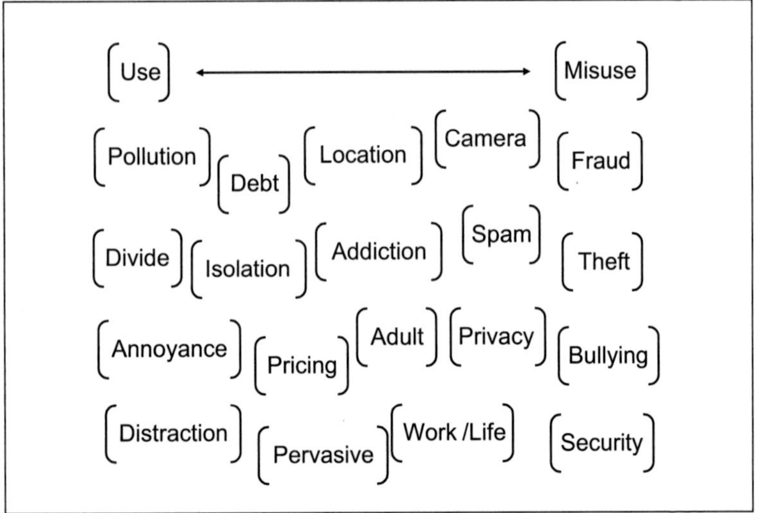

We invited 300 experts from academia, research institutions and the telecommunications industry to take part and to answer a first online questionnaire. Fifty percent of the invited experts answered these questions in the first wave (see Table 1 for details on demographics). To validate the effects of mobile phone use, we provided statements (and short scenarios), and it was the participants' task to estimate these 'everyday situations' in the light of their likeliness to happen in the near future (i.e. 2005-2007). Therefore, a six-point Likert scale was applied to all the statements.[1] These statements were then bundled into thematic entities. The experts were asked to estimate the likelihood of a specific scenario occurring in the near future. The online questionnaire in the first wave of the survey consisted of 54 closed and seven open questions. The wording of questions and statements was kept simple and designed to get distinct opinions about the effects of mobile phone usage in everyday life.

1. The scale description is followed by abbreviations used in this chapter's figures: Very unlikely (VU 1), Unlikely (U 2), Somewhat unlikely (SU 3), Somewhat likely (SL 4), Likely (L 5), Very likely (VL 6). We did not provide a neutral 'middle position', in order to force the experts to give clear predications.

Table 1: Survey demographics (percentages).

		Wave 1	Wave 2
Response rate		n=153	n=117
Gender	Female	22.9	23.1
	Male	77.1	76.9
Age	20-29	6.2	6.0
	30-39	39.7	38.8
	40-49	28.8	27.6
	50-59	19.9	21.6
	60+	5.5	6.0
Origin	Europe	75.8	76.1
	North America	18.3	17.1
	Asia/Oceania	5.9	6.8
Workplace	University/College	51.0	52.1
	Telecom industry	17.0	17.1
	Consultancy/Market research	11.8	10.3
	Private research institute	8.5	6.8
	Public research institute	6.5	7.7
	Other	5.2	6.0
Expertise	Low	4.1	4.4
	Medium	28.1	28.3
	High	67.8	67.3

The second questionnaire consisted of those 27 closed-ended questions which evoked dissent among the panel in the first wave. In the second wave, the participants were encouraged to build on or revise their replies in the light of the other replies. To be able to reconsider the first reply we provided mean value, standard deviation, and the expert's own opinion for every statement. After considering this information the participants were asked to confirm their previous answer or to revise/alter the answer. Three-quarters of those who concluded the first questionnaire were willing to answer the questionnaire of the second wave as well. The Delphi technique used is a subjective-intuitive method and builds on the experience that participants are more likely to revise their answers if they are not fully convinced about them.

Unfortunately, the Asian sample is too small to draw relevant conclusions about this region. Still, it is possible to state that there are no significant differences as to participants' origin or workplace: Americans and Europeans are equally distributed among progressive and conservative views, whereas a certain type of 'cultural critique bias' is slightly visible among German participants; surprisingly, industrial members are equally as critical as academics. Cross-testing showed that self estimated 'higher level' experts tend to change less to the direction of mainstream answers and are more likely to remain with their opinions in the second wave. In general, changes between the first and second wave were not that significant. Despite a certain (methodologically given) movement towards the mean value of the first wave, changes between the two opposite opinions (unlikely vs. likely) were minimal. The chapter ends with a list of those participants who agreed to be mentioned and a full data table (see Table 2).

Social relationships

As has been clear from the preceding chapters, an important aspect of recent research has been establishing how mobile phones will determine social relationships in the near future. However, the experts do not agree on the statement that the mobile phone will be important for 'making new friends' (Q 4.1). Sixty percent indicated that it might be likely to do so but half of them said that it will only be somewhat likely. Despite future technology seeming to enable complex social interactions, as discussed by Paul Golding in this volume, there is still no convincing answer as to whether the mobile phone will allow users to make new friends, but there is first evidence of users exchanging numbers readily as they become some kind of personal ID. There may be potential in offering services like a mobile 'friendster' to get to know friends of your friends as they are in the same bar or club for example. The answer is rather different if asked whether mobile phones will be important to maintain existing relationships (Q 4.2). Almost all of the experts agreed to this statement with more than half of the experts saying that this is very likely. The experts are convinced that it is very likely that social consequences of mobile phone use—as they are shown throughout this volume and the Delphi chapter—will affect everyday culture a great deal (Q 17.1). But they do not think that such consequences are likely to pose a threat to the telecommunications industry in general (Q 17.2). Because the mobile is 'attached' to its user (as Jane Vincent lays out in her chapter in this volume) it allows an easy and always accessible connection to stay in touch with loved ones—'Research so far has demonstrated that mobile phones are most often used to maintain contact with existing social networks, rather than make entirely new contacts'. Most experts agree with the statement that mobiles are an important means of maintaining relationships (see Hans Geser's chapter in this volume).

The results after the first wave showed that participants were discordant but that they tend to see it as more likely that 'people who do not use mobile phones will risk losing contact with mobile phone users' (Q 4.3). Some of them adjusted their answer in the second wave. According to the experts, it is still likely that possession of a mobile phone will divide the haves and the have-nots in the near future. Three quarters of the experts assume that this scenario is to some extent likely to happen. One expert is convinced that this is 'only true among the young' and if people are not present in other way (WLAN, landline phones etc). Most respondents do not think that relationships will become more superficial (or less committed) as a result of mobile phone usage (Q 4.4). Three quarters of the experts assume that this scenario is unlikely to happen. It is interesting to see that experts who already had an extreme opinion tend to stick to their first estimation. It was mentioned that all of these five scenarios are dependent on age, gender, different cultures and geographic regions: 'The debate will rage on around the lack of sensitivity and impact on social values as consumers withdraw into their devices and ignore the public settings they find themselves in. This is already very apparent in Japan and Korea.' Mobile telephony not only connects people but 'mobile telephonic practices run the risk of forging walled communities within already established social groups'.

Figure 2: Social life will become less predictable.

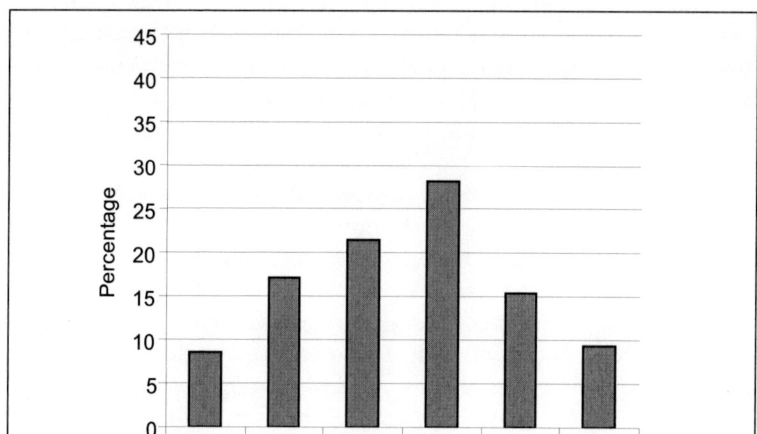

The last and most interesting aspect seems to be if social life will become less predictable because of the mobile phone (Q 4.5). After the first wave of our Delphi survey there was distinct uncertainty among the experts (aggregated values: 50 percent unlikely vs. 50 percent likely). This is also shown by the fact that all possible options were chosen at significant levels. After the second wave it seems to be somewhat likelier that social life may become less predictable because of spontaneous mobile phone use (47 percent unlikely vs. 53 percent likely, see Figure 2). It is acknowledged by experts that mobile phones will increase the flexibility in social life and shorten planning time scales from days to hours or minutes. It was quoted that the mobile 'will allow (and even encourage?) people to be less committal' and that 'social life will become different because of the mobile phone.'

Non-users and mobile phones

We wanted to understand what problems non-users are going to face. The Delphi participants are (slightly) undecided as to whether non-users of mobile phones will be confronted with an information deficit (Q 12.1). The statement presumes that more and more information gathering will take place via mobile devices (this will probably not be the case in the near future, according to 54 percent of the experts). In general, experts do not seem to pay too much attention to the phone as a source of information ('because people always will have an (additional) online access via PC'). But, 'the mobile phone will very likely eliminate the information divide in due time' (because they are affordable, portable and can be bought second hand in many developing countries, see Jonathan Donner's chapter in this volume). The problems that non-users may encounter 'may be much more about their social relations than a lack of information.' There is some connection between this and another expert's opinion: 'One should not underestimate the informational effect coming from spontaneous and flexible use of a device that offers access to sources or coordination with others.'

It seemed likely that not having a mobile phone could limit people's mobility (Q 12.2). But similar to the previous statement, experts are undecided (aggregated values: 44 percent unlikely vs. 56 percent likely). Usually, 'non-users have strategies for not having a mobile phone, it is more likely to be a conscious decision not to have a mobile.' How much this is a cultural issue is showed by one expert's opinion: 'In the US, I do not foresee mobiles becoming the necessity they seem to have become in Europe or Asia.' One respondent has drawn the following conclusion in the second wave: 'It is interesting that I found myself thinking, the core value of mobile phones is not the mobility'. But the answer to another question shows that more than eighty percent of the Delphi participants think that it is likely that the mobile phone will increase its user's mobility (Q 16.1). Still, we would have expected the likelihood to be higher. This may have to do with the fact that 'the mobile phone became a mass consumer item at least in part because the population was already very highly mobile.'

The detachment of the mobile phone user, in contrast to the non-user, is clearly shown by the significant likelihood (almost eighty percent) of problems with the planning of everyday life and coordination with other people's lives (Q 12.3). Taking into account that so many contacts already occur on mobile communications (see Leslie Haddon's chapter in this volume), it does not seem unrealistic that non-users 'may not be able to do as many things simultaneously, which is not necessarily bad.' According to respondents, not having a mobile phone in the future should not be more of a problem than it is now.

Dependence on mobile phones

To reveal how much users will depend on their mobiles we assumed and tested the following statement: 'If the mobile phone gets lost or stolen, it will affect the user's daily life a great deal.' (Q 2.1) Even though a few experts claimed that there will be backup solutions for personal data stored in mobile phones, the opinion dominates that it really is affecting people's lives if they are separated from their mobile phone (and the data like contacts, messages, photos it carries). More than ninety percent of the experts think that this scenario is to some extent likely to happen. One expert's quote ('I think we should not overestimate dependency as it relates to objects.') can be partly refuted because there seems to be more than just a 'material object' involved. Most experts do not acknowledge that people's dependence on mobile phones is problematic, as long as it is defined as reliance (as depicted in the statement and not as some psychological dependence or addiction). The idea of 'dependence' sometimes implies a negative effect, with which the participants do not necessarily agree.

The mobile phone will become more and more important. This can be seen in the increasing dependence that is predicted by the Delphi participants. Ninety percent agree with the statement that this dependence will increase dramatically (Q 2.2). A few experts point out that dependence will not increase much more as people already depend a great deal on their mobile phones (see Jonathan Donner's chapter for information on the importance of mobile phone usage in developing countries). On the other hand, the expert sample is undecided as to whether dependence on a technological device like the mobile phone will mobilise the broad public and lead to a public debate (Q 2.3). The outcome almost equates to a normal distribution or so-called bell curve. It is finally a question of people's awareness of what kind of issue this will be in the future. According to one participant, 'the public debate depends on transparency regarding health risks and social status of the mobile phone'.

The survey then introduced a concept of addiction and asked to what extent mobile phone addiction will be a genuine problem. The experts agree with the assumption that mobile phone addiction will only affect very few people (Q 3.1). Three quarters are convinced that this scenario seems likely to happen. Still, some participants criticised our definition and stated that it is difficult to separate addiction from dependence. One expert made clear that 'addiction is a clinical condition, dependence is not.' The question would 'assume that there is such a thing as mobile addiction' and would 'portray an impending crisis which does not exist, even though understanding the psychology of mobile attitudes is very important'. Or, as another expert stated, 'the mobile phone becomes the scapegoat for larger issues about decay in society'.

Even though only few people might be affected by some kind of addiction, it is likely to lead to a debate in the media (Q 3.2). Because of this topical nature of the controversy over mobile addiction, the participants assume that it will be covered by the media (see Figure 3). Some experts point out that it is the logic of the media to search and display ambivalent and controversial issues ('perceptions of addiction rather than realities often drive media debates'). One expert suspected that 'this debate in the media will be relatively short lived'. Another expert is convinced that the 'media debate will not affect the problem.'

Figure 3: Addiction will lead to a debate in the media.

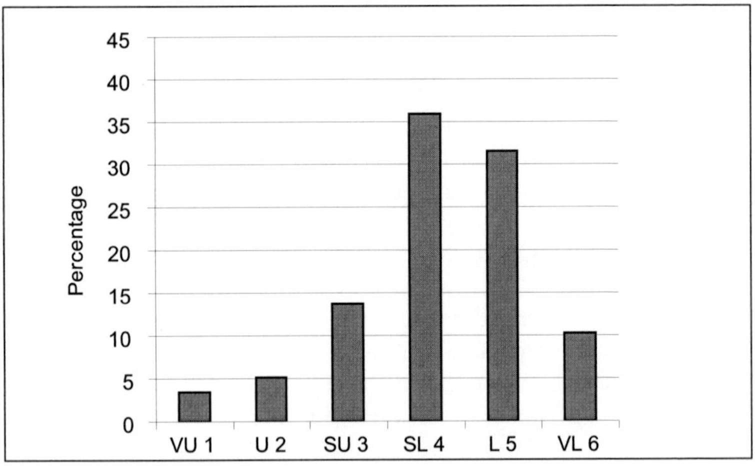

Children and mobile phones

The only strictly normative question in our survey asked at what age children should get their first mobile phone (Q 6.1). Most experts specify an age between ten and fourteen years which they consider as being appropriate (with a mean value of 11.4 years). We were surprised how broad the distribution was (it spans between the age of six and sixteen years). According to one expert, the appropriate age depends on the functions available. Another respondent answered the question more generally: 'When they earn enough money and have enough media competence to buy and run a mobile phone!'

According to the experts, the average age of first mobile phone possession will get lower (Q 6.2). Almost all of the experts indicate that this scenario is likely to happen in the near future. Safety and security are benefits of children's mobile phone usage mentioned most, followed by the ability to stay in touch with parents, family and friends. Potential health hazards and surveillance (with different characteristics) have been mentioned as negative aspects of children using mobile phones, followed by cost, responsibilities in general and peer pressure. Because of this confirmed probability that children using mobile phones are getting younger, it seems likely to very likely that the public, and especially the media, will cover the issue. Ninety percent assume that it is to some extent likely to happen that children's possession of mobile phones will lead to a debate in the media (Q 6.3). One of the experts made clear that 'parental choice should be a primary determinant not government regulation'.

The same may apply to the following aspect. Because at the time of the survey it is easy to access adult content (such as porn or gambling) with a mobile phone, we were interested what this will mean for the protection of minors. Experts are undecided as to whether the mobile phone will erode the protection of minors (Q 7.1). The answers were almost equally distributed after the first wave (aggregated values: 51 percent unlikely vs. 49 percent likely) and changed slightly during the second wave of the survey (i.e. 48 vs. 52, see Figure 4). It can be rated as a highly controversial issue. According to one respondent, 'access to adult content is limited by the network operator's mutual agreement, so the actual statement in this [the main] question is false'. Still, it may be questioned if such an agreement will be sufficient to protect minors. Some experts claim that 'technical filters will be needed' but others are unsure 'if we would be able to regulate what gets transmitted from phone to phone.' The worst fear is seen in 'unsolicited porn (spam) showing up on a child's mobile phone.'

There is also significant uncertainty as to whether we will need stronger legal regulation on minors' use of the mobile phone (Q 7.2). However, more than half of the experts assume that this scenario is likely to happen in the near future. A few respondents are convinced that we will get more regulation but that stronger legal regulation 'will not help much'. One expert believes that 'network operators will be forced to take legal responsibility for the content (of images) transmitted on their networks'. The solution, according to two experts, is parental control, not legal limitations, and teaching media competence is more important than regulation.

Teenagers and families

Because such effects are already visible we assumed that there may be peer pressure among teenagers to have the latest device and to use new services (e.g. games, ringtones, video). The responses to the statement that the mobile phone will be important for teenagers to display their own lifestyle (Q 9.1)—99 percent of the experts indicated that it is to some extent likely to be true—show strong evidence that the mobile phone is more than a means of person-to-person communication. Even though the answers are related to teenage usage, the question of taste and environment of usage determine what kind of phone a person possesses and what kind of abilities or services are used ('symbolic value'). In many places and for some years now, it is true to say that 'the mobile phone is already an important part of a teenager's identity', but it is dependent on culture as well: 'American teenagers are far less likely to see their phones as a reflection of themselves than are teens in Europe or Asia.' It looks as if 'the phone is the fashion item rather than the services or contents.' (See Leopoldina Fortunati's chapter in this volume.)

Figure 4: Mobile phones will erode the protection of minors.

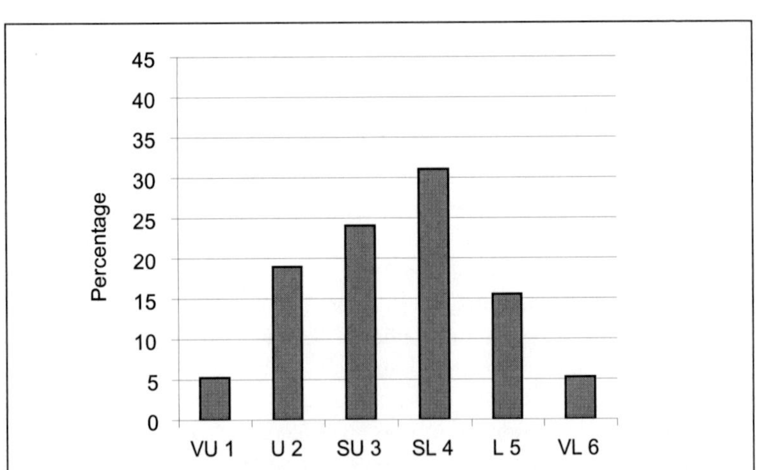

The widespread use of ringtones and wallpapers already indicates that the ability to use a certain service leads to strong usage. Ninety percent of the participants think that it is likely that new services and contents will put pressure on teenagers to use them (Q 9.2). Services which are able to make the phone more unique and personal are seen as important drivers. In the near future it is likely that this finding will apply to pictures, music and games. 'My phone is better than yours' could be an expression that leads back to the statement above. One expert points out that it is more probable that new services attract usage and evoke pressure among peers. Usually these factors will 'be tempered by the negotiation of economic cost (especially with parents), and also by the role of novelty in the expression of identity' (see both the chapters by Leslie Haddon and Richard Harper in this volume).

Closely related to teenage usage of mobile phones is the belief that very intensive use may lead to indebtedness. Whereas there is no doubt that the amount of money spent on mobile phone use will increase (Q 10.1) and that higher costs will be connected to more extensive uses, it seems a little less likelier that an increasing number of people will spend more money on mobile phone use than their budget allows (Q 10.2). It may soon happen 'that the expense for mobiles will be considered a necessity rather than a luxury' and that 'families prioritise these costs in their budgets'. 'People are much more aware of how much they spend on their mobile phone than on other household and personal expenditure.' This aspect is highly dependent on culture and development. It was mentioned that 'kids often do not spend their own money'. Unclear tariffs or pricing plans are given as a likely reason for people's problems with cost control (Q 10.3). According to some experts, prepaid or pay-as-you-go options (or specific family plans) will decrease the risk of losing cost control. Additionally, consumers seem to be more sophisticated, 'changing tariff and pricing plans relatively frequently to establish what works for their call usage.' According to one expert, the 'intelligence of billing systems allows operators to monitor usage, and increasingly allows users to control usage.' Service providers who offer ringtones etc. with unclear cost policies and paid subscription offers are mentioned as well. It is not surprising that the Delphi participants see a distinct likeliness that consumer protectionists will increasingly address indebtedness (Q 10.4). In some countries they have already been criticising prices for mobile phone usage (especially for text messaging). One expert points out that this kind of indebtedness is 'a problem of the lower classes', and that these problems never find much real attention in the public debate.

To assess the mobile phone's effect on family relationships we assumed that parents do not know what their children are doing with their mobile phone and therefore they might lose authority (Q 8.1). Almost three quarter of the experts state that it is unlikely that such a scenario will take place. Participants' remarks indicate that this issue, as well as the two following, is dependent on context, like relationships and social practices within each individual family, and on the specific culture in place; thus, problems are not caused solely by the presence of the mobile phone. There is evidence that 'parents use the mobile, and prepaid or pay-as-you-go vouchers in particular, as a reward or punishment tool for their children'. Seventy percent of the experts agree with the statement that because of the mobile phone, people will feel closer (more intimate) to their family members (Q 8.2). Still, it is in some way surprising to see that family bonds are not expected to be more strengthened by intense contact over distance (see Figure 5). The mobile phone may allow people to keep in touch more often, but according to some experts, 'this will not make the relationship more intimate or closer because it does not replace physical closeness'.

Figure 5: People will feel closer to their family members.

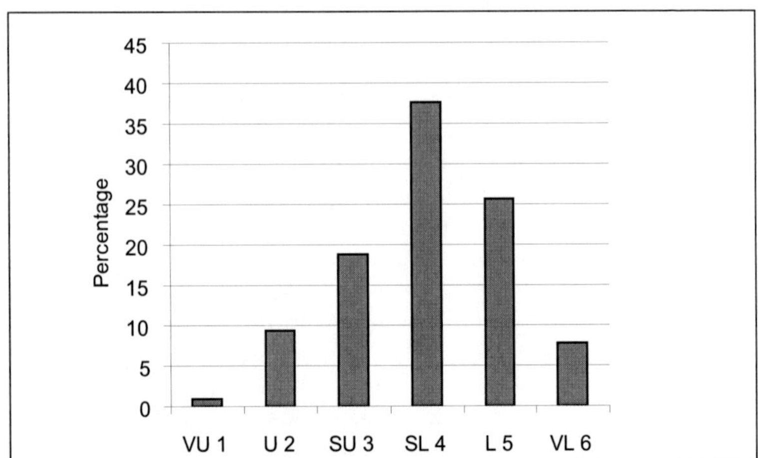

The phenomenon shown here—in the previous and the following scenario, saying that the mobile phone will be used as a means of social control and surveillance (Q 8.3)—is Janus-faced: Where there is a likelihood of closer relations, there is the same likelihood of control and surveillance (as assumed by more than eighty percent of the experts). Children like the mobile phone because they can call their friends away from parental ears, but it also allows parents to call them anytime, anywhere. Even surveillance can have a positive connotation, so long as parents can assure themselves that their children are alright and not in any danger. Some experts point out that 'children already have strategies to avoid surveillance'.

Communication and the mobile phone

The scenario that 'mobile phones are going to compensate increasingly for face-to-face contacts' (Q 5.1) led to a wide distribution of the values on the scale (aggregated values: 44 percent unlikely vs. 56 percent likely). There is a slight likeliness that distant communication compensates for direct communication. This effect can not solely be attributed to the mobile phone, and this may explain the experts' answers. According to one respondent, it is more likely that the 'quality of face-to-face contacts may decrease due to the presence of mobile devices (checking incoming mails etc)'. In Japan, 'it has been shown that mobile phone usage increases the instances of personal interactions with friends'. It is a rather widespread opinion that mobiles 'tend to add to and facilitate face-to-face communication, rather than replace it'.

Three out of four experts in our sample think that there is a likeliness that people will spend more time communicating because of new services (pictures, video etc). If there are more opportunities to communicate, it is quite certain that people will use them (Q 5.2). But as the comparison with the foregoing answer shows, these communications will probably not replace established forms of mobile (or even human) interaction. Finally, it is quite obvious that the variety of mobile communication possibilities is growing. But according to the Delphi participants, this will not apply so rapidly to pictures (Q 5.3). It seems to be unlikely that pictures will increasingly replace words in a mobile communication setting (as indicated by more than sixty percent of the experts). This is implied in the statements that 'pictures work with text' and that it needs 'special situations, where the picture can replace words or where the context is known'.

The Delphi participants are convinced that the social pressure to communicate anytime and anywhere will increase (Q 5.4). More than ninety percent think that this will most likely happen in the near future (see Figure 6). Current research already shows that instant reaction to mobile communication attempts is expected by some people. Still, it is not fully known 'if social pressure to communicate with others is a function of age or exacerbated by the technology'. One expert is convinced that 'we will see a more conscious use of mobiles in the near future'. The following statement is connected to this: 'As a non-user of mobile phones I am very conscious of social pressure to be available anytime and anywhere, and have made a lifestyle choice to reject it'.

Whereas it seems rather unlikely that the specific language of mobile text messaging will worsen young people's orthography and grammar skills (Q 13.1), it is likely that mobile phone language will change standard language, according to the experts (Q 13.2). It was mentioned 'that text messaging provides a creative means of expression that may disregard conventional grammar and is more closely associated with oral/aural language (as opposed to written language)'. But seventy percent of our experts agree that a new mobile language, which is adjusted to the device (small amount of characters, poor typing interface) and the lifestyle of the user, will interfere with standard language. Experts are not worried about such a change because languages, 'in order to be relevant to cultures, need to evolve, change and transform'. The rather extraordinary hypothesis—'Through mobile messaging near-illiterate population groups will be reintroduced to literacy' (Q 13.3)—is not thought to be true, nor will it have a distinct impact in the near future. But it can be said that text messaging 'gives people an incentive to write and formulate their ideas, so in places with a low literacy rate, it may even boost literacy.'

Figure 6: The social pressure to communicate anytime and anywhere will increase.

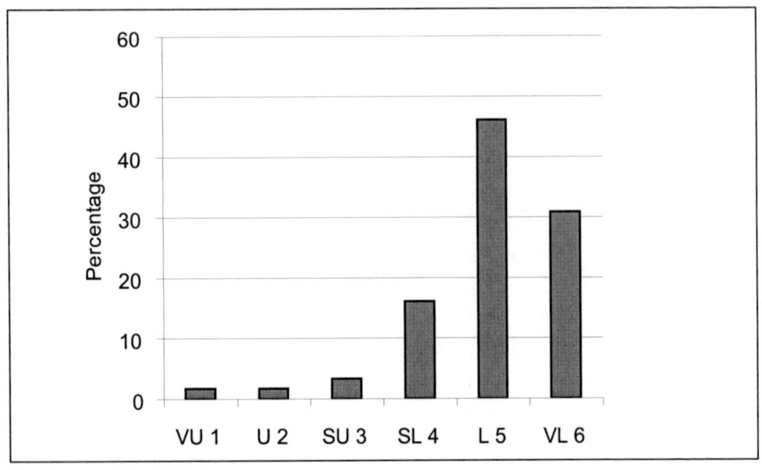

Privacy and camera phones

Mobile phone use leaves data traces (e.g. shopping, downloads). Therefore we wanted to know if people will lose control over their personal data (Q 14.1). Data protection is a highly important issue with mobile devices. Our respondents obviously predict that it is likely for mobile phone users to lose direct control over their personal data (more than eighty percent think so). 'Many companies so-called privacy policies outline exactly how individuals sign away many of their rights to control over their data.' This can be contrasted with another expert's notice: 'People give away a lot of personal information if you offer them bonus or incentives.' It is even possible that the mobile phone may shift what is considered private. It is not surprising that ninety percent of the experts say that it is to some extent likely that misuse of personal data will lead to a public debate (Q 14.2). There is an issue which rather hinders debate: 'Users are beginning to be aware of privacy concerns on the Internet, but I think awareness of issues related to the mobile lags behind.' As soon as a new condition builds awareness for its impacts and is reflected as potentially dangerous, people may ask for stronger legal regulation. Even though regulations of some kinds already exist, there is high probability of such a thing happening: According to eighty percent of the experts, we will need stronger legal regulation mandating privacy (Q 14.3), and most likely 'we will get stronger regulation'. Legal regulation will strengthen service providers' obligations to make personal data collection an opt-in activity. It is obvious that regulation is dependent on countries and markets: In Germany (and other parts of Europe) legal regulation is sufficient but needs to be controlled. In general, regulation in Europe is already more strict than in the US. This leads experts to demand stronger privacy laws.

We assumed that one potential impact of (the increasing number of) mobile phones with built-in cameras can be seen in a substantial invasion of people's privacy (Q 11.1). According to two thirds of the experts, this is likely to happen to some extent. Camera phones will probably continue to gain in popularity but will not be at the centre of public debate. Findings among young Norwegians indicate that people do tend to behave according to acceptable standards when they take photos. Therefore, 'camera phones will invade a few people's privacy intensely but there will not be widespread invasion of privacy'. Use and misuse of camera phones will be dependent on the culture in a specific society: In Japan there are already issues of concern—mostly around porn and copyright violations. In Europe, video phones have been misused in a phenomenon called 'happy slapping'. Furthermore, we assumed a certain positive effect of increasing camera phone usage. But more than sixty percent of our experts think that it is unlikely that people will rediscover their surroundings and their environment because of camera phone use (Q 11.2). It was mentioned that 'people will rather use pictures increasingly to communicate about fashion, share time-tables etc.' There is huge consent among the experts that if camera phones are massively misused legislation will be necessary (Q 11.3). Less than a fourth of the experts are saying that such a scenario is unlikely. 'The Data Protection Agency in Italy has already legislated against the misuse of camera phones.' Similarly it has already lead to legislation in the US but after all, legislation seems more likely to happen in Europe. One respondent adds that it could be handled similarly to smoking, others object that it is unlikely that many governments will legislate for this (also because it is difficult to enforce), and that it is more likely that 'control will happen at the organisational, local level (in individual buildings and facilities).' An exception can be seen in the 'moves by some governments requiring a shutter click on camera phones'.

Work/life balance

According to our experts, there is no denying that mobile phone usage increases its users' accessibility. What may be surprising is the fact that almost all of the respondents predict an ongoing increase in accessibility in the near future (Q 16.2). To have a closer look at this issue we asked the following questions again in the second wave of the Delphi survey. The balance between work and life seems to be endangered (see Figure 7). There is a significant prediction shown in this figure that users of mobile phones increasingly face losing leisure time because they will always be accessible to their employer (Q 16.3). But accessibility needs to be adjusted as 'mobiles can both facilitate working practices, as well as become an interference in leisure time'. Having to be accessible for employers is already a fact for most professionals known to one of the experts, but they seem 'to be attracted to the idea that they 'have' to be 'always on' because they are anxious to be seen to be indispensable'.

Figure 7: People will lose leisure time because they will always be accessible to their employer.

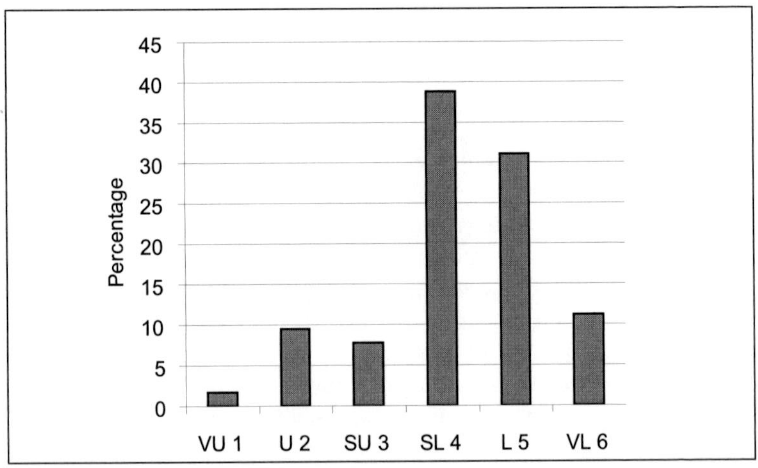

Even though a potential loss of leisure time seems likely, almost three quarters of the experts do not assume that people will not be able to do what they like with their leisure time (Q 16.4). An expected change in quantities does not have to be followed by changes in the quality of people's life planning. Mobile phone users will still have control over their own leisure time. It could even be easier to organise both spheres and their interactions. It was mentioned that 'people are very good at negotiating their public and private lives even as they continue to blur.' One expert objects that leisure time has already been eroded and that 'the mobile has become embedded in these changes, rather than causing them.'

It is an important insight from our survey that almost ninety percent of the experts predict that people will develop an awareness of the influence of mobile phones on their everyday lives (Q 16.5). According to a respondent, 'people are already aware of the influence of the mobile phone in their everyday lives, as witnessed by their reactions when the phone is lost or stolen.' Another pointed out that 'the intense battle between addiction and awareness will go on.' In the second wave two respondents greatly doubted the outcome of this question, because 'people have not demonstrated an awareness of the influence of other technologies on their lives, so why should the mobile phone raise awareness?', and because 'mobile phones will drop into the background and people are not likely to realise what has changed.'

Conclusion and outlook

In a second part of the Delphi survey we asked the participants what they think were the most positive and negative effects of the mobile phone, and what effects it will have in the near future (i.e. 2006-2007).

The most important positive effect the mobile phone has had on people's lives so far is "connectivity and connectedness" (36 votes or 15 percent). Increased 'social connectivity' or connectedness includes the easiness to keep in touch with people (mostly defined as friends and family). The mobile phone is seen as 'the most important channel in social life' because it facilitates interactions. Especially for young people the mobile phone provided new experimental grounds. The second most frequently quoted effect is summarised and coined as "flexibility, efficiency and convenience" (counted 35 times, 15 percent of experts, where convenience accounts for half of this number). First of all the mobile phone allows ease of communication in an as yet unknown way. Furthermore it improves life quality because of an 'increase of flexibility in an environment with increasing demand for flexibility'. Through mobile phone use the user can achieve more efficient lifestyles and convenience in handling practical matters. Not only that 'work has become more efficient' via the 'ability to handle daily business on the fly', but the mobile phone allows people with restricted time (blue collar workers) or place (construction workers) to have more efficient control over what they do, and maybe over a certain balance between work and life. We find "security, safety and emergency" (32 mentions, 14 percent) as the third positive effect significantly brought up by our experts. Next to the mobile phone's ability to save lives (because it can be used in the case of emergency anywhere), it has increased the sense of safety in all kind of threatening situations.

The most important positive effect the mobile phone will have in the future remains to be "connectivity and connectedness" (35 mentions or 18 percent of experts). The possibility to share experiences (via pictures and video) will grow, and there will be an overall increase in mediated social connectivity. This will allow the 'strengthening of social relations between groups of friends, family or business colleagues', or even change the ways in which people interact. Mobile data services are the second most frequently quoted positive effect (27 mentions, 14 percent of experts) from communication tools (like e-mail), access to services and exchange of data to entertainment services, because of the mobile phone's ability 'to be increasingly in touch with data assets'. Its ability to easily communicate data 'will be beneficial both for work and leisure'.

Data services are a rather new phenomenon in the Western hemisphere (compared to Asia where this has a longer tradition, see Genevieve Bell's chapter in this volume). Therefore the first Delphi questionnaire opened with a question on important drivers of mobile phone usage in the near future. Accessing (or surfing) the Mobile Internet is not yet clearly seen as a major driver of mobile phone usage (compared to the other drivers, see Q 1 in Table 2). Using the wording of an expert, 'Mobile Internet will not be a driver in the next 2-3 years as it will still be slow, inconvenient and very expensive'. But it has the potential to become a driver in the longer run (almost eighty percent of the experts indicate a likeliness of some kind, see Figure 8).

Figure 8: Surfing the Mobile Internet will be an important driver of usage.

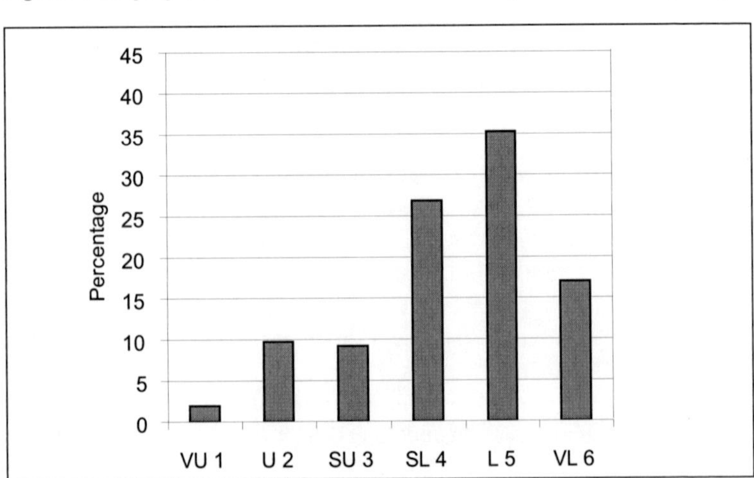

As soon as the mobile phone gets other technical capabilities, like more precise location awareness, information gathering of different kinds could be a widely used application (mobile commerce was mentioned in this context as well). The significance of this driver will largely depend 'upon the degree to which the services offered meet the mobile lifestyle'. Downloads (games, ringtones, music etc) are a kind of data service as well and they are already an important driver, especially among young people. Our experts predict that it will be even more important in the next two or three years. Like the ringtone example indicates, all of these drivers 'will depend on market segments', their symbolic value and cultural backgrounds. There is no doubt that voice communication and messaging will remain important drivers. Some experts pointed out that they would give a 'very likely' for text messaging and a 'somewhat likely' for picture messaging. Nevertheless our survey indicates that people-to-people communication is seen as the main driver of mobile phone usage (see Nick Foggin's chapter in this volume). But data services are winning ground in this race.

"Flexibility, efficiency and convenience" are seen as some of the remaining effects the mobile phone will have on people's lives in the near future (counted 27 times, 14 percent of experts, where convenience accounts for a third of this number). One of the experts sees 'the greatest benefits going to populations that are not a part of the mainstream and to white-collar workers'. New data functionalities will increase the ability to work and communicate nearly everywhere and according to people's own schedule, and will therefore lead to new and increased flexibility. One benefit in terms of efficiency can be seen in saving transportation time and costs (see Michael Hulme's and Anna Truch's chapter in this volume). According to another expert, the mobile phone will 'allow in many places the continuation of important cultural practices (see for instance the spread of Islamic applications on cell phones in the Middle East)'.

The most important negative effect the mobile phone has had on people's lives so far has been coined as "accessibility and the balance of work and life" (40 votes or 25 percent of experts). This threat emerges from the expectation of constant availability and pressure on social life emanating from the mobile phone's intrusiveness. It includes the demand for immediate response which is part of people's 'feeling of always being on call' and which is 'leading to difficulties separating work and leisure'. The effect summarised as "privacy, stress and distraction" was frequently quoted by our experts as well (37 mentions, 23 percent). They complain about a loss of privacy and intimacy, and criticise surveillance, increased stress and distraction which accompany a life supported by mobile communication. The invasion and loss of privacy, the 'control within personal relationships about whereabouts (and development of mistrust)' may lead to friction and stress. According to one expert, the mobile phone 'has made people more insular and rude within their environment'. There are some wider effects applied by experts as well: The mobile phone 'has reduced time to reflect and to adjust to situations', led to a lack of concentration and to a reduced 'ability/readiness to contemplate and rest without external contact'. Finally, there is the aspect of 'distraction' by mobile phone use. Opinions range from 'we have many distractions but this one seems particularly pernicious and ongoing' to an even more discerning statement seeing the introduction of a 'new opaque and aggressive industry and an overpriced consumer distraction from more important issues'. "Inappropriate usage" of mobile phones was mentioned 27 times (or by 17 percent of experts). This effect is connected with the issues of increased ambient noise and disturbance, the blurring of the public and the private (see Joachim Höflich's chapter in this volume) and a decline in social etiquette (see Lara Srivastava's chapter). Inconsiderate use in meetings, cinemas, restaurants etc and its negative effects on people's environments is not only connected with simple annoyance. But even 'barriers where cell phone use was considered a faux pas are gradually being eroded' and the same is happening to the 'social permission regarding interruption' (where inappropriate use directly leads back to accessibility).

The most important negative effect the mobile phone will have in the future is seen in "privacy, stress and distraction" (56 votes or 39 percent of experts). This category of effects was already important in the past, but now it is mostly extended with 'intensified' or 'increasing', such as intensified loss of privacy. The risk of easy access to specific information may lead to an abuse of personal data and an intrusion of integrity; and 'privacy issues will become more significant with location-based services' (increasing quality of camera phones, where pictures will be taken in all kinds of situations, is mentioned by some experts as well). According to one expert, users need to become more aware of the dangers provided by data collections and their potential misuse. Another effect, increasing 'mobile spam' (Q 15.1) and mobile advertisements, account for eight of the mentions in this category. In general, experts are convinced that technological solutions will develop to keep mobile spam under control (Q 15.3). The increasing loss of intimacy has a second face to it, loss of attention. According to one respondent, the mobile phone could be used as a means of not-being-excluded, and this could 'encourage the proliferation of the public use of mobile phones' to avoid loneliness within public life, or to avoid being ignored (see Hans Geser's chapter in this volume). The mobile phone 'will test the bounds of security, privacy, and social and behavioural taboos'. However, to quote one expert, one can 'reckon that people will learn to actively manage the technology'. Far behind with a mere of 18 votes (or 13 percent of experts) ranks "accessibility and the balance of work and life", the most negative effect seen in the past (which of course will be important in the future as well, thinking about next generation mobile network infrastructure; see Paul Golding's chapter in this volume). According to respondents, mobile phone use will 'further abolish the borders between business and leisure life'. Control over accessibility is more and more eroded. The issue of "cost and indebtedness" was mentioned by twelve experts (or eight percent). 'People will be more and more lured into expensive no-value-services.' This especially applies to younger people who have problems affording mobile phones and services.

Beside the fact that already established effects will continue to be important, one can see that positive effects are more widely distributed in the experts' views and that negative effects come to a head more precisely (compare given percentages). In fact, one of the experts' statements is rather conclusive: 'Mobile phones are essentially a fulfilment of a universal need that has always existed!' The present volume has tried to cover most of the identified aspects and issues and therefore—in the combination of invited chapters and Delphi survey—provided a variety of topics on the meaning of mobile phones for society. However, the future will show how accurate the estimations in the Delphi survey are and will be.

List of participants

Participants who agreed to be listed in the Delphi publication (116 out of 153 experts)

- Matthias Adam, Eventmanager, Deutsche Telekom Foundation, Germany
- Tomi Ahonen, Author and Consultant, associated with Oxford University, UK
- Jouko Ahvenainen, President, Xtract Ltd, Finland
- Mikael Anneroth, Manager Usability and Interaction Lab, Ericsson Research, Sweden
- Urs von Arx, Head of Section Mobile and Satellite Services, BAKOM, Switzerland
- John W. Bakke, Research Scientist, Telenor, Norway
- Alexandru Balog, Senior Researcher, National Institute for Research and Development in Informatics, Bucharest, Romania
- Boldur-Eugen Barbat, Professor, Lucian Blaga University, Romania
- Louise Barkhuus, PhD Student, IT University of Copenhagen, Denmark
- Naomi S. Baron, Professor, American University, Washington D.C., USA

- Andreas Becker, Consultant, Solon Management Consulting, Germany
- Viktor Bedö, Junior Researcher, Institute for Philosophical Research of the Hungarian Academy of Sciences, Hungary
- Genevieve Bell, Senior Researcher and Anthropologist, Intel Research, USA
- Steffen Binder, Research Director, Soreon Research, Switzerland
- Torsten Brodt, Researcher, University of St.Gallen, Switzerland
- Hans-Bernd Brosius, Professor, Ludwig-Maximilians-University, Munich, Germany
- Günter Burkart, Professor, University of Lueneburg, Germany
- John Byrne, Wireless Industry Analyst, Comcast Corporation, USA
- Mads Christoffersen, Assistant Professor, Technical University of Denmark
- Elizabeth Churchill, Senior Research Scientist, Palo Alto Research Center, USA
- Tony Crabtree, Principal Analyst, Juniper Research, UK
- Ken Crisler, Research Manager, Motorola, USA
- Kathleen M. Cumiskey, Assistant Professor, The College of Staten Island, City University of New York, USA
- Isaac van Deelen, CEO, TIMElabs Management Consulting GmbH, Germany
- Roland Deiser, Senior Fellow, Center for the Digital Future, Annenberg School of Communication, USA
- Veit V. Dengler, Vice President, Marketing Strategy, T-Mobile International, Austria
- Jonathan Donner, Post-Doctoral Research Fellow, Columbia University, USA
- Nicola Döring, Professor, Ilmenau University of Technology, Germany
- Gregor Dürrenberger, Head, Swiss Research Foundation on Mobile Communication, Switzerland
- Thomas Fellger, Managing Director, iconmobile GmbH, Germany
- Andrew Finn, Professor, George Mason University, USA
- Peter Fleissner, Professor, Vienna University of Technology, Austria
- Einar Flydal, Senior Adviser, Telenor, Norway
- Nick Foggin, Independent Consultant, Spain
- Leopoldina Fortunati, Professor, University of Udine, Italy
- Oliver Gerstheimer, Manager, Lecturer and Researcher, chilli mind GmbH, University of Kassel, Germany and HGK Zurich
- Markus Giordano, Partner, iconmobile GmbH, Germany
- Randy Giusto, Vice President, IDC, USA
- Klaus Goldhammer, Managing Director, Goldmedia GmbH, Germany

- Paul Golding, Consultant and Author, Magic E Company, UK
- Janey Gordon, Senior Teaching Fellow, University of Luton, UK
- Nicola Green, Lecturer, University of Surrey, UK
- Michael Häder, Professor, Dresden University of Technology, Germany
- Janos Heé, Consultant Business Development, bmd wireless, Switzerland
- Peter Heinzmann, Technical Director, cnlab/ITA-HSR, Switzerland
- Per Helmersen, Research Psychologist, Telenor, Norway
- Larissa Hjorth, Lecturer, University of Melbourne, Australia
- Joachim R. Höflich, Professor, University of Erfurt, Germany
- Matthias Horx, Futurist, zukunftsinstitut, Austria
- Michael Hulme, Professor, Lancaster University, UK
- Ken Hyers, Wireless Industry Analyst, In-Stat/MDR, USA
- Kaarina Hyvönen, Researcher, National Consumer Research Centre, Finland
- Christina James, Director, Tegic Communications, USA
- T. Erik Julsrud, Researcher, Telenor, Norway
- Euichul Jung, PhD Candidate, Rutgers University, USA
- Stefan Kaltenberger, Head of Direct Marketing and Special Media Department, mobilkom austria
- Bo Karlson, Manager, Royal Institute of Technology, Sweden
- James Katz, Professor, Rutgers University, USA
- Turkka Keinonen, Professor, University of Art and Design Helsinki, Finland
- Tim Kelly, Communications Policy Analyst, International Telecommunication Union, Switzerland
- Castulus Kolo, Researcher and Consultant, Ludwig-Maximilians-University Munich, Germany
- Dieter Korczak, Senior Researcher, GP Forschungsgruppe, Germany
- Ilpo Koskinen, Professor, University of Art and Design Helsinki, Finland
- Nalini P. Kotamraju, PhD Candidate, University of California at Berkeley, USA
- Jürgen Kuhn, Auditor, KPMG, Germany
- Heikki Leskinen, Director, Strategy and Business Development, Starcut, Finland
- Louis Leung, Associate Professor, Chinese University of Hong Kong
- Sun Sun Lim, Assistant Professor, National University of Singapore
- Rich Ling, Researcher, Telenor, Norway
- Chris Locke, Strategist, T-Mobile International, UK
- Niels Logemann, Scholar, German Sport University Cologne, Germany

- Santiago Lorente, Professor, Universidad Politécnica de Madrid, Spain
- Steve Love, Lecturer, Brunel University, West London, UK
- Paul May, Writer and Consultant, verista, UK
- Cai Melakoski, Principal Lecturer, Tampere Polytechnic, Finland
- Hitoshi Mitomo, Professor, Waseda University, Japan
- Christian Neuhaus, Researcher, DaimlerChrysler AG, Germany
- Kristóf Nyíri, Director and Professor, Institute for Philosophical Research of the Hungarian Academy of Sciences, Hungary
- Britta Oertel, Head of Department, Institute for Futures Studies and Technology Assessment (IZT), Germany
- Virpi Oksman, Researcher, Tampere University, Finland
- Leysia Palen, Assistant Professor, University of Colorado at Boulder, USA
- Fernando Paragas, Assistant Professor, PhD Student and Fulbright Fellow, University of the Philippines and Ohio University
- Woong Park, Assistant Professor, Soongsil University, Korea
- Per Egil Pedersen, Professor, Agder University College, Norway
- Carina Pettersson, Lecturer, University of Gävle, Sweden
- Arnold Picot, Professor, Ludwig-Maximilians-University Munich, Germany and Georgetown University
- Sadie Plant, Independent Writer, UK
- Gary Pöpl, Director Mobile Solutions, BBDO InterOne GmbH, Germany
- Costin Pribeanu, Researcher, National Institute for Research and Development in Informatics, Bucharest, Romania
- Petri Pulli, Professor, University of Oulu, Finland
- Ronald Rice, Professor, University of California, Santa Barbara, USA
- Tommi Rissanen, Project Manager, eBRC, University of Tampere, Finland
- J. P. Roos, Professor, Dept of Social Policy, University of Helsinki, Finland
- Jessica Sandin, Editorial Director, Informa Telecoms Group, UK
- Raimund Schmolze, Head of Market Research, T-Mobile International, UK
- Mike Short, Vice President, mmO2, UK
- Ralph Simon, Chairman, Mobile Entertainment Forum, USA
- Richard Smith, Professor, Simon Fraser University, Canada
- Lara Srivastava, Telecom Policy Analyst, International Telecommunication Union, Switzerland
- Gitte Stald, Assistant Professor, University of Copenhagen, Denmark
- Katarina Stanoevska, Project Manager, University of St.Gallen, Switzerland

- Charles Steinfield, Professor, Michigan State University, USA
- Richard Tee, Researcher, University of Maastricht, Netherlands
- Bas Verhart, CEO, Media Republic, Netherlands
- Lars Vestergaard, Wireless Research Director, IDC, UK
- Jesus Villadangos, Teacher and Researcher, Universidad Publica de Navarra, Spain
- Jane Vincent, Research Fellow, DWRC, University of Surrey, UK
- Roberto Vitalini, Conceptualist, Switzerland
- Yuichi Washida, Research Affiliate, The Comparative Media Studies at MIT, Japan
- Arnd Weber, Researcher, Forschungszentrum Karlsruhe, Institute for Technology Assessment and Systems Analysis (ITAS), Germany
- Barry Wellman, Professor, University of Toronto, Canada
- Dagmar Wiebusch, General Manager, Informationszentrum Mobilfunk e. V., Germany
- Rolf T. Wigand, Professor, University of Arkansas at Little Rock, USA
- Marc Ziegler, Managing Director, TIMElabs Management Consulting GmbH, Germany
- Hans-Dieter Zimmermann, Temporary Professor, University of Muenster, Germany
- Michael M. Zwick, Sociologist, University of Stuttgart, Germany

References

Borg, I. (1977), 'Some basic concepts of facet theory', In: J. C. Lingoes et al. (Eds.), *Geometric representations of relational data: Readings in multidimensional scaling*, Ann Arbor, MI: Mathesis Press.

Linstone, H. A. and Turoff, M. (Eds.) (1975), *The Delphi Method: Techniques and Applications*, London: Addison-Wesley.

Table 2: Complete data table (percentages, mean and standard deviation).

	Wave 1									Wave 2								
	1	2	3	4	5	6	n	M	SD	1	2	3	4	5	6	n	M	SD
1.1 Drivers: Mobile Internet	2.0	9.8	9.2	26.8	35.3	17.0	153	4.4	1.3									
1.2 Drivers: Downloads	2.0	3.9	2.6	17.8	36.8	36.8	152	4.9	1.2									
1.3 Drivers: Voice communication	0.7	2.0	0.7	6.6	14.6	75.5	151	5.6	0.9									
1.4 Drivers: Text and picture messaging	0.7	0.7	1.3	3.3	38.4	55.6	151	5.5	0.8									
2.1 Dependence: Life	0.7	3.3	1.3	9.2	38.2	47.4	152	5.2	1.0									
2.2 Dependence: Increase	0.7	2.0	5.9	24.2	33.3	34.0	153	4.9	1.0									
2.3 Dependence: Public debate	3.3	15.1	23.0	24.3	23.0	11.2	152	3.8	1.3									
3.1 Addiction: Few people	5.3	9.9	10.6	21.2	38.4	14.6	151	4.2	1.4	3.4	6.8	13.7	28.2	35.0	12.8	117	4.2	1.2
3.2 Addiction: Media debate	4.0	7.3	16.6	29.1	32.5	10.6	151	4.1	1.3	3.4	5.1	13.7	35.9	31.6	10.3	117	4.2	1.2
4.1 Relationships: New friends	6.0	18.5	15.2	28.5	21.2	10.6	151	3.7	1.4	5.2	19.1	13.9	33.0	20.0	8.7	115	3.7	1.4
4.2 Relationships: Maintain relationships	0.0	1.3	0.0	10.5	30.9	57.2	152	5.4	0.8	0.0	0.9	1.7	7.8	34.5	55.2	116	5.4	0.8
4.3 Relationships: Losing contact	1.3	14.5	13.2	27.0	20.4	23.7	152	4.2	1.4	1.7	9.4	15.4	26.5	33.3	13.7	117	4.2	1.2
4.4 Relationships: Superficial	13.1	37.9	23.5	14.4	5.9	5.2	153	2.3	1.3	12.8	35.0	26.5	16.2	4.3	5.1	117	2.8	1.3
4.5 Relationships: Social life	7.8	23.5	19.0	22.9	15.7	11.1	153	3.5	1.5	8.5	17.1	21.4	28.2	15.4	9.4	117	3.5	1.4
5.1 Communication: Face-to-face	5.9	22.2	15.0	30.7	17.6	8.5	153	3.6	1.4	3.4	17.9	23.1	31.6	19.7	4.3	117	3.6	1.2
5.2 Communication: More communication	2.6	11.2	11.8	29.6	32.2	12.5	152	4.2	1.3									
5.3 Communication: Pictures	9.8	26.1	27.5	20.9	11.1	4.6	153	3.1	1.3	8.5	23.1	33.3	23.1	10.3	1.7	117	3.1	1.2
5.4 Communication: Social pressure	1.3	5.2	5.9	15.0	40.5	32.0	153	4.8	1.2	1.7	1.7	3.4	16.2	46.2	30.8	117	5.0	1.0
6.1 Children: What age							141											
6.2 Children: Lower average age	0.0	2.0	1.3	15.0	47.1	34.6	153	5.1	0.8									
6.3 Children: Media debate	0.7	2.6	5.3	20.4	40.1	30.9	152	4.9	1.0									
7.1 Minors: Erode protection	4.8	23.8	22.4	26.5	15.6	6.8	147	3.5	1.3	5.2	19.0	24.1	31.0	15.5	5.2	116	3.5	1.3
7.2 Minors: Stronger regulation	7.4	23.0	14.9	20.3	20.9	13.5	148	3.7	1.5	6.0	20.5	17.9	27.4	16.2	12.0	117	3.6	1.4
8.1 Family: Losing authority	9.9	31.1	25.2	22.5	7.9	3.3	151	3.0	1.2	11.2	30.2	31.9	19.8	5.2	1.7	116	2.8	1.1
8.2 Family: Closer relationship	2.0	14.5	12.5	30.9	28.9	11.2	152	4.0	1.3	0.9	9.4	18.8	37.6	25.6	7.7	117	4.0	1.1
8.3 Family: Social control	1.3	3.9	9.9	34.9	38.2	11.8	152	4.4	1.0									
9.1 Peer: Teenager lifestyle	0.0	0.0	1.3	6.5	41.8	50.3	153	5.4	0.7									
9.2 Peer: Services and pressure	1.3	2.6	5.3	19.2	43.7	27.8	151	4.9	1.1									

	Wave 1									Wave 2								
	1	2	3	4	5	6	n	M	SD	1	2	3	4	5	6	n	M	SD
10.1 Indebtedness: Increased spendings	0.7	2.6	5.9	27.0	38.8	25.0	152	4.8	1.0									
10.2 Indebtedness: Budget control	0.7	4.0	12.6	38.4	32.5	11.9	151	4.3	1.0	0.0	2.6	10.3	37.1	42.2	7.8	116	4.4	0.9
10.3 Indebtedness: Unclear tariffs	3.3	10.5	15.1	30.3	25.0	15.8	152	4.1	1.3	3.4	7.8	12.9	34.5	30.2	11.2	116	4.1	1.2
10.4 Indebtedness: Consumer protection	2.0	3.4	8.1	39.2	33.8	13.5	148	4.4	1.1									
11.1 Camera phones: Invade privacy	2.6	13.7	15.0	34.6	26.1	7.8	153	3.9	1.2	2.6	11.1	18.8	31.6	29.1	6.8	117	3.9	1.2
11.2 Camera phones: Rediscover surroundings	10.5	25.7	26.3	25.7	7.9	3.9	152	3.1	1.3	11.1	31.6	23.1	25.6	6.8	1.7	117	2.9	1.2
11.3 Camera phones: Governments	2.0	10.5	10.5	31.6	29.6	15.8	152	4.2	1.3									
12.1 Non-user: Information deficit	9.3	22.5	22.5	25.8	13.9	6.0	151	3.3	1.4	6.0	21.4	26.5	28.2	13.7	4.3	117	3.4	1.2
12.2 Non-user: Limitation of mobility	4.6	21.2	21.9	21.9	19.2	11.3	151	3.6	1.4	4.3	17.9	21.4	29.9	21.4	5.1	117	3.6	1.3
12.3 Non-user: Problems coordinating life	3.3	11.3	10.6	31.1	23.2	20.5	151	4.2	1.4	2.6	8.5	11.1	32.5	30.8	14.5	117	4.2	1.2
13.1 Writing: Young people	5.9	22.4	26.3	23.0	11.8	10.5	152	3.4	1.4									
13.2 Writing: Change language	2.6	10.5	16.4	34.2	25.0	11.2	152	4.0	1.2									
13.3 Writing: Reintroduce near-illiterate	11.4	20.8	34.2	22.8	8.1	2.7	149	3.0	1.2									
14.1 Data protection: Lose control	1.3	8.6	10.6	38.4	27.8	13.2	151	4.2	1.2	0.9	5.2	8.6	37.9	31.0	16.4	116	4.4	1.1
14.2 Data protection: Public debate	0.0	1.3	9.9	25.2	41.1	22.5	151	4.7	1.0	0.0	0.9	7.8	21.6	50.9	19.0	116	4.8	0.9
14.3 Data protection: Stronger regulation	3.3	2.0	12.7	24.0	37.3	20.7	150	4.5	1.2	2.6	0.9	12.2	24.3	40.0	20.0	115	4.6	1.1
15.1 Mobile spam: Increase	0.0	2.7	2.7	14.7	36.0	44.0	150	5.2	1.0									
15.2 Mobile spam: Media debate	0.0	0.7	4.0	15.2	38.4	41.7	151	5.2	0.9									
15.3 Mobile spam: Filters	1.3	1.3	5.3	21.2	37.1	33.8	151	4.9	1.0									
16.1 Life: Increase mobility	1.3	7.3	8.6	22.5	33.8	26.5	151	4.6	1.2									
16.2 Life: Increase accessibility	1.3	0.0	3.3	10.0	36.7	48.7	150	5.3	0.9									
16.3 Life: Lose leisure time	3.3	7.9	14.6	33.1	27.2	13.9	151	4.2	1.3	1.7	9.5	7.8	38.8	31.0	11.2	116	4.2	1.2
16.4 Life: Control leisure time	14.0	26.7	28.0	15.3	11.3	4.7	150	3.0	1.4	10.3	31.0	31.9	18.1	7.8	0.9	116	2.8	1.1
16.5 Life: Develop awareness	0.7	6.0	8.0	28.0	37.3	20.0	150	4.6	1.1	0.0	6.1	7.0	30.4	40.0	16.5	115	4.5	1.0
17.1 Wider effects: Everyday culture	0.0	2.7	4.7	24.0	42.7	26.0	150	4.9	1.0									
17.2 Wider effects: Telecommunications industry	18.1	38.2	27.1	8.3	4.2	4.2	144	2.6	1.2									

M = Mean, SD = Standard Deviation

Notes on Contributors

Genevieve Bell is a Senior Researcher and Principal Research Scientist at Intel, USA. In 2003, she completed a three year multi-sited ethnographic research project in urban Asia. She is currently the director of a small interdisciplinary team of researchers working in the Digital Home space. She holds a PhD in Cultural Anthropology from Stanford University, and a BA/MA from Bryn Maw College.

Stefan Bertschi is a Sociologist and Scholar of Literature; he is Project Manager at the Institute for Media and Communications Management, University of St. Gallen, Switzerland. His latest research focused on tendencies and prospects within the mobile media culture. He is founder of loginb.com, a research-based consultancy specialising in understanding social and cultural processes. Current interests include post-structuralist theory, semiotics and cultural theory.

Jonathan Donner (PhD in Communication, Stanford University) is a Post-Doctoral Research Fellow at the Earth Institute at Columbia University, USA. His research focuses on information and communication technologies in economic development, and particularly on applications of mobile telephony. Prior to joining the Earth Institute, Jonathan worked with Monitor Company and with the OTF Group, both management consultancies in Boston, MA. E-mail: jd2210@columbia.edu.

Nicola Döring is Professor of Media Design and Media Psychology at Ilmenau University of Technology, Germany. Research interests: design and psychology of online and mobile communication; learning and teaching with new media; gender research; evaluation research. Personal homepage: http://www.nicola-doering.de.

Nick Foggin is an independent telecommunications, media and technology consultant, specialising in corporate strategy. Formerly Group Director of Strategy for Orange, Nick has spent twelve years in the telecommunications arena, in senior strategy and planning roles. His clients include mobile operators, broadcasters and publishers. He has a

BA (Hons) from Manchester University and an MSc from Strathclyde Graduate Business School, UK.

Leopoldina Fortunati teaches Sociology of Communication and Sociology of Cultural Processes at the Faculty of Education of the University of Udine, Italy. She has conducted many research projects in the field of gender studies, cultural processes and communication technologies. Professor Fortunati has published several articles on mobile phone use and recently edited, together with J. Katz and R. Riccini, *Mediating the Human Body. Technology, Communication and Fashion* (2003). E-mail: fortunati.deluca@tin.it.

Hans Geser is Professor of Sociology at the University of Zurich, Switzerland. He is co-editor of *Local Parties in Political and Organizational Perspective* (1999). His latest research focuses on the sociocultural implications of computer networks and digital communication where he develops a sociological theory of the mobile phone. Main interests include the sociologies of work, organization, politics, and international relations.

Peter Glotz is Professor Emeritus for Media and Society at the Institute for Media and Communications Management, University of St. Gallen, Switzerland. His past responsibilities include Director of the University of Erfurt, Germany, and Professor for Communication Sciences; Professor for Media Ecology and Communication Culture at the Ludwig-Maximilian University Munich. He was member of the German Bundestag (Parliament) and Federal Manager of the Social Democratic Party. Amongst many other books, his publications include *Die beschleunigte Gesellschaft: Kulturkämpfe im digitalen Kapitalismus* (1999), *Von Analog nach Digital: Unsere Gesellschaft auf dem Weg zur digitalen Kultur* (2000), and most recently together with Robin Meyer-Lucht *Online gegen Print: Zeitung und Zeitschrift im Wandel* (2004).

Paul Golding is an independent consultant renowned for his extensive expertise in mobile application technology. Through writing, training and consulting, he has actively promoted the transformative potential of 3G within many companies, such as Vodafone, Motorola, O2, Three, and Virgin Mobile. Not just a theoretician, Paul has built many real mobile solutions and his recent book *Next Generation Wireless Applications* (2004) surveys the entire spectrum of technologies that are converging in the 3G era. Not just a technologist either, Paul draws from a wide range of subjects to form mobile business strategies, including management science, sociology, psychology, economics, linguistics and others (http://www.paulgolding.me.uk).

Peter Gross is a Professor and Head of the Institute of Sociology at the University of St Gallen, Switzerland. In addition to his academic activities, he is involved in a number of other educational and consultancy organizations. His most recent publications include *The Multi-option Society* (*Die Multioptionsgesellschaft*, 1994) and *Ego Hunt—In the Century of Independence* (*Ich-Jagd—Im Unabhängigkeitsjahrhundert*, 1999).

Axel Gundolf is a Student of Applied Media Science at Ilmenau University of Technology, Germany. Research interests: intercultural communication, journalism research, online and mobile communication.

Leslie Haddon is a Visiting Research Associate at the University of Essex and a Part-time Lecturer at the London School of Economics, UK. He has conducted a range of studies on the social shaping and consumption of information and communication technologies. His most recent book is *Information and Communication Technologies in Everyday Life: A Concise Introduction and Research Guide* (2004).

Richard Harper is a Senior Researcher in Microsoft's Interactive Systems Group, in Cambridge, UK. He has spent twenty years developing sociological tools and techniques for understanding user behaviour that lead to the design of more innovative computer technologies. Before coming to MSR Cambridge, he ran his own digital technology companies, prior to which he led an interdisciplinary research centre at the University of Surrey, where he was also appointed the UK's first Professor of Socio-Digital Systems. He commenced his research at Xerox EuroPARC, after completing his PhD at Manchester. He has published over 130 articles, eight books, and has three patents.

Larissa Hjorth currently lectures in the BA in Games in the Creative Media Department at RMIT University, Melbourne, Australia. Hjorth has been researching mobile telephone customisation and gender in the Asia-Pacific. Examples of published research include '"Pop" and "Ma": The Landscape of Japanese Commodity Characters and Subjectivity' in Fran Martin, Audrey Yue and Chris Berry (Eds.), *Mobile Cultures* (2003) and 'Kawaii@keitai' in Nanette Gottlieb and Mark McLelland (Eds.), *Japanese Cybercultures* (2003).

Joachim R. Höflich is Professor of Communication Sciences and Media Integration at the University of Erfurt, Germany. His research interests include interpersonal and mediated communication, media use and its consequences. He published several articles on mobile communication and recently edited together with Julian Gebhardt *Mobile Kommunikation. Perspektiven und Forschungsfelder* (forthcoming).

Michael Hulme is a Professor and Associate Fellow of the Institute for the Advanced Study of Management and Social Sciences at Lancaster University, UK, Director of the Centre for the Study of Media, Technology and Culture, and Chairman and founder of Teleconomy Group, a commercial research company specialising in organisational and consumer behaviour research in relation to strategic futures.

James E. Katz is Professor of Communication and Director of the Center for Mobile Communication Studies at Rutgers University, New Brunswick, NJ, USA. He is the author of *Connections: Social and Cultural Studies of the Telephone in American Life* (1999) and editor of *Machines that Become Us: The Social Context of Personal Communication Technology* (2003).

Chris Locke started his career as an academic, eventually becoming the Xerox Lecturer in Electronic Communication and Publishing at University College London, UK. He then moved into the internet and telecoms industries as a strategist, and has held senior roles at companies such as the Virgin Group, Freeserve, Hutchison 3G and T-Mobile International. He is currently working for AOL. He has a MA in Critical Theory from the University of Sussex, and his published works include 'Digital Memory and the Problem of Forgetting' in Susannah Radstone (Ed.), *Memory and Methodology* (2000). He can be contacted via chris@feeshes.freeserve.co.uk.

Kristóf Nyíri studied mathematics and philosophy. He is Member of the Hungarian Academy of Sciences, and Director of the Institute for Philosophical Research of the Academy. Main interests: philosophy in the 19th and 20th centuries; the impact of communication technologies on the organization of ideas. Latest book: *Vernetztes Wissen: Philosophie im Zeitalter des Internets* (2004). Further information: http://www.phil-inst.hu/nyiri.

René Obermann was born in March 1963 in Düsseldorf, Germany. He has been the CEO of T-Mobile International, the worlds 3rd largest mobile operator today, since December 2002 and is also a member of the Board of Management of Deutsche Telekom AG. René Obermann was one of the pioneers of the mobile communication business. In 1986 he founded ABC Telekom, a mobile start up company. In 1991 he became Managing Partner of Hutchison Mobilfunk GmbH, successor of ABC Telecom, and in 1993 Chairman of the Management Board before joining T-Mobile in 1998.

Raimund Schmolze, PhD is Head of European Customer Insights at T-Mobile International and Part-time Lecturer at the London School of

Economics, UK. His research team supports T-Mobile's product development and marketing through detailed studies of consumer needs and behaviour.

Lara Srivastava is Project Director of the ITU New Initiatives Programme and Telecom Policy Analyst at the International Telecommunication Union (ITU), Geneva, Switzerland. Lara is responsible for monitoring and analysing trends in information and communication technologies, policy, and markets, with a focus on mobile communication. She manages and drafts publications, and is in charge of organising and advising on workshop and symposia content. Lara holds an MA, LL.B., and M.Sc. and is a qualified barrister and solicitor (Canada).

Anna Truch is a Research Fellow at the Centre for the Study of Media, Technology and Culture at Lancaster University, UK. Since graduating from Oxford University with a degree in politics, philosophy, and economics, her career has spanned both the commercial and academic worlds (IBM Telecommunications Consulting Group and Henley Management College). Anna is completing a PhD that explores the impact of personality on knowledge sharing within organisations.

Jane Vincent is a Research Fellow at the University of Surrey's Digital World Research Centre, UK. Specialising in the social shaping of mobile communications, she is also studying for a PhD. Prior to joining DWRC in 2001 she worked for twenty years in the European mobile communications industry. E-mail: j.vincent@surrey.ac.uk.

Laura Watts is a Research Fellow in the Department of Sociology at Lancaster University, UK. She is currently completing her doctorate, in the field of Science and Technology Studies, on the archaeologies and futures of the mobile telecoms industry, which also draws on her prior career as a designer and business strategist inside the industry.

Die Neuerscheinungen dieser Reihe:

Henry Keazor,
Thorsten Wübbena
Video Thrills the Radio Star
Musikvideos: Geschichte,
Themen, Analysen
Oktober 2005, ca. 500 Seiten,
kart., ca. 250 Abb., ca. 31,80 €,
ISBN: 3-89942-383-6

Joanna Barck, Petra Löffler
Gesichter des Films
Oktober 2005, 388 Seiten,
kart., zahlr. Abb., 28,80 €,
ISBN: 3-89942-416-6

Andreas Becker, Saskia Reither,
Christian Spies (Hg.)
Reste
Umgang mit einem
Randphänomen
Oktober 2005, 278 Seiten,
kart., ca. 27,80 €,
ISBN: 3-89942-307-0

Heide Volkening
Am Rand der Autobiographie
Ghostwriting – Signatur –
Geschlecht
Oktober 2005, ca. 300 Seiten,
kart., ca. 27,80 €,
ISBN: 3-89942-375-5

Julia Glesner
Theater und Internet
Zum Verhältnis von Kultur und
Technologie im Übergang zum
21. Jahrhundert
Oktober 2005, ca. 270 Seiten,
kart., ca. 26,80 €,
ISBN: 3-89942-389-5

Christoph Ernst
**Essayistische
Medienreflexion**
Die Idee des Essayismus und
die Frage nach den Medien
Oktober 2005, 508 Seiten,
kart., 29,80 €,
ISBN: 3-89942-376-3

Jürgen Straub, Carlos Kölbl,
Doris Weidemann,
Barbara Zielke (eds.)
Pursuit of Meaning
Advances in Cultural and
Cross-Cultural Psychology
November 2005, ca. 500 Seiten,
kart., ca. 30,00 €,
ISBN: 3-89942-234-1

Natascha Adamowsky (Hg.)
**» Die Vernunft ist mir noch
nicht begegnet«**
Zum konstitutiven Verhältnis
von Spiel und Erkenntnis
September 2005, 288 Seiten,
kart., 26,80 €,
ISBN: 3-89942-352-6

Christina Bartz,
Jens Ruchatz (Hg.)
**Mit Telemann durch die
deutsche Fernsehgeschichte**
Kommentare und Glossen des
Fernsehkritikers Martin
Morlock
September 2005, ca. 220 Seiten,
kart., ca. 25,80 €,
ISBN: 3-89942-327-5

**Leseproben und weitere Informationen finden Sie unter:
www.transcript-verlag.de**